The Golden Key to Heaven

An Explanation of the Spiritual Exercises of St. Ignatius

by
St. Anthony Mary Claret

Immaculate Heart Publications

This work, in its original Spanish and in the edition from which it was translated, bears the following:

Ecclesiastical Approbation:

Nihil obstat:
Juan Maria Gorricho, C.M.F., Censor.

Puede reimprimirse:
Pedro Schweiger, C.M.F., Superior General.

Nihil obstat:
Dr. Andrés de Lucas, Censor.
Imprimatur:
†José Maria Lahiguera
Madrid, 15 March 1955

In addition, since the author is a canonized saint of the Catholic Church, all his writings, including this one, have undergone a most rigorous examination and have been deemed, by the authorities of the First See of the Church of Rome, "the Mistress and Mother of all the other Churches", to be in conformity with Catholic Truth.

ISBN 1-896384-01-3

St. Anthony Mary Claret's Introduction to the Reader

Having already given the spiritual exercises of Saint Ignatius both publicly and privately, we have been asked many times for a book explaining these exercises with the purpose of profiting further, so that individuals can meditate thoroughly and carefully on them, book in hand, and even repeat aloud what they have heard. Not only for this reason, but also when no spiritual director is available, the exercises can be performed without him. Acceding therefore to such wishes, we have determined to make available to the public meditations distributed over ten days; we should recognize that there are eight complete days and two incomplete days, those being the eve of the Communion day* and the concluding day.

The first day has merely one meditation, and the last day two; the other days have four: two in the morning and two for the afternoon and evening.**

But it must be understood that the spiritual masters divide the material of the meditations into three orders, according to the three states of those meditating.

(1) Some are sinners who want to get away from their sins, and they walk on the road called the "Purgative Way." The aim of this road is to purify from the soul all its vices, sins, and faults.

---

*NOTE — It must be noted that Saint Anthony wrote this previous to the decrees of Pope St. Pius X who encouraged frequent, even daily, reception of Holy Communion.

**NOTE — Also see the outline of the schedule of these 35 Meditations for 10 days as proposed by St. Anthony Mary Claret on page iv of this book. Also see the hourly schedule suggested on pages 354 and 355 to complete all these meditations.

(2) Others go further and increase in virtue and walk on the road called the "Illuminative Way," whose aim is to enlighten the soul with the splendor of the many virtues and increase significantly in them.

(3) Others are already perfect, and they walk in the "Unitive Way," so called because the purpose of this state is to unite our soul with God in a union of perfect love.

St. Ignatius distributes this same matter of the three ways into four weeks: he places the material dealing with the "Purgative Way" in the first week; the "Illuminative Way" is dealt with during the second and third weeks, and the fourth week handles that of the "Unitive Way".

Following therefore, in the explanation of these holy exercises the thought of spiritual masters and the words of St. Ignatius, we have decided for greater clarity to divide the total plan and material into five sections as follows:

Section 1 The Purgative Way — This section and the next are taken from the first week of St. Ignatius' Spiritual Exercises. These two sections dwell on the Purgative Way. The first section comprises more suitable meditations designed to inspire sorrow for and confession of sins, and help us keep clear of them.

Section 2 — Consists of meditations fostering the resolution not to fall into sin again and always to preserve that cleanness acquired through the meditations of the first section.

Section 3 The Illuminative Way — This section embraces meditations on the virtues which we should learn and possess from Jesus Christ, spoken of by St. Ignatius in the second week of his spiritual exercises.

Section 4 — Consists of the meditations on Our Lord, but considered in a more elevating and perfect manner, according to the spirit in which St. Ignatius drew up his holy works. In this section we consider Jesus as He suffered so much pain and practised all the virtues. These are the meditations which St. Ignatius places in the third week.

Section 5 The Unitive Way — contains meditations which St. Ignatius calls the fourth week.

This then is the plan we have proposed in explaining these holy exercises; and as we hold the words of the saint in such high esteem, we put them as headings in each meditation, as he wrote them, preserving even the style of his period, and then we follow the explanation of the text.

As for the number of meditations, we should like them to be used as designed for each day; and if this is not possible when they are performed publicly in a church, do them privately at home, for which this book will serve most effectively.

May everything be done for the greater glory of God, in praise of Most Holy Mary and for the salvation of souls.

Amen.

Madrid, January, 1859.
Antonio Maria, Archbishop of Cuba.
(Saint Anthony Mary Claret)

Plan of the Meditations of the Exercises

Table of Contents

SECTION IV - The Illuminative Way (continued)

SECTION V - The Unitive Way

APPENDICES

Time And Method
of Making the Meditation

(1) Each meditation is to last one hour.

(2) Each meditation usually has three points[1], and each point has two affective acts or affections[2], with the time distributed as follows: at the beginning the Holy Spirit is invoked; next the preparatory prayer and corresponding preludes; then the first point is read, and when finished, silence is kept while meditating on what was read. After ten minutes, the first affective act is read, after fifteen minutes the second affective act is read.

In a short time the second point is read, and after ten minutes the first affective act, and after fifteen minutes the second affective act.

In the third quarter (after 30 minutes) proceed as in the first two quarters.

(3) The last quarter hour will be employed in colloquies, conclusion, thanksgiving, offering of intentions and resolutions, in the examination of the meditation itself, in going over all the points of the meditation and choosing what has made the greatest impression, so that we may ruminate and meditate on that point. If the opportunity presents itself, jot it down briefly so as never to forget it, and it will be the sweet bouquet to extract from the meditation.

---

1 Some meditations have only two points because they have topics which have to be meditated upon more slowly.
2 The term "affective act" or "affections" refers to an act of the will that follows or results from some reflection on some mystery of the faith. Acts of faith, hope, charity, contrition and humility are examples of affective acts. Henceforth, we shall use the term "affective act" since "affection" has also other connotations.

(4) During the meditation one should meditate and contemplate: one meditates when one uses discursive reasoning from one truth to another; one contemplates when interiorly one sees or grasps a truth in a simple glance, without a variety of discourse; when one produces great affections or affective acts of admiration, love, sorrow for sins, etc., etc.

(5) Meditation is done with the application of the three powers of the soul. The memory recalls and keeps in mind the matter of the meditation. When the memory is unfaithful and has no retentiveness, it must be supplied with slow and thorough reading of the same meditation.

The understanding discourses about the material of the meditation, penetrates deeply into the truth it contains, sees the riches resulting from the practice of that truth and the damage and harm which follow from abandoning it or working to the contrary.

Then comes the will, and as it sees the good which the understanding proposes to it, it makes the intention to follow it and put it into practice, and for the same reason it resolves to remove from itself everything it knows to be harmful. In order to assist the will, one applies one's imagination and feelings, for example, as if one sees, hears, touches, etc., the persons and things contained in the meditation. This work of the imagination and senses kindles the affections of the will in an admirable way, and the will resolves finally to separate from evil, to do good, to seek peace and follow after it.[3]

---

3 Diverte a malo, et fac bonum; inquire pacem, et persequere eam.
  (Ps. 33:15)

Morning Prayers

We begin each day in this way:

Kneeling we say — Through the sign of the Cross deliver us from our enemies, O Lord, our God.

☦ In the name of the Father and of the Son and of the Holy Spirit. *Amen.*

Veni, Creator

Come, O Creator Spirit blest! And in our souls take up Thy rest; Come with Thy grace and heavenly aid, To fill the hearts which Thou hast made.

Great Paraclete! To Thee we cry, O highest gift of God most high! O font of life! O fire of love! And sweet anointing from above.

Thou in Thy sevenfold gifts art known, The finger of God's hand we own; The promise of the Father, Thou! Who dost the tongue with power endow.

Kindle our senses from above, And make our hearts o'erflow with love; With patience firm and virtue high, The weakness of our flesh supply.

Far from us drive the foe we dread, And grant us Thy true peace instead; So shall we not, with Thee for guide, Turn from the path of life aside.

Oh, may Thy grace on us bestow, The Father and the Son to know, And Thee through endless times confessed, Of both the eternal Spirit blest.

All glory while the ages run, Be to the Father and the Son, Who rose from death; the same to Thee, O Holy Ghost, eternally. *Amen.*

V. Send forth Thy Spirit and they shall be created.
R. And Thou shalt renew the face of the earth.

Let us Pray. Lord, Thou have instructed the hearts of Thy faithful by the brilliant light of the Holy Spirit. Give us the grace, under His divine inspiration, to have a sense of the true and a taste for the good, and always to find our consolation and our joy in Him. This we ask of Thee through our Lord . . . in the unity of the same Holy Spirit. *Amen.*

Following, three *Hail Marys* are said to the Most Holy Virgin.

We fly to thy patronage, O holy Mother of God,

despise not our petitions in our necessities: but deliver us from all dangers, O ever glorious and blessed Virgin.

Then an *Our Father* and a *Hail Mary* in honor of the Holy Angels, one each in honor of Saint Ignatius and again in honor of some other saint to whom you are devoted, as patrons of the holy exercises.

Come Holy Ghost fill the hearts of Thy faithful and kindle in them the fire of Thy love.

V. Send forth Thy Spirit and they shall be created.

R. And Thou shalt renew the face of the earth.

Let us pray. Lord, Thou hast instructed the hearts, etc.

Say three *Hail Marys* in honor of the purity of Our Lady.

Preparatory Prayers Before Each Meditation

First Prelude, preparatory prayer — My Lord and My God, I believe most firmly that Thou art here present.

I adore Thee, my God, with complete surrender and affection of my heart, and I humbly beseech Thee to pardon all my sins.

I offer Thee, my Lord and Father, this meditation, and I hope that Thou will grant me the graces necessary for making a good meditation. For this same purpose, I turn to Thee, Most Holy Virgin, to the angels and saints, so that Thou wilt intercede for me and obtain for me what I need in order to make this meditation fruitfully. Amen.

Second Prelude or petition prayer — consists in asking for the grace, not in general, as in the preparatory prayer, but for the special grace, according to the matter of the meditation. This prayer is found at the beginning of each meditation.

Afterwards — the reading of the designated meditation, with frequent pauses, of the meditation, looking at it as coming from God, and applying its contents to the present state of the soul, from which will be seen those points that should be amended, reformed or improved. Thus seeing oneself one makes practical resolutions, and following these, the supplication and colloquies, now to Our Lord, the Son of God, now to the Eternal Father, now to Our Lady, in order to obtain the suitable grace for doing what is intended and for everything desired.

Concluding Prayers at end of each Meditation

Thanksgiving — I give Thee thanks, my God, for the good thoughts, affections and inspirations which Thou hast communicated to me in this meditation.

Offering — I offer Thee the resolutions which I have formed in the meditation, and I beseech Thee, grant me the most efficacious grace to put them into practice, and to this purpose I beg Thee, Mary, my Mother, the angels and saints, especially those to whom I am particularly devoted that They intercede for me and obtain for me this grace. *Amen.*

Examination after each Meditation

1. Before beginning the meditation, have I reflected on where it was going and for what purpose?
2. Have I begun it with the efficacious desire to perform it well, and profit from it?
3. Have I anticipated beforehand the resolutions I should have been making and the special graces for which I should have been asking?
4. Have I strengthened my faith in the presence of God, believing that I was going to speak with the same God?
5. Have I offered the meditation to Him and have I

asked for the grace to perform it fruitfully?

6. Have I neglected the composition of place? (pg.2)
7. Have I read with care the points, thinking that God was speaking to me, and have I applied what I was reading to the present state of my soul?
8. Have I drawn up practical resolutions?
9. Have I kept suitable composure of body?
10. Have I allowed myself to be overcome by drowsiness or laziness?
11. Have I given place to useless thoughts?
12. Have I become over-proud from feeling holy?
13. Have I become anxious through dryness or desolation?
14. Have I omitted colloquies or supplications?
15. Have I dwelled upon discursive thoughts or other operations of the intellect for too long a time?
16. Have I paused too little in motions of the affections?
17. Have I shortened the meditation for reasons of dryness, temptations, or other pretexts?
18. What resolutions have I drawn up?
19. Have I asked for the grace and other necessities for this purpose?
20. Have I omitted to pray for those to whom I am obligated and for the whole Church?

If we find that we have failed, we should seek forgiveness and make a firm purpose of amendment; and if we do not discover any faults, we will give thanks to God for that. Finally, let us recall whatever in the meditation moved us most, and place it in our heart to be recalled throughout the day.

Examining oneself after the meditation is most useful, in order to gain fruit from our prayer and to learn the practical way of doing it; consequently it is always wise to make this examination, not only at the time of the Exercises, but also every day of the year.

SECTION I

Meditation 1

Preparatory Meditation

Explanation — Christian soul, you should be convinced that you are fortunate in being called to these holy exercises, and that nothing is so important as that you make them well. Reflect that this might be your last chance of making them well, either because no other opportunity will be offered to you, or because death will overtake you before you can make fruitful use of them. Who knows whether your salvation or damnation depends on them?

So you ought to make them with full attention, care and devotedness as though this were the last retreat of your life, as though they were for your quickly forthcoming death when you must make an accounting of yourself to God.

This preparatory meditation has three points: 1) the need of these spiritual exercises; 2) their advantages and excellence; 3) the disposition you should have in order to make them well.

Preparatory Prayer — My God and Lord, I firmly believe that Thou art present. I adore Thee, my God, with all the reverence and affection of my heart and humbly beg pardon for all my sins. I offer this meditation to Thee, my Lord and Father, and hope and anticipate that Thou will give me the graces I need to make it well. With that aim before me I appeal to Thee, Holy Virgin, my Mother, and you angels and saints, to intercede for me and gain for me what I need in order to make this meditation fruitfully. *Amen.*

First Prelude

Composition of Place — Imagine that you see glorious Saint Ignatius with the book of these Exercises in his hand and that he has around him countless upright souls who are now forever to remain in God's friendship, including converted sinners, souls who changed from lukewarm to whole-hearted in a warm eagerness to please God. Imagine that, addressing His words to you, he says, "Take this book, my son, and think seriously on the truths contained in it."

Then imagine that you see that great throng which no one can count, belonging to all nations, tribes, peoples, and tongues, standing before the throne and before the Lamb, and dressed in white robes with palms in their hands, with which they give evidence of the victory they have gained — victory over tyrants, victory over their own passions — and that they are shouting in loud voices, We owe ". . .salvation to our God, Who sitteth upon the throne, and to the Lamb," and to the Exercises of Saint Ignatius! (Apoc. 7:10).

Second Prelude

I beg Thee, my God and Lord, for the grace to know the need I have for these Exercises, and how much I ought to make good use of them.

First Point

Need of the Holy Exercises — One of the great and extraordinary favors which God gives a soul is to allow it to make the holy Spiritual Exercises. In order to have more fitting gratitude for this favor and appreciate your need of it, you ought to know first of all what the Spiritual Exercises are. According to Saint Ignatius, the Spiritual Exercises are nothing else than a method of examining your conscience, of meditating and putting the mind on Divine things, of praying mentally and vocally, and of other spiritual operations.

Just as to walk, to pace, and to run are bodily exercises, likewise we call spiritual exercises every method of conditioning, rousing, preparing, enabling the soul to rid itself of feelings and attractions that are out of place, and once rid of them, to seek and find the Divine Will in all circumstances of life, for the sake of the soul's salvation.

Once the essential point in the exercises is known, you will easily know the need you have for them.

If you are just — you need the Spiritual Exercises to keep upright, to grow more, and to purify yourself more, as you ought to, and as God commands. (". . .He that is just, let him be justified still: he that is holy, let him be sanctified still." Apoc. 22:11).

No matter how good you may be, without such recollection and reflection made according to your need, you will not continue good to the end. Just as plants die when left without water, likewise souls going without suitable reflection undergo the death of sin.

Just as good soil is more productive when it is cultivated, fertilized, and watered, likewise an upright soul is better and richer in good works, when it gives good attention and care to examining itself, to repenting, praying, and meditating and doing the other things that are done in the Holy Exercises.

Therefore we see that spiritual people and those wanting to make headway in perfection are not satisfied with doing each day their spiritual reading, mental and vocal prayer, particular and general examen; but in addition every year they spend a number of days doing this with added hours devoted to it, engaging exclusively in this holy undertaking.

If you are living in sin — you also need the holy Spiritual Exercises; for the sinner, in order to become converted, needs them no less than the upright person needs them in order to continue in God's friendship. In the solitude of the holy Exercises, God speaks to the heart.

When the Christian has drawn himself aside from the noise and the business of the world, he hears the voice of the Lord, Who says to him: O Christian soul, where do you come from? Where are you going? — You come from Me, Who have created you and have redeemed you and have planned and intended you for Heaven. So that you may gain salvation I have given you laws and Sacraments, helps and special graces.

And you — what is your present state? Alas! You are in the state of sin, stripped of grace, unworthy of Heaven, and you have been found guilty and sentenced to death. Where are you heading? Alas! You are proceeding to hell! At every step you keep taking, you are approaching those eternal torments.

Surely on hearing the Lord's voice, you will not harden your heart. You will confess your sin, and God, Who wills not the death of the sinner, but that he be converted and live in grace and hereafter in glory, will forgive you as He forgave the prodigal son, and will admit you to His friendship and favor as He did Mary Magdalene, and in this way you will find happiness.

If you are lukewarm — you have even more need of the holy Spiritual Exercises than the upright person does, for his continuance in grace; more need also, than the sinner does for conversion. God Himself says to you, "Would that you were either hot" — in grace and charity — "or cold" — in sin. "But because thou art lukewarm, . . . I will begin to vomit thee out of My mouth." (Apoc. 3:16).

O lukewarm soul, you are the one who has most need of the holy Spiritual Exercises; they alone can awaken you from the sluggishness you are now in! You, O lukewarm soul, are that unfruitful tree that only produces leaves, as the Gospel says. (cf. St. Luke 13:6ff). The landowner Who is God, commands that it be cut down with the axe or cutting instrument of death, and be cast into the fire of hell, as you have been so uselessly taking up soil space.

But the Gardener, Who is Jesus Christ, has made the request and obtained the favor of another year's delay in the hope that you will soon bear fruit; for now a new and special gardening treatment is applied to you by means of the holy Spiritual Exercises.

The soil will be turned; the soil of which you (that is, your body) are made, will be an object of your reflection. The rubbish and trash of your sins and faults will be under your mental gaze and consideration. With the knowledge of yourself, of your miseries and sins, you — like a tree given good gardening treatment — will bear much fruit, fruit consisting of humility and repentance.

In this holy solitude you will know where you have gone astray, how you have separated from God, and the steps you have gone through to develop the lukewarmness which is your present condition.

5

You will know that you are this way because you have neglected mental and vocal prayer, the frequent reception of the Sacraments, or you have received them carelessly, or you have neglected other practices of piety; and if you do anything at all, it proceeds in a neglectful, half-hearted way, with little care and much sluggishness and laziness.

You have gotten bored and displeased with the heavenly manna. You have grumbled at everything; with all that is worthwhile you are bored and displeased. You have regarded God's law not as a sweet yoke and a light burden (which it truly is), but as something unbearable.

You have regarded perfection as something impossible, even though Jesus Christ tells you to be perfect as your Heavenly Father is perfect. Therefore instead of achieving perfection, you have drunk down iniquity like water. Oh, what grumbling! What lying!

What wild uncontrol of your feelings and desires! What faults of every kind! Like one afflicted with leprosy, you are diseased from head to foot with sins. Only the holy Exercises can deliver you from so many evils.

Affective Acts

(1) Gratitude — I am now beginning to experience the great benefit that God has bestowed on me in attracting me to these Holy Exercises. May You be blessed my God, for having given me this probatic pool (cf. St. John 5:2) where a cure is given for every sickness, not just to the first one to enter, but for all who present themselves with a genuine desire for a cure.

(2) Humble Appeal — Oh Lord, till now there has not been any man who would show compassion for me; but now I have found such a Man. Yes, now I have found Thee, my Jesus, Who, without ceasing to be God, are true Man. Thou art my Savior, and I trust that in these holy Exercises Thou wilt heal my soul, for that is something it greatly needs. "Create a clean heart in me, O God, and renew a right spirit within my bowels." (Psalm 50:12).

Second Point

Excellence and Usefulness of the Holy Exercises — Oh, how excellent and precious are the Spiritual Exercises of Saint Ignatius!. . . Their teaching is Heavenly and Divine. They are inspired by God, and are something taught by the Blessed Virgin Mary. They have been approved by the Popes. They have received honors and recommendations from prelates. Instructors in the spiritual life have urged their use and their value is upheld by experience.

Just as a tree is known by its fruit, likewise the great value, the excellence and profitableness of the holy Exercises of Saint Ignatius can be clearly known by the plentiful and precious fruits which they have always produced and are producing. In order to convince our mind better and move our will more and more, and give the Exercises the rating they deserve, it will be well here to bring forward some evidence.

Therefore we report that Pope Paul III in his Bull of approval issued on the last day of July 1548, says: "Ignatius of Loyola. . . has written certain papers or Spiritual Exercises taken from Holy Scripture and from experience in the devout life, and worked out according to a very good method suited to move the souls of the Faithful in a holy way: and these Exercises are of great profit, well suited for spiritual encouragement and advancement."

He says in closing, "Acting on our certain knowledge, and with Apostolic authority, We approve, We praise, and with the support of the present letter We lend Our backing to the above-mentioned writings or exercises and to each and every thing contained therein, while We earnestly urge in the Lord that all the Faithful of both sexes, regardless of their station in the world, make use of these very edifying and uplifting Exercises."

Pope Alexander VII states: "We, who know well how profitable these Exercises are for guiding the souls of the Faithful and for placing and keeping them on the path of serving God, etc." Besides praising and recommending the Exercises, he enriched them with a plenary indulgence which he granted to all the Faithful who make these Exercises for eight days.

Clement XI recommended them and exhorted their practice and Clement XII, besides recommending the Exercises of Saint Ignatius and granting them a plenary indulgence for those who make them for ten days, excuses parish priests from the law of residence during the Exercises, and grants a privilege to Canons, Beneficiaries, and others obliged to assist at choir during the Exercises, as is stated in the Bull addressed to Prelates dated at Rome, August 30, 1732.

In the Process documents of the canonization of Saint Ignatius, the Judges of the Rota declare, "Considering the fact that these Exercises were written at a time when the favored Father (Ignatius) was un-educated and unlettered, we find ourselves forced to admit that the light whereby he wrote was not something he gained in a natural way, but in a supernatural way it was shed into his mind."

These same judges told Pope Gregory XV that the saint had written the Exercises from what he had learned from Divine instruction. For this reason Father Diego Lainez and Father Juan Polanco, noted for their holiness and great knowledge, and wise in the secrets of the saint, declared that when he was writing the Exercises, Saint Ignatius was able to say what Jesus Christ said in St. John's Gospel (7:16), ". . .My doctrine is not Mine but His that sent me;" for it was not so much the teaching of Ignatius as it was that of the Divine Wisdom, Who was his only instructor.

Also something quite comforting and proven by reliable documents, is that the Holy Virgin, as a fond Mother of Saint Ignatius and a central object of his affections, revealed that She had been Patroness and Foundress of these holy Exercises, that She helped him and was like a teacher to Saint Ignatius so that he might write as he did.

So excellent, useful, and profitable are the Exercises of Saint Ignatius, that one can say that for three centuries all the saints and men of outstanding goodness have been formed in the Exercises of Saint Ignatius, to fill the parts they have played.

In proof of this, one need do no more than read history, and there he will find a Saint Charles Borromeo, Cardinal and Archbishop of Milan, who from the retreat he made in Rome in the house of the Society of Jesus, gained that apostolic perfection that made him an example and model among higher churchmen. In the Exercises of Saint Ignatius, Saint Francis de Sales, Bishop and Prince of Geneva, learned the gift of governing and guiding souls in a gentle and sweet way to the highest perfection.

Where did Saint Philip Neri learn the way of prayer except in the Exercises of Saint Ignatius, as he himself asserted? Fashioned and perfected in the workshop of the Exercises of Saint Ignatius, were Saint Francis Xavier, Saint Francis Borgia, and the Venerable Louis of Granada, eminent member of the order of Saint Dominic on account of his good character, his learning and fine preaching; and once called the Spanish Cicero.

This can likewise be said of the Venerable Louis Blosius, that great master of mystical theology of the order of Saint Benedict; and of the venerable master, Saint John of Avila, Apostle and glory of Andalusia; of the most pious Father Louis Estrada of the Holy Cistercian order; and of the glorious and noted John Camus, Bishop of Belley, who, overjoyed at the good fruits which he felt within himself from the Exercises of Saint Ignatius, burst forth with these words:

"O book all golden, more precious than all the riches which the world holds dear! O Divine book, written with a special light from God! O book which hides within itself the manna and the best portion of Libanus, and the grain of mustard seed of the Gospel! O book which can never be valued as much as it deserves, because it can never come about that it be sufficiently praised!"

To the testimony of so many wise and holy men and of others who are omitted, one can add that of Saint Vincent de Paul, Founder of many pious and charitable institutions and organizations, in particular of the missionary clerics.

With great effectiveness he persuaded these men to often make use of these Exercises as the one means of reforming people's morals and restoring the spiritual life. In view of this, in order to carefully form his spiritual sons to be true and zealous fathers of souls, he made it a rule that they make the Exercises of Saint Ignatius.

It will not be in vain to mention here some wise and holy ladies who greatly valued the Exercises of Saint Ignatius. These ladies include Saint Teresa of Jesus, Saint Mary Magdalene de Pazzi, Lady Marina de Escobar, and others. Concerning Lady Marina, we read in her life that her mind became so enlightened from the Exercises of Saint Ignatius which she made, that very learned men believed she possessed the richest treasures of wisdom.

After the Exercises her heart was so enkindled with love for God that words cannot explain it, and so brave and willing in suffering and in pain, that for a period of thirty years she was afflicted on a bed of pain without ever being heard to complain, as she underwent very great sufferings not only with unconquerable patience, but also with a very sweet peace.

In view of the excellence of the Holy Exercises, of the advantage and profit which have always been gained from them when they were made in the right way, you will not wonder, Christian soul, at our final comment, that the little book of the Exercises of Saint Ignatius is like the grain of mustard seed which the Gospel tells us about; that it is small in appearance but great in power.

Chew well, that is, ponder well this little book as one might chew well a grain of mustard seed, and you will then experience how its sharp taste will make your eyes open, its fragrance will strengthen you, its blaze will set you on fire, and you will be astonished that in so small a volume there can be so much light and fire.

Affective Acts

(1) Admiration — Blessed be God, Who has deigned to teach men the Exercises of Saint Ignatius in this period of history, in order to make souls holy by a special method! Oh, what heroes the Exercises have produced in the Holy Catholic Church!

(2) Resolution — I resolve to make the exercises in the best way I can, and I hope to gain from them, by the Lord's help, the grace that others have gained, for I well understand that the time of the Exercises are the days of salvation. ". . .Behold, now is the acceptable time; behold, now is the day of salvation." (cf. 2 Cor. 6:2).

Third Point

Disposition and Method Needed for Making the Holy Exercises Well — It is desirable that before everything else you form the high appreciation that the task you have undertaken deserves from you. It is truly a task that not only serves the good of the soul, but serves the soul's entire and only interest. It is an undertaking that strives to put your conduct in good order, to cure the sickness of your soul, to make the good habits perfect which until now you have been practising, to influence you so that you will be growing daily in perfection, increasing each day your treasure of merit and adorned with good qualities, you can enter the kingdom of Heaven.

Now you see how this is something that cannot be of greater importance. . . What obedience, what pains, will a sick man not agree to, in order to gain lost health or correct a defect or unsightliness on his body? He keeps his mind on his business and away from foolishness, he keeps quiet, and goes on a diet, he takes his medicines, no matter how bad they taste, he undergoes operations and treatments at the hands of doctors, even when they are painful. And will you not do something just as great for the health of your soul? Imagine on these days of the Exercises that you are ill, and therefore you send for the Lord your God Who is your Doctor, Who has the care of your spiritual health, or salvation. "Salvation is of the Lord. . ." (Psalm 3:9).

Imagine that you tell Him with great earnestness, "Cure my soul, Lord, for I have sinned and have offended Thee." ("Here burn, here cut, here in this life do not spare, so that you may spare me in eternity." - Saint Augustine). Tell Him that you are ready to take all the medicines which He prescribes for you, that you are willing to suffer any operations, any cutting of bodily limbs, in order that your soul may be saved and not perish. (". . .O Lord, be Thou merciful to me, heal my soul, for I have sinned. . ." Ps. 40:5).

Again, imagine that you are a great merchant who has a large amount of business at hand that keeps you occupied. While you are making clever and shrewd transactions, you receive a telegram. In the telegram one of your agents informs you that it is necessary and urgent that you go where he is without further loss of time, for your enterprises threaten to suffer a heavy bankruptcy, and if you go promptly and work on certain transactions with which he is familiar, your enterprises will not only be saved, but you can make a large profit. What do you do about such a message? What indeed?

It is clear that you would undertake the journey at once, setting aside other affairs. You leave your parents and your wife and children, your friends and associates. You give up the conveniences and comforts of your home, your amusements, the local sights and social pastimes about your town. You give it all up, and without stopping to worry whether this is a desirable time to be away, without thinking about the risks and inconveniences of travel, you go tend to your business.

Apply the illustration. I am your agent. The telegram is the advice about the holy Exercises, and I tell you that your greatest possession and your only business is in danger of being lost, and if you arrange to come and make these Exercises with seriousness and care, not only will you deliver your soul from being lost — for eternal damnation hangs over it, menacing it — but you will also make a great profit, the greatest that can be made, which is the gaining of grace and afterwards of glory in Heaven.

What will you do about this message? What indeed? You will, we hope, set aside ten whole days and make these holy Exercises well, as you should, and in this way you will deliver your soul from eternal damnation and you will provide it with grace and the glory of Heaven.

In order to make the holy Exercises well, you

should carry out the following recommendations fully and conscientiously:

(1) Keep your attention away from other things and stay in your room, the more the better. Have the shade down, and only let that light enter which you need in order to read or write when you have to; otherwise, stay in the dark. Meditate, examine and go back over things in your mind a great deal.

When you are sick in bed, for the health of your body you do as much as this. Why not do it now for the health and salvation of your soul? The hen does it to hatch and bring life to her eggs. And will you not do it to bring life to your soul — your soul which is now lifeless and cold because of sin?

(2) Keep your eyes mortified; that is, do not peer from one side to another, nor gaze, nor read things that can turn your mind away from what it should be thinking about; and even avoid reading things, no matter how good they are, if they are not suited to your present plan.

I likewise urge that you entertain no wish to know or read the meditation that follows the one you are making. Avoid satisfying your curiosity, and mortify it. You should let your whole care be on the meditation that you are making, and on the ones that you have made up to this time — for the more you think back over them, the better; and the more you repeat them, the more fruit you will gain.

(3) Mortify your tongue; that is, do without talking. If you were seriously and gravely ill, and the doctor ordered you to keep absolutely quiet, you would do it for the health of your body. Do it, then, for the health and salvation of your soul.

Silence, silence — I urge it and order it for you;

the more, the better. Let yourself talk only with God, with Jesus Christ, with the Blessed Virgin, the angels and saints, and with your spiritual director. Your conversation must be heavenly.

But if, due to some necessity, you must say something, if you can say it in two words, do not speak three, and let your voice be low. This recommendation about silence is the hardest to fulfill, and because it is not fulfilled as it should be, many people consequently do not complete the Exercises as profitably as they should have.

Therefore I repeat to you again: silence, silence; for during this time every word you may utter, will not only be idle, for which you will one day have to render an account, but also highly dangerous, and would deprive you of many graces already prepared for you, and which you would even lose until you have received them here.

(4) Mortify your hearing, listening to no one except God alone, Who will cause you to feel His voice through inspirations, meditations, and through your spiritual director, who will advise you in everything, and will tell you how to mortify yourself in eating and drinking and other things.

(5) You will make a general confession of your whole life, or since your last general confession, or from whatever time your spiritual director tells you.

(6) If you wish to profit a great deal from these Exercises, put yourself entirely in the Hands of God, and surrender completely to Him, so that He might do whatever He wishes with you, like the mud in the hands of the bricklayer, or wood in the hands of the sculptor: In all these moments you will repeat often and with all your heart some of these ejaculations:

1) May Thy Will and not mine be done. 2) Lord, what dost Thou want me to do? 3) Lord, grant that I may know Thy Will and help me with Thy Grace to fulfill it. 4) Speak, Lord, for Thy servant is listening. 5) Lord, grant that I may know the road through which You want me to travel. 6) My God, my heart is prepared and disposed to complete fully Thy most holy Will.

(7) You will have to carefully note every illustration, inspiration, and other knowledge which God will give you, and communicate everything to your spiritual director, and then you will put into effect what he has approved. In addition, during the holy Exercises, you should write out a plan of your life to be always observed from that time onwards.

(8) Each day of the holy Exercises you will examine these points to see if you are indeed fulfilling them, since the fruits of these Exercises depend greatly on their faithful observance.

Intimate Conversation with Our Lady

My Mother Mary, Thou Who had the consolation of seeing the Apostles and disciples united in the Upper Room for the space of ten days, and finally Thou didst have the enjoyment of seeing them all filled with the Holy Ghost; I, dear Mother, have the great honor and good fortune to find myself at these holy Exercises under Thy direction, and thus I hope with complete confidence that Thou wilt obtain for me all the graces needed in order to make them well. I, on my part, am resolved to do everything possible for the greater Glory of God and for the welfare of my soul, and so, my Mother, help and protect me now and always. *Amen.*

Now pray the Our Father and the Hail Mary and the Concluding Prayers as on page xi.

Meditation 2

On The End of Man

Principle and Foundation
of all the Meditations

Notice to the reader — Before everything else, Saint Ignatius proposes for our consideration a most important truth which he calls principle and foundation. He calls it principle because just as sciences have their basic principles which are undeniable truths whence other truths are inferred, so too in the science of salvation the first truth proposed by Saint Ignatius is a principle from which one reaches conclusions and resolutions that plan a life that is good.

He also calls this truth a foundation, because just as in the construction of a building, the first thing to do is pour the cement which supports the building; similarly on this underlying basic truth is built not only the structure of the Exercises, but also the whole moral and spiritual life of the Christian who strives to save his soul.

Hence one easily discovers how important is the attentive, careful consideration of this great truth; for if a science is not understood without well-established principles, and as a building is not constructed without a firm cement foundation, neither will the Spiritual Exercises be made with lasting fruit if we do not provide and firmly lay this very solid foundation which we are going to talk about.

Let us, then, probe and penetrate it; for the more deeply we think on it and instill it into our souls, the more abundant and lasting will be the fruit we will obtain.

First Point

Preparatory Prayer as on page x

Composition of Place or first prelude — Imagine that you see God full of majesty and grandeur seated on His throne, and that you hear a voice that says: "I am the Beginning and the End." (Apoc. 22:13) You can also imagine that you see a vast ocean from which many rivers come forth and return, and that this ocean represents the goodness of God, from Whom come forth all creatures and to Whom they return, and that you are one of them, who has come from Him, and to Him you must return.

Second prelude — My God and Lord I ask Thee that Thou let me know my end, that I may seek it and attain it, and I beg that Thou give me the grace to make myself better than I am and overcome all the obstacles that can hinder me.

Foundational Principle — In the words of Saint Ignatius, "Man was created to praise, honor, and serve God our Lord, and thereby save his soul."

Explanation — What is my origin? Who is author of my being? This knowledge is so important that I cannot excuse myself from it without forsaking common sense and the religion which I profess. This knowledge guides me by the hand, as it were, to the accomplishment of my essential duties. All nature shouts to me that I owe submission, respect, obedience, acknowledgment, and love to the Author of my being.[1]

Now Who is the Author of my being? I exist. There was a time when I did not exist. Twenty, thirty,

[1] "Heaven, earth, and all things tell me to love Thee." (St. Augustine, Confessions, L. xi. c.4.)

sixty, eighty years ago, I did not exist. Where was I then? I was nothing. How have I come into the world? Who has created me? Did I give being to myself? No; for since I was nothing, I could do nothing. Was it a force called chance that formed me? No; for such a chance is a deceptive dream. Did my parents produce me out of nothing? No; they have been instruments which God has used.

But God is my Creator, not they, although I should always honor them. Ask yourself if the following is not so: The non-material, spiritual, eternal and immortal soul which you have, which makes you above all animals and almost equal to the angels, and this soul is an image of God — could anyone have made this, but God Himself? Right reason declares the answer, and faith teaches it when God states, "Let Us make man to Our image and likeness. . ." (Gen. 1:26).

The same thing is to be said of your body, which is material. Something material is changeable, and does not independently exist of its own power nor does it possess existence of itself. It possesses it from the Supreme Being, Who is God. Thus you see that you ought to raise yourself — even the less important part of you — to God as your first Principle Who created you, drew you from your parents, and keeps you in existence.

Furthermore, the complex structure of your body, the coordination and movements of the numerous parts which form its wonderful machinery, are not familiar knowledge to our parents.[2]

2 The mother of the seven Machabee children who were martyred, said to them in order to encourage them: "I know not how you were formed in my womb, for I neither gave you breath, nor soul, nor life, neither did I frame the limbs of every one of you. But the Creator of the world. . ." (2 Mach. 7: 22, 23)

God alone, Who is the First Intelligent Cause, Mover and Ruler, formed your body and preserves it whole. Indeed, preserving is continuous creating. He lets secondary causes operate, but even they would not function without the cooperation, the order, and the movement of the First Cause.

You ought, then, to be well convinced that God has given you all you have — the soul with its powers, and the body with its senses. It is He and no-one else who preserves you. Indeed if He withdrew His Almighty Hand you would at once return to the nothingness from which you came.[3]

God has given you existence and preserves by His Goodness and Mercy the existence you have.[4]

He has preferred you to others whom He could have created and will never create. He has given you the noble existence of a man, and not that of a beast, nor of a plant, nor of a stone; although you had no right to such a noble and privileged existence.

And what did He do this for? Ah, an Infinite Wisdom cannot make anything without assigning it an end that matches its greater or lesser excellence. And this holds true here. The final end for which this Immense Being drew you out of nothing is simply this: that you know Him here on earth, and that hereafter you enjoy Him eternally in Heaven.[5]

Are you persuaded about this, my soul?. . . Do you believe it? In all the moments of your past life you should have glorified and loved God, and in every

---

3 "Thy hands have made me and formed me. . .Thou hast laid Thy hand upon me." (Ps. 118,73; 118, 5)
4 ". . .I have loved thee with an everlasting love: therefore have I drawn thee, taking pity on thee." (Jer. 31:3.)
5 "I have created him for My glory. . ." (Is. 43:7.) "You have your fruit unto sanctification, and the end life everlasting." (Rom. 6:22).

moment remaining to you, you will have to serve Him, glorify and love Him. . . and why?

(1) Because the Goodness of God requires it. Imagine that you had come to the world in the same state in which you now find yourself, except that you were completely speechless, without the power to utter one word; and that today God should come down from Heaven, loose your tongue and give you speech, adding at the same time, this command: "In recognition of the kindness I have shown you, you shall not utter a word except what is in My Honor."

Could anything ever be more proper than that a tongue, to which God has given the power of speech, should praise Him?. . . Now look at yourself, and tell me, do you find any part of your body, no matter how small, which you have not received from God? Is there in you some power which He Himself has not given you?[6]

Is it not, then, very just that God be loved by that heart which you have received from Him, and that those hands which He has fashioned be engaged in working for God?

(2) Because God's supreme Ownership calls for it. It is He Who created you and brought you out of nothingness. One who plants a garden gains an ownership of the garden and is owner of all its fruits. A person who chooses to take a single apple against that owner's will, would commit a theft and an injustice.

God has created you and is your owner, and of all there is in you, so that every affection which is not directed to Him, every word that is not to His praise, every deed that is not done for love of Him, is a theft and an injustice.

6 "What hast thou that thou hast not received?. . ." (1 Cor. 4:7.)

Do you understand now, oh! my soul, how right it is that you serve God and that you honor and love Him with all your heart? How have you complied with this obligation? A master receives a bad service in two ways: First, by our loafing and utterly neglecting the duties we owe to him as master, or by our doing them carelessly. Second, by your doing things with evil intent so that the master is offended. Up to now how have you served your God and Lord? What does your heart say?

Affective Acts

(1) Confession — Oh my God! I am well aware of the disorders of my life so far. My only goal and pursuit should have been to love Thee, to serve Thee, and to glorify Thee with all my heart. I should never have used one moment, nor uttered one word, nor performed any work, except for Thy Honor and Glory. . . But, how have I behaved?

How many thousands of hours there have been in my life, how many thousands of words my lips have uttered, thousands of deeds my hands have performed, and to what purpose have they been directed? Oh, how many times it has been to creatures, and how few times to Thee, oh my God!. . . But that is not so important as this; How many days have passed in which I have not committed new outrages and new offenses against Thee? What a wretch I am! How neglectful, how ungrateful and how perverse I have been, Lord!. . .

(2) Act of sorrow — I cannot do more, oh! my God, except implore Thy Infinite Mercy, humbly asking for forgiveness. I detest and abhor with all my heart and all the powers of my soul, as much as I can,

all the moments that I have not used for Thy Honor and Glory ... Oh, if I could recover as many precious hours as I have wasted and used badly! Pardon, Lord, pardon; already I am weighed down by my sins. Have mercy, my God and my Father.

Second Point

Nothing is more profitable than living for the Last End by serving, glorifying and loving God with one's whole heart.

The Final End for which God has created you has not been merely that you serve Him and love Him solely for His glory, but also that you gain eternal blessedness and come to enjoy it in the next life. By serving God you will, after a while, go to enjoy Him in Heaven. This is as sure as it is that you are now alive on earth. Pause here a bit, my soul, to reflect on the benefits that await you.

(1) In Heaven there is an immense blessing for the soul. To comprehend fully the blessing that the soul will enjoy in Heaven is as impossible as it is to swallow the ocean. The only idea that in any way lets us understand its greatness is this: As God is an Infinite Being, His Blessedness must be, as a consequence, infinite; for an inferior blessedness cannot match an Infinite Being.

Oh, what a marvellous fact! God's Blessedness, His happiness, is infinite, and this very same happiness is your last End. God wants you to enjoy the same object of happiness by which He is happy and the same delights that He enjoys.

(2) In Heaven there is a blessing beyond measure for the body. — The soul cannot serve God in the things He commands it, in His holy law, unless it has

cooperation from the body. Just then, as the soul will gain blessedness, the body will likewise gain the same favor. Now what will this happy state be for the body and how great will it be?

Faith tells us this much: It will be of such a nature and such greatness that eye has not seen nor ear ever heard the like, nor can any imagination ever picture it nor any mind comprehend it. To put it in a few words, God engages all His Almighty power in order to make the body happy in all its senses.

(3) In Heaven the blessedness of both body and soul are eternal. Oh how empty is all the glamor and pleasure of earth! A hundred years ago there were kings and queens; and millions of their citizens humbly bent their knee to acknowledge the royal authority. Everyone was awed at the splendor of these rulers, and their power made kingdoms tremble.

Where are these rulers now? They have rotted under the ground. Their bones have changed into dust, and this dust is now trampled underfoot. Likewise today on earth are kings and queens who are honored like gods. But let a century pass, and what will be left of them?

Nothing more than a heap of dust that wind will scatter. . . The kingdom that awaits you is of a very different kind. Everything in it is everlasting. That infinitely delightful enjoyment of the Holy Trinity is eternal. Those sweet exchanges with Jesus Christ are eternal. That tender love and close friendship with the Mother of God and with the other saints and angels is eternal. The beauty of paradise is eternal.

That overflowing measure of joy that engages all the powers of the soul is eternal. That river of delight that floods all the senses of the body, is eternal. Everything there is without any lessening, without change, without interruption, without end — eternal, eternal...

Affective Acts

(1) O God! O Infinite Goodness! How consoling this truth is to me! Heaven is my homeland! Heaven is my inheritance! Heaven is my reward! It is my last end. Yes, it is really true. God has made it for me. If I serve Him and love Him, a day will come when I will shine with a loveliness greater than that of the sun and moon, when I will behold paradise with my own eyes, when I can embrace my beloved Jesus, and when my body and soul will be plunged into a sea of delight.

Oh happy day! Can I expect this? Indeed I do expect this, and I expect it with assurance. Jesus Himself has promised it to me. For all this, it is enough that I keep His law, that I act according to the end of my creation.[7]

(2) Detachment from temporal things — If Heaven is mine, then how is it that I do not make light of this world and all that this world can give?.. Why do I get upset and make myself sad because of the aches and pains of my body, if a day will come when my body will have nothing but pure delights for all eternity? Why do I feel so badly when men treat me as of no account, if for all eternity I am to be loved and honored by God and all the saints?.. Oh how blind I have been up to now. O my God, in

---

7 "...If thou wilt enter into life, keep the commandments." (Matt. 19:17). ...Fear God, and keep His commandments: because for man everything depends on this." (Eccles. 12:13.)

27

valuing so highly the vile goods of this world!.. From now on I choose and resolve to treat the things of this world as of no account, and to love what belongs to eternity and Heaven.

Third Point

Nothing can be more necessary than to hope and strive for the last end by loving, serving and glorifying God with all our heart. Here is a fact, O my soul: In creating you, God's goal was His honor and glory, and He ought to obtain it and unfailingly will obtain this goal of His. This is as certain as it is that God is God. Therefore consider and reflect.

(1) God is infinite Goodness and infinite Justice — O my soul, let these truths sink deeply into your heart. As God is infinite Goodness, it is absolutely certain that He must love and reward eternally all those who have glorified Him, served Him, and loved Him. And as He is infinite Justice, it is impossible that He not hate and punish eternally all those who treat Him disrespectfully. Have you understood these truths well? Let us proceed further.

(2) As God is infinite Goodness, He has created paradise; and as He is infinite Justice, He has created hell. In paradise God will love and reward forever the souls that have been faithful, and they, in return, will praise and bless Him forever. In hell, He will oppose and punish forever the unfaithful souls, and they will curse and blaspheme Him forever. In paradise, His Infinite Goodness and Mercy will be praised for all eternity; in hell, His Majesty will be upheld and His Justice fulfilled. . . What is the consequence of this? The consequence is. . .

(3) God always and unfailingly will achieve His

28

goal. Very well, then, regardless of what you do, it will always turn out that you will serve God's glory. If you serve Him and love God on earth, you will love and praise His Mercy forever in Heaven. If you do not serve Him on earth, you will forever glorify His Justice in hell.

It equally honors a Lord of infinite Majesty, namely God, to reward for all eternity His faithful servants, as well as to punish forever those who rebel. Now picture to yourself, O my soul, on one side Heaven opened and those immense joys that the saved experience there, and on the other side, picture hell with the immense torments which the damned suffer there; and say within yourself: I must of necessity glorify God for all eternity; this is His decree, and it is as impossible for it to be cancelled or changed as it is for God to cease to be God.

Oh frightening truth! One of these two things will come upon me: either I will live forever in Heaven, or I will live forever in hell; — for we understand that in the other world all is eternal (after Purgatory). This soul of mine will praise or blaspheme, will love God or hate God forever, for it is eternal. My body will be forever plunged in heavenly delights or it will wail in the torments of hell; for it will also be eternal. These hands of mine will embrace Jesus as I please forever, or they will be bound with the chains of hell; for they are eternal.

My eyes will contemplate forever the resplendent bodies of Heaven's citizens, or will forever see the horrifying phantoms of hell; for they will be eternal. My flesh and all senses of my body will forever have a matchless happiness, or will forever burn in fire, and in the midst of flames; for all these things are eternal. What an awesome and frightening affair, but certainly real! What is my choice to be? It is for me to choose to follow the one or the other. One of the two is to be my lot for eternity, and it will be what I myself pick.

Affective Acts

(1) Fear — What a serious affair, O my God! Shall I go to Heaven or to hell? What a frightening question, which makes my heart pound! Will I go to paradise? I cannot know if that will be my fortune, but I know Thou hast said, "He that loveth his life (in this world) shall lose it; and he that hateth his life in this world, keepeth it unto life eternal." (John 12:25).

These are Thy words. To love one's life in this world means to surrender oneself to bodily pleasure and sin, to obey one's self-will, to run away (from duty) in order to escape contempt, to hold bitter resentment against people who offend us. To hate one's life means to practise (dutiful) mortification generously, to deny one's self-will, to hunt contempt (when to do so is in accord with duty,)[8] to return good for evil. Have I done this? Alas for me!

Alas! Jesus' lips condemn me! Have I failed to be counted among those who hate their own life?

(2) Resolution — And how much, my God, I have failed! If an endless and happy eternity depends on gaining my End, and an unhappy eternity comes from losing it, how is it possible for me to be so negative about pursuing it? If it were necessary, should I not gladly sacrifice my life this minute to

8. This is to be taken in the sense explained by St. John of the Cross in Ascent, Bk. 1, 13.

gain Heaven? Should I not shed all my blood in a moment to escape hell? Yes, gaining an infinite Good, avoiding an infinite evil — these are two objectives for which one can never do too much or put up with too much.

In the presence of Thy Divine Majesty, I now resolve to go about pursuing my Last End at all costs, O my God! And in order to safely gain it I also resolve to faithfully follow everything in these holy Spiritual Exercises which I recognize to be needful and profitable for success.

(3) Prayer of Petition — How many times have I made these resolutions, and later been unfaithful and failed to fulfill them? I realize well that if Thou dost not help me by giving me greater strength, I am lost. I turn to Thee, O my God, and with a heart contrite and humbled I cry: Forgive me, O Supreme Good! Forgive my sins and neglects! Look not on my lack of merit, but on Thy Mercy, and deal not according to the rigor of Thy Infinite Justice, but according to the kindness of Thy Infinite Mercy.

Grant me new lights that enable me to clearly understand the importance of my End, new promptings that deeply move my heart. Grant me new graces that make me constant in my (right) resolves. How would the creation of me profit me, O my God, if I perish forever? How would Thy shedding Thy Blood for me help me, O Son of God, if I am lost? How would my having become an heir by grace benefit me, O Divine Spirit, if I am damned?

Now pray the Our Father and the Hail Mary and the Concluding Prayers as on page xi.

Meditation 3

Concerning Indifference to Created Things

Preparatory Prayer as on page x

First Prelude

Composition of Place — "Imagine you see God in His majesty and greatness seated on a throne, and that you hear a voice which says: I AM THE BE-GINNING AND THE END (Apoc. 22:13). Like-wise you can picture an immense sea from which many rivers flow and into which all the rivers return. This sea represents God's goodness, from which all creatures come, and they return to Him. You are one of these creatures which has come from God and you must return to Him."

Second Prelude

My God and Lord, I beg Thee to give me grace to behave always with a holy indifference regarding objects of our senses, and to select and prefer only what better serves Thy honor and glory and the salvation of my soul. Amen.

Words of Saint Ignatius: "Other things on earth were made for man's sake and to help him in pursu-ing the end for which he was created."

"Thou hast subjected all things under his feet. . ." (Psalm 8:8) They are like a step-ladder, like rungs for climbing. God put them under our feet, and man has placed them higher than his heart and above shoulders and head, and they cause his downfall.

(Continuing with Saint Ignatius): "Consequently

one should use them to the extent that they help him reach his end, and he should withdraw from them to the extent that they hinder him in that pursuit. One must become indifferent to everything created wherever a scope of free will is allowed and is not prohibited; so that for our part we no more want health rather than sickness, riches rather than poverty, honor rather than the experience of being dishonorable, a long life rather than a short one — and so in all other things, desiring only and choosing only what better leads to the end for which we were created."

Explanation — One who fails to attain his last End, loses it either because he is very attached to certain things of the world, or because he hates other things too much. I say attached — referring to comforts, satisfactions of the body, good things of life, riches, the honor and esteem of men. Such things attract us to pursue them, even by offending God, so that one loses his last End.

The loathing refers to discomforts, troubles, pains, poverty, suffering of contempt, abuse, sickness, death. These cause a man sadness and dread, and also get him to turn from God and thus fail to attain his last End.

My soul, as you want to play safe about your last End, you must put your heart in a condition of proper balance and indifference, so that you are always prompt and ready to get rid of even the best liked things, whenever they serve to obstruct your reaching your last End, and when things help you gain it, you must always be prompt and ready to embrace them, even things most arduous and distasteful.

First Point

The supreme ownership God has over me calls for this total indifference of heart toward all things that are not of God — Your end, O my soul, on this earth is nothing else than that you love and serve God with perfection. But to so love and serve Him, is nothing else than to fulfill the Divine Will with perfection. Indeed this is true, my soul; to love and serve God perfectly is no more than to perfectly fulfill His Will. Now this cannot be accomplished unless you are ready and willing with complete indifference and proper balance to have health or sickness, honor or contempt, riches or poverty. Weigh this truth well.

(1) It is not your business to determine the way of serving God. It belongs to His Divine Majesty to determine that. It is your business to serve Him according to His wishes, not according to your own. He is Master and you are servant. It belongs to the Master to command, to the servant to obey. Even in Heaven this order is observed.

Among the angels some are always before God's throne praising Him, adoring Him, and blessing Him. Others hover about the earth as guardians of men. This angel is assigned to a powerful king, that one to a poor laborer. Each one serves God the way he is commanded. Will God perhaps have less authority on earth than He has in Heaven? When you have grasped this truth well, let us take a step further.

(2) God's ownership is without limits. He has authority to order this or that way of serving Him, as suits Him best. He is your God and you are His creature. Who will have the boldness or even the

ability to limit His Power? A potter follows his own wishes in disposing of the vessel he has made. Is it not right for God to be able to dispose of the man that is His creature, just as a potter disposes of his vessel?

God has an owner's right to put one in the state that suits His Divine Majesty best; and wherever He may put you, you are bound to honor, serve and love Him.

(3) Serving God as His Majesty wishes is simply to love Him and serve Him with perfection, and as a result attain our last End. Everything else is wasted business. If some duty or office has been assigned to you, you ought to fulfill your obligation with care and love for God, and not turn aside to other cares. This is serving God according to His Will.

If your inner self is all wrapped up in darkness, in temptation, in affliction, in desolation, it is necessary for you to adjust yourself to this arrangement of Providence and do so out of love for God. This is serving Him according to His pleasure. If the world hates you, criticizes you, insults you with abuses, suffer it in silence out of love for God. That is serving Him as He wishes. The more you part from this way of life, the more you part from your last End.

Affective Acts

(1) Acknowledge God's supreme dominion — It is true, O Sovereign Good! Thou art my God and my supreme Lord. Thy role is to command, and mine is to obey. I am obliged to serve Thee, but in the way that pleases Thee. I acknowledge Thy supreme ownership and I adore it profoundly. Alas for the self-willed servant! To choose to serve God according to

our impulses and not as He wants to be served, is treating God as the servant and wanting to be His master. What reward might one expect for a disorder of this kind? Or rather, what punishment should one not expect and fear?

(2) Repentance — How is it possible, O Infinite One, that there should be a single person who strives to serve Thee and love Thee according to his own wishes and not according to Yours? Sad to say, there are many, many such fools, and I see that I am obliged to admit with shame that up to now I have been one of them. I want to love Thee and serve Thee with health, by no means with sickness.

I wish to serve Thee and love Thee, but just when I am loved and honored, not ever in the midst of experiencing contempt, insults and persecutions. I want to serve Thee and love Thee, but as long as things go my way and tender feelings of devotion delight my heart; but not in any state of darkness, desolation, or trial. Is this serving and loving God as His Majesty wishes? Ah! What sad shape I am in! What have I been doing?

Second Point

God's Providence demands that I have a heart of holy indifference — As it is arduous and difficult to gain one's last End without complete and holy indifference, it is likewise so much the easier to gain this End with it. To thoroughly convince yourself of this, weigh this truth:

(1) God is Infinite Wisdom and Knowledge. He knows and understands the means that lead with all security to the attainment of your last End. There are all kinds of means serviceable for the gaining of your last End — health and sickness, honor and dishonor, an honored calling and a lowly occupation — provided they are put to good use.

Now if you know the answer, tell me: What will lead you most securely to your last End? Is it the enjoyment of robust health, or is it a sickly condition? Is it a state of being honored and loved, or one of being insulted and hated? Is it holding a high post, or having a humble employment? This is something you do not know, nor do I, nor does anybody else in the world. All those things are mysteries that no perception can penetrate except only the perception of Him Who is Almighty.

(2) God is Infinite Love, Who always arranges for souls the surest means for reaching their last End — surest, provided they always keep themselves in this holy indifference and proper balance. God deals with souls as a mother who fondly loves her tender child.

As a true mother is incapable of giving poison to her beloved child, even more so is God incapable of providing anything harmful for a soul that surrenders itself to Him with indifference. O my soul, become for once fully convinced that if God visits you with illness, that is the surest way then for leading you to reach your last End; when He allows you to be despised and belittled, when He places you in darkness, in desolation, in trials, that is the surest way for you to advance to your last End.

(3) God is Infinite Power, and He leads infallibly to its last End the soul constant in holy indifference and proper balance. And who will be so bold and so daring that he can put an obstacle before God?

Neither an angel, nor a man, nor Heaven, nor earth, nor all hell can fight against Infinite Power.

You alone, O my soul, you alone can obstruct and can defeat His loving designs by withdrawing from the order He has arranged concerning you by your turning away from holy indifference. But if you stay firm in it, it is as certain that you will reach your last End as it is certain that God is a God of Infinite Love, of Infinite Wisdom and of Infinite Power.

God is your Father Who loves you from eternity. A father naturally loves his son; but though he loves him and desires every benefit for him, he does not know what is most suitable; and if he does know this, he cannot always do what he wants and what he knows would benefit his son. But God, Who is such a loving Father, has the wish, the knowledge and the power to do what is best suited for you. And will you fail to conform yourself? Will you resist? Will you murmur? Will you complain to His Fatherly Providence?

Affective Acts

(1) Confidence — Oh, how consoling is this truth! He Who rules over me is Infinite Wisdom, Who knows and understands the means that are most suitable for me. He Who guides me is Infinite Power, and there is no one who can push me down if He holds me up and strengthens. He Who loves me is Infinite Love, Who from hour to hour provides the means best for me. With this knowledge, can I admit any mistrust into my heart?

Let that never happen, O my God. I surrender myself completely to Thy Fatherly Providence; and fully confident, I make this assertion: Thou seekest me for Thy company in Paradise, and wish me to be in a high rank of glory. Thy goodness is so great as to wish all this for me and so I also hope for the same thing. Thou art my Father and Thy Love will lead me to that wonderful happiness.

(2) Self-doubt — But how can I hope for something so wonderful? No one can get an assurance that he will gain something so wonderful, so great, except the souls which serve and love God as He wishes and who walk in His presence with perfect and holy indifference. Am I one such soul?

Oh how far removed from me is such a good disposition! What joy do I not show amid praises and honor, amid prosperity and riches! What sadness do I not feel when I suffer contempt, poverty, and misery! How much satisfaction my heart gets in time of tender devotion and consolations! With what pleasure does it carry out what is commanded, if it is according to my wish and inclination; and with what displeasure, if it is what I do not like!

Is this perhaps that holy indifference which is required for perfect love? O Jesus, have pity on me! A heart so poorly disposed is not capable of loving Thee, and one can say that the first stone of the building of holiness and salvation has not yet been laid. . .

Third Point

Divine Justice calls for holy indifference and a proper balance in my heart — If you, O my soul, do not submit to the provision of Divine Providence, and if you do not embrace in humble submission the means that Providence keeps providing for your last End, you will fall into the hands of Divine Justice.

And what will be the result? A heap of misfortunes for which you cannot weep enough. Reflect well on this and what follows.

(1) It is quite certain that such a soul must of necessity suffer in this world much more than another soul. You greatly deceive yourself, my soul, if you imagine you can escape the troubles which God's Love holds in store for you as means to your last End. You will never be able to. You will suffer, and you will necessarily have to suffer the pains and ailments, the contempt and other mistreatment which from eternity God has assigned for you to suffer.

"You will either fulfill what God wants, or you will suffer what you do not want." - Saint Augustine.

If you maintain an indifferent heart and bear everything with patience, you will give God pleasure and He will fortify you with an inflow of His graces. He will give you a continual peace and calm and will make the way of the cross something easy and sweet for you. If you neglect this holy indifference and bear troubles impatiently, you will displease God and He will deny you all His strengthening, supporting help and every kind of peace and consolation, letting you fall under the weight of your cross.

(2) It is very certain that for all eternity you will lose that high degree of glory unless you adopt the means God has appointed. If your heart is not indifferent and you do not use such means, adopting them willingly, you will weary yourself in vain and will lose your last End. It is certain that you are in danger of not gaining your eternal salvation, not even a lower grade of glory.

A soul that has not this holy indifference, falls out

of (moral) necessity into many grave temptations. In such circumstances, who is not drawn downward by anger, by resentment, by faintheartedness and melancholy, by pride and fear of contempt? And who is not moved by impulsiveness and self-will, by interior upsets and disorder, and by the rebellion of uncontrolled passions?

Ah, to overcome these problems requires a particular help of God. Now will He give it to a soul unwilling to submit to His plans, to a soul who, full of anger, rejects the means which God had provided, a soul unwilling to serve except in its own way, unwilling to acknowledge Him as Master and Lord, and who insolently resists God's designs? Let a man place his hopes in the One Whom he can trust, for the struggle is quite dangerous.

Affective Acts

(1) Humiliation — O Sovereign Good, my God and my Lord! How many faults I find in my soul at this hour! What blindness there is in my thinking! What disorder in my will! I regard pains and ailments as the greatest of evils, and Thou valuest them as most effective means for my sanctification. When I'm treated with contempt I count it to be the worst thing in the world, and Thou dost rate it as the best means for my exaltation in Heaven.

I call desolation and trial my ruin; and Thou sayest that they are to fashion the greatest part of my glory in paradise. So it is: My judgment has deceived me and the blindness of my intellect has reached this extreme. ("I have gone astray like a sheep that is lost. Seek thy servant. . ." Psalm 118: 176). But alas! My misery does not end here; for the blindness of my intellect matches the corruption of my will.

Concupiscence, comfort, honor, esteem from creatures, sweet peace and tranquility of heart, obedience agreeing with my wishes — these are the only things to which I am inclined. Everything else repels and frightens me. I'm always stretching out both hands to poison, and withdrawing from the medicine that could cure me.

(2) Resolution — What is the remedy for this? I have learned two things today, O my God. The first is that it is necessary to serve Thee and love Thee in the way Thou dost desire, not in the way I wish. The second is that I cannot serve Thee nor love Thee that way if I have an indifferent heart and if I do not make use of the means that Thou assigns to me. Without those means, I cannot serve Thee nor love Thee, nor become holy, nor be saved.

Considering how true this is, I surrender at this moment before Thy Divine Majesty, my fondness for the creatures I like, as well as my distaste for what I do not like. Honor and contempt, health and sickness, consolation and grief, this or that occupation — these will be indifferent matters for me.

Let nature groan and complain as much as it wishes, grace is to win from now on. This, then, is my resolve, O my God and Lord. I choose to serve Thee and love Thee in the way Thou dost will, not in the way I like. This is the way I will employ the days, the hours, and all the minutes that remain in my life.

(3) Prayer for grace — Oh how fortunate is the soul with these dispositions! It has the basis of holiness; it has in fact the true essence of it, which

is perfect charity. It is travelling the right way that leads to union with God. Oh, who will preserve me in this state? Not I, O my Jesus! I cannot do so much! My weakness is too great. My fickleness is too deep-rooted. Only Thy Almighty Power can remedy my misery and keep me upright.

I turn the most ardent sighs of my heart to Thee, O my Jesus! Take from me all desire and love for those creatures that just appeal to my selfishness. Rid me of all fear and opposition to what displeases my selfish temper. Put me in a state of total holy indifference, and grant that I will desire nothing but to please Thee, and fear nothing but Thy displeasure, O Jesus. O Father of mercies! Assist me with Thy powerful grace.

Now pray the Our Father and the Hail Mary and the Concluding Prayers as on page xi.

Meditation 4

The Sin of the Angels and of Our First Parents, Adam and Eve

Preparatory Prayer as on page x

Commentary — After a consideration of our End, Saint Ignatius puts before our minds the malice of mortal sin, so that we will flee from it as from the sight of a serpent, since sin is the only thing that can prevent us from reaching our last end.*

First Prelude

Composition of Place — Imagine you see the Eternal Father seated on His throne of majesty and grandeur, Who, as Judge, passes sentence against the rebellious angels, against Adam and Eve, and against Jesus Christ, His Son, Who has assumed the figure of the sinner. Imagine that one of the angels who stand before the Lord's throne approaches you and says, "Know and understand how evil and bitter it is to have offended your God." (". . .Know thou, and see that it is an evil and a bitter thing for thee, to have left the Lord thy God" Jer. 2:19.)

Second Prelude

Petition — My God and Lord, I beg light and grace to know the malice of sin, to grieve at the faults I have committed, and to firmly resolve to die rather than sin again.

*NOTE — The meditation on the malice of sin is the first reflection that is structured upon the foundation described in Meditation 2. During the days of the meditations of Sections I — i.e., Meditations 1 through 9 — one will read in his free time on the need and advantage of general confession and will make an examination of conscience.

44

First Point

Words of Saint Ignatius — "The first point will be to recall to memory the first sin, which was that of the angels, then to apply the understanding by considering this sin in detail, then the will by seeking to remember and understand all, so that I may be the more ashamed and confounded when I compare the one sin of the angels with the many that I have committed. Since they went to hell for one sin, how many times have I deserved it for my many sins. I will recall to mind the sin of the angels, remembering that they were created in the state of grace, that they refused to make use of their freedom to offer reverence and obedience to their Creator and Lord, and so sinning through pride, they fell from grace into sin and were cast from Heaven into hell. In like manner my understanding is to be used to reason more in detail on the subject matter, and thereby move more deeply my affections through the use of the will."*

Explanation — From the punishment given the angels, one can gather the infinite malice of sin. Turn back a little in your thoughts, O my soul, to those marvelous times when God created Heaven and peopled it with angels. Who could ever imagine a happiness greater than what was given those spirits? So remarkable was their beauty that no man could have gazed at it without being overcome with joy. So astonishing was their wisdom that compared to it, Solomon's could be called pure and genuine ignorance. Their essential blessedness was such that they were not capable of suffering any pain. Their

*NOTE — Tr. Anthony Mottola, p. 55 of *The Spiritual Exercises of St. Ignatius;* Garden City, N.Y.: 1964.

dwelling was as lovely as a paradise could be. In spite of the greatness of their gifts of nature, their gifts of grace were too great to compare. They had a very perfect knowledge of God; a most ardent charity was infused into them; and their friendship and union with God was very intimate. Also they had a certain promise that after a few moments they were to enter into His glory to enjoy it forever.

Then all at once some angels abused this great kindness. They were unwilling to serve God in the way His Majesty wanted. They sinned, and received punishment. (". . . I will be like the most High." Isaias 14:14.)

Reflect, now, with all the powers of your mind, on the circumstances of this punishment.

(1) This punishment deprived them of all good. — These very unfortunate angels were transformed in a moment from the extremely beautiful spirits which they were, into horrible demons. From preferred sons of God they became objects of everlasting hatred and were cast like a lightening bolt from the height of Heaven to the depths of hell-fire. (". . . I saw satan like lightning falling from Heaven." Luke 10:18.)

(2) This punishment was the sum-total of all possible misfortunes — In their memory there remained the very distressing recollection of the past. In their minds was extreme storminess. In their wills was supreme despair; and very painful flames afflicted all their powers of perception.

(3) This punishment was without a remedy. — More than four thousand years had passed in which these miserable spirits burned in these flames, when Jesus Christ came into the world to destroy sin. But

of what help was His coming to them? That merciful Jesus, Who shed so many tears over wicked Jerusalem, shed not one tear for them. That loving Jesus, Who gave all His Blood for His treacherous enemies, offered not a drop to His Eternal Father for them. It took but a single moment to commit the sin, but the punishment will last for all eternity.

Pause here a little while, my soul, and go in thought down into that prison of fire. Picture to yourself the misery of those condemned spirits. Observe what a horrible, terrifying appearance it has, which no mortal man could gaze upon without dying of fright. Their dwelling place is a dreadful prison, confined and blazing all around with fire. The torments which they suffer are so very painful that no mind can grasp it. After you have observed these things, ponder with me as follows:

These monsters were once very beautiful spirits, very dear sons of the Most High God, masterpieces of the Divine, Almighty Power, first occupants and very beautifying sights in the heavenly mansion. What evil have they done, to have fallen into such great misfortune? All their guilt comes down to a single thought, consented to in an instant, a single act of disobedience, one single sin. For this single sin they have been burning for at least six thousand years, and will burn for all eternity. And who is it Who has pronounced this horrifying sentence against them? God. O awesome truth! It is God! We must say, then, either that God is not Infinite Wisdom, Infinite Justice, Infinite Mercy, or that sin is truly an infinite evil. The first is unthinkable. Therefore we must admit the second and declare that sin is an infinite evil.

Affective Acts

(1) Admiration — O my God, I know not which I should marvel at more, the strict justice with which Thou treated the rebellious angels, or the greatness of the mercy Thou hast shown me. Those very noble spirits, those beautiful likenesses of Thy Divinity, committed a single sin, and for this sin alone they were damned for all eternity. I, who am a heap of dirt and dust, have committed many sins. And Thou hast borne up with me!. . . I have abused Thy Mercy, and after I had been pardoned for earlier sins, I committed others. And Thou forgavest me again. Even now at this very moment Thou dost look on me with fatherly eyes and stretch out to me the arms of Thy mercy. O sovereign spirits, O blessed souls who are in Heaven, cast a glance down on me and in me you will see as many evidences of God's mercy and long suffering as there are sins which I have committed. Ah! Supply for me what I ought to do, but cannot. Praise and bless God, for He is good, and great is the mercy He has had for me.

(2) Repentance — This mercy is what fills my heart with grief. I have offended a God Who has loved me more than so many thousands of millions of very noble spirits, a God Who, at the very time I committed the greatest offenses, clasped me to the bosom of His Mercy; a God Who, in spite of my sins, wants to love me for all eternity. And I, an ungrateful person, how could I make light of such great love and offend such great kindness? How can I now remember such malice without breaking down into sad, bitter tears? O my Jesus, I recognize and admit my sins. I am repentant and hate them all.

Second Point

Words of Saint Ignatius — "The second point is to use the three powers of the soul to consider the sin of Adam and Eve. Call to mind how they did such long penance for their sin and what corruption fell on the human race, causing so many to go to hell. Call to mind the second sin, that of our first parents. Recall that after Adam had been created in the Plain of Damascus and placed in the earthly paradise, and Eve had been formed from his rib, they were forbidden to eat the fruit of the Tree of Knowledge, and eating it, they committed sin. After their sin, clothed in garments of skin and cast out of paradise, without the original justice which they had lost, they lived all their lives in much travail and much penance.

"The understanding is likewise to be used in considering the subject matter in greater detail and the will is to be employed as already explained." (Tr. Anthony Mottola, pp. 55-56, op. cit.)

Explanation — Perceive the infinite malice of sin from the punishment imposed on our first parents. Never in the world has a happiness been seen like that in which God created our first parents.

(1) How pleasant their dwelling place was, this earthly paradise! It was not subject to cold, nor to hot, nor rainy nor windy weather, but there was the continuous, peaceful enjoyment of the sight of the sun. Needing no one's toil, some trees of themselves bore excellent fruit, vines bore tasty grapes, and the soil yielded wonderful sprouts of plants and flowers.

(2) How perfect their dominion was over the animals! At first call, birds would descend from the sky and show them their dependence. At a word,

animals would run up and halting at their feet, would give them proof of their obedience. At a signal, fish would come swimming through the water to the bank and show their joy.*

(3) How marvelous was the condition of their body! It was not subject to exhaustion, nor weariness, nor pain, nor sickness, nor old age, nor even death. In order to always keep the flower of youth, it was enough that they eat fruits from the Tree of Life.

(4) How wonderful was the good condition of their soul! It had perfect control over all the passions. No melancholy, nor envy, nor hatred, nor any other disorderly movement dared rise up against reason. Their soul was endowed with a plentiful knowledge of God, a very ardent love for Him, a tender fondness for His Divine Majesty.

Finally, a promise had been made to our first parents that after a long and happy life, without first undergoing sickness or death, they would be transported body and soul into Heaven, to reign there forever with God. But if God's generosity to our first parents was enormous, no less was their monstrous ingratitude towards Him. They were unwilling to serve Him in the way He wanted to be served. They sinned and received the punishment. Reflect now on the circumstances of this punishment, and the seriousness of the sin in their case.

(1) For this single sin, Adam was left deprived of all happiness. The ground is under a curse. Henceforth it would produce nothing else but thorns and

*NOTE — We have seen these teachings in the Roman Catechism of the Council of Trent and in writings of the Holy Fathers. Original sources cited for them were certain profound passages of Scripture and continuous and persistent tradition. — Translator.

thistles. The human body is under a curse and condemned to pain, sickness and death, and as God's enemy, is in this valley of tears as a place of exile from paradise.

(2) For this single sin, all of Adam's descendants are condemned alike to these misfortunes. Imagine a piece of land, for instance (let us say) one league square and completely piled about half a league high with corpses, and say to yourself: All these thousands of millions of men had to undergo death for this single sin.

(3) For this single sin all infants who die without baptism are deprived of paradise for all eternity. Let us suppose that every year in all the world ten million infants die. This would be saying that from the time of Jesus Christ's birth, probably over eighteen thousand million have died. All these are kept out of Heaven for this single sin.

(4) For this single sin, a majority of adults are damned for all eternity. Everyone who is damned is damned on account of the uncontrolled passions of his heart which draw him to sin. This vehemence of his bad inclinations is a punishment of that disobedience which our first parents committed. . . Here is something more frightful: If, by an impossibility, the world were to last forever in the present state, every year for all eternity millions of men would fall into the fire of hell on account of this single sin.

(5) For this sin Jesus died on the Cross. Oh, amazing miracle! The Supreme Lord of Heaven and earth, Who by essence is Holiness, and is the Only-Begotten Son of God, was condemned by His own Father to the disgraceful death of the Cross! And this was on account of that sin.

51

(6) In spite of this death, the Heavenly Father continues to punish us poor men for that sin.*

Thus, having lost paradise, we are pilgrims in a valley of tears with life plentiful in bitter things, with death full of anguish and terror and eternal salvation in doubt, and no other way to enter Heaven except a way of penance and tears.**

Affective Acts

(1) Fear — O Holy Faith, how amazing are the truths you bring to my view! The most beautiful angels are cast down to hell! The whole human race is exiled from Heaven! Millions of souls are condemned to hell! Jesus, Son of God, has died on a Cross, and so died by the Will of His Eternal Father! And all this on account of one thing, namely, sin! O sin, how great is the evil hidden within you! If the

*TRANSLATOR'S NOTE — Four points in the Traditional Patristic teaching will answer in advance certain difficulties:

1. Sin is truly so terrible as to deserve all these unhappy consequences, and one doubting this while appreciating the good authority for it, would not have this doubt if he appreciated how terrible sin is.

2. In casting aside God's friendship, Adam lost all title to further protection from Providence and God would have been justified in damning him at once. If God had, we would not be here. But God gave him another chance, and us a chance to exist, on condition that we be earmarked to share with Christ in a reparation wherein, if we would cooperate, we would be rewarded a hundredfold in this life and the next.

3. God does none of this haphazardly but in all things follows principles of wisdom and fitness, which our glimpses often recognize to be beautiful, though their depths stay beyond our grasp.

4. This fitness demands that children inconvenience themselves to practise gratitude to their parents as instruments of their existence which they would not otherwise have. In so inconveniencing ourselves by suffering for Original Sin, we will be rewarded by God many times over and see ourselves obliged to praise God for His goodness. . .

**In Meditation 16, Saint Anthony will develop the sweetness of patiently, willingly bearing one's appointed share of reparation in company with Christ.

Eternal Father dealt in such a severe way with His beloved, only-begotten Son on account of sin, with how much rigor will He deal with me, who has committed so many sins? — with me, who, after receiving pardon, has fallen back into sin so many times?

(2) Repentance — I see very well, O my God, that there can be no other way open for me except Thy Infinite Mercy on Thy part, and on my part true and persevering repentance. So I kneel down before Thee, hating with all the powers of my spirit, all the sins I have committed. I have done evil. I know it and confess it. I should never have offended Infinite Goodness. I ought rather to have died, and even given up a thousand lives, than have done so much evil. Ah! Who will give a spring of bitter tears to my eyes and an intense grief to my heart, such as I need. . . ?

Third Point

Reflections on the foregoing truths — Gather your thoughts again, my soul, to comprehend well the following reflections:

(1) If a single sin is so hateful in God's sight, how hateful should my soul be in His presence? If I have committed one single (mortal) sin, I have sinned as much as one rebel spirit. If I have done a hundred, I have sinned so much that alone I am like a hundred rebel spirits. Again, if I have committed a single (mortal) sin, I have made myself as displeasing to God as each one of the rebel spirits. If I have committed a hundred, I have made myself, taken alone, as displeasing as a hundred of those spirits taken together.

(2) If one who (mortally) sins once, deserves hell, how obliged am I to bless God's Infinite Mercy! If

I have committed a single sin, I have deserved hell, just like all the reprobate spirits. If I have committed more than one, I have deserved it more than any of them. And why do I not find myself where those unhappy creatures are? Ah! That very God Who used all the strictness of His Justice with them, has used with me all the riches of His Infinite Mercy. Oh, what goodness! What love! What long suffering!

(3) If for a single sin God gave such a terrible punishment to angels and men, with what good reason should I not fear His Justice? For just one sin God damned so many thousands of millions of angelic spirits to burn forever in the fire of hell, leaving no remedy, no grace, no period to do penance. If I were to boldly sin again, could He not do, and perhaps will He not do, the same with me? O my God, I see my duty to confess that now I could not sin again without extreme boldness, and that Thou couldst not forgive me now if Thy Mercy were not Infinite.

Affective Acts

(1) Repentance — Heaven and earth bear me witness that Thou hast an infinite hatred for sin. Ah! Would that a single drop of that holy hatred would descend into my heart! Unfortunate as I am, what have I done? There is nothing so deserving of my love as Jesus. Nothing ought to be hated by me so much as sin. And I, a fool, have abhorred Jesus and loved sin. By my works I have said: long live sin! Give life to Barrabas and death to Jesus!... Crucify Him! Or rather, I have crucified Him by the sin I have committed! Oh, impiety that deserves to be punished forever in hell! I know it, O my God, and I weep for

it! How much better it would have been for me to have rotted under the ground before sinning! But these sighs of regret come very late. I have sinned! I have sinned, oh, so many times! I have sinned enormously! Forgive me, my Jesus. I do repent.

(2) Thanksgiving — But my great malice calls to my mind Thy Mercy. Without fear and trembling I cannot reflect on that unhappy hour in which I sinned for the first time. O wretched hour! Ah! Would that it had never come! O God, if Thou hadst treated me then as Thou treated the angels, oh, for how long a time I would have been in hell! Ah! Just the recalling of it makes me tremble — of that great peril in which my precious one and only immortal soul stood at that time. Thou hast had mercy on me and have given me time to do penance. Oh, what praise, what blessing, what thanks I owe Thee!

(3) Prayer of Petition — Have mercy on me, O my God, have mercy! I know now the infinite evil that sin contains. I know it by the hell fire of the rebel spirits. I know it by the fate of man exiled from paradise. I know it by the sufferings and torments Jesus underwent dying on a Cross. O awesome mystery! The Son of God had to die, and die in this way, for my sins! Could I have committed a greater wrong than this, of leading Jesus to the Cross? I am Jesus' executioner! O sin, O accursed sin! How is it you have seemed sweet and agreeable to me? O Jesus, by the Blood Thou shed for my sins, I beg Thee to grant me the special graces I need in order to bitterly weep over my past sins and avoid them in the future and hate them more than death.

Now pray the Our Father and the Hail Mary and the Concluding Prayers as on page xi.

Meditation 5

The Malice of Mortal Sin

Preparatory Prayer as on page x

First Prelude

Composition of Place — Imagine you see God seated on a throne of majesty and grandeur as Judge, and yourself, guilty sinner that you are, with hands bound standing before the Judge, and an account concerning yourself is read of all the sins that you have committed in the whole course of your life, with all the circumstances of places and persons, with mention of your state in life and your age at the time. You cannot excuse yourself nor deny anything.

Prayer of Petition — My God and Lord, I beg that I may know the number and gravity of my sins, and may be sorry and repentant for having committed them.

First Point

The text of Saint Ignatius: ". . . Recall to mind. . . the particular sin of any person who went to hell because of one mortal sin. Consider also the countless others who have gone to hell for fewer sins than I have committed. . . We speak of this as the third particular sin (the first being of Lucifer, the second of Adam and Eve).

Call to mind the grievousness and malice of sin against our Creator and Lord. Let the understanding consider how in sinning and acting against Infinite Goodness, one has justly been condemned forever. End this reflection with acts of the will, as we said above. . .

"I shall call to mind all the sins of my lifetime, considering them year by year, period by period. Three things will help me to do this: first, I will recall the place and home where I live; secondly, the associations I have had with others; thirdly, the positions I filled.

"The second point is to weigh my sins, considering the loathsomeness and malice which each mortal sin committed has within itself, even if it were not forbidden.

"Next, consider who I am. . . Let me see myself as a sore and an abscess from which there have come forth so many sins, so many evils and very vile poison.

". . . Next consider who is God, against Whom I have sinned, recalling His attributes and comparing them to their contraries in me."

Explanation — (1) In the very moment in which sin is committed, the soul, from being a likeness of God, becomes transformed into a very horrible monster. It is not possible for a man to comprehend the wonderful beauty with which a soul which enjoys God's grace, is adorned. When in that state it is a portrait and a copy of the Divine Beauty. For its formation, nothing less is required than Infinite Wisdom and Power.

One day, when God had enabled her to see this beauty, a great saint, Teresa of Avila, declared that she would gladly give a thousand lives and suffer a thousand deaths, to preserve the beauty of a single such soul. But just as grace makes a soul lovely, sin makes it ugly. A soul in sin and a condemned spirit are quite equal in ugliness. Just as a man could not see a demon in any vision that would fairly represent it, without dying of fright, neither could he see a soul that is in sin without dying of terror.

(2) In the moment in which sin is committed, a soul becomes extremely repulsive to God. It is not possible for any intelligence in Heaven or on earth to come to a comprehension of how great the abhorrence is, how profound the hatred is, with which God regards sin. Yes, indeed! God hates sin and necessarily abhors it. Just as it is not possible for Him to cease loving Himself as the Supreme Good, likewise it is not possible that He cease hating sin as the supreme evil.

(3) The moment one sins, his soul, from being a child of God, becomes a slave of the devil. The condition of a possessed person moves us to compassion; for he is compelled to make room day and night within his body, for a demon from hell. But much more pitiful is the condition of someone's soul who, by sin, becomes a slave of the devil and is constrained to live under his tyrannical power.

Someone possessed may happen to be a child of God and enjoy His grace, having full confidence that he will succeed in enjoying Him forever in Heaven. But one in sin is God's enemy, is without His grace, and is liable to fall into hell at any time, with the same slave-master accompanying him to torment him there forever.

(4) The moment one sins, his soul falls into the vilest, most deplorable condition. There is nothing more shameful than sin, nothing more blameworthy than the sinner. Imagine, O my soul, that God opened everyone's eyes so that they could look into your heart clearly and see all your vices, all the sins you

have committed during your lifetime by thought, word and deed. Oh God! What embarrassment! What shame you would have!

Would you not first seek a hiding place in the grottos and caves of deserts rather than appear before men? Even in the judgment of the same natural right reason, there is nothing more shameful than sin, nor anything more vile than the sinner. Ah! How much you ought to blush before God, in Whose presence you have committed so many sins and before Whose eyes all the hideous things of your life continually lie bare!

Affective Acts

(1) Shame — Oh my God, how many sins I have committed! There is not a faculty of my soul nor a sense in my body that has not offended Thee. O unfortunate memory! How many unworthy recollections you have fed to yourself! O unhappy mind! How many bad thoughts have you not produced! O wretched will! How many bad desires you have entertained!

O unhappy tongue! How many loose words have you not uttered! O unworthy hands! How many forbidden acts have you not performed! O disorderly heart! How many objects have you not wrongfully loved or wrongfully hated!

O my God, if a single sin arouses in Thee a nausea, a horror and an infinite displeasure, how in Thy sight does my soul appear in which nothing else is seen but sin? Where shall I flee to hide myself and conceal my shameful guilt! O sin! How lovable you seem to one who commits you! How bitter and hateful you are after you have been committed! Truly, if everybody knew me as God does, there would not be a saint in Heaven nor a man on earth who would not look away in greatest horror...

(2) Prayer of Petition — O my God, as I consider my madness I am ashamed and completely horrified. Ah, my God! To whom shall I turn but to Thee, O God of Eternal Goodness and Infinite Mercy! In Thy Pity deign to grant me a sorrow that will penetrate my whole heart and will have power to successfully purify my soul of all uncleanness. I cannot have this sorrow without a special help of Thy grace. Grant it to me, O Lord! And Heaven and earth will have another reason to praise and bless Thy Mercy.

Second Point

The evil of sin is something supreme by reason of the supreme meanness and lowliness of the man who offends God... O my soul, reflect attentively on what you are, and then make your judgment about sin.

(1) You are a creature who possesses, of yourself, nothing good. For, what goodness can a creature possess — a creature which can be called nothingness? A few years ago such a creature was nothing. Now, as to the body, it is a handful of clay. In a little while it will be put in a grave, to change into powdery substance, to serve as food for very disgusting worms, and change back into dust.

Who can have an existence so contemptuous, the low status of which no mind can comprehend, and whose nothingness not even sovereign (angelic) intelligence, not even the Blessed Virgin's intelligence, can fathom and measure? For that is something for God's intelligence alone to do ... And yet this handful of dust, this worm of the earth, this wretched creature, has dared to be bold against God and oppose His Will, and its rashness has gone so far as to treat God lightly and say in deeds, if not in words, "Who is the Lord, that He should want me obedient to His voice? I know no master who is superior to myself. . . "

(2) *You are a creature* with whom God has shown Himself to be infinitely generous. O my soul, God has loaded you with countless benefits and in all the course of your life there has not been a single moment in which you have not experienced some new effect of His loving kindness; and (if there is no failure on your part) in the future for all eternity there will not be an instant in which He will not do you some new favor.

He has shown this generosity toward you with an eternal love; for the Lord has not loved Himself at a time before He loved you. He has loved you with a love you did not deserve; for He had no need of you nor your works. He has loved you with a magnanimous love. He could have given the same graces to others who would have used them better than you have.

And in spite of this you have been so rash and ungrateful, O my soul, and have had the boldness to offend a God so kind to you, and offend Him so many times with so much shamelessness! How monstrous it would be for a son, in the sight of his father, to commit every kind of depravity and then spit in his father's face! Ah! Have you not done something just as bad, O vile creature, against your God Who has ever shown Himself to be your loving Father?

(3) *You are a creature* who owes all of himself to

God. Indeed, my soul, for all there is in you, you are indebted to your Creator. He it is Who gave it to you and Who preserves it for you. Oh, what impiety, to abuse the benefits and graces received from God and to use them in a way that is bold and outrageous toward His Infinite Majesty!

Would not it be a monstrous thing if someone whose paralyzed hand Jesus Christ had miraculously cured, were to use that very hand later to give Christ a beating? Would it not be a great example of unworthiness, if somebody who had been miraculously cured of muteness by Jesus Christ were to break out later into blasphemies against Him on the Cross? Ah, turn your eyes to yourself, my soul. Who gave you that tongue? those eyes? those ears? those hands and all other members of your body and powers of your soul, which you so often have used to offend your God? Is this how you have paid Him back for such great favors?

(4) You are a creature whom God has drawn from hell by the operation of His Power and Mercy. ("Thy mercy is great towards me: and Thou hast delivered my soul out of the lower hell." Ps. 85:13) My soul, if you forsake God's friendship just once, you have deserved hell and are indebted to God's pure Mercy for not being plunged into hell. Faith teaches you this.

Now does this circumstance not make your sins appear the more grievous? If today God delivered a damned soul from hell and gave it time to do penance, and in spite of this great favor it blasphemed Him again tomorrow, what would you think? God has delivered you from hell, ten, twenty, perhaps more times, and after having such extraordinary

Mercy toward you, what have you done? Alas! to the dismay of Heaven, you have sinned!

Affective Acts

(1) Humility and sincere confession of guilt before God — My most lovable God, I tremble before Thy Divine Majesty, ranking myself as one belonging to the depths of hell. Indeed a more proper place for me could not be found. Am I any more than dust and ashes? Yet I have dared to treacherously rebel against the Most High God, from Whose Hand I have received all. All that I am, all that I have, all that I can do, is a gift of God, Who, like an immense river, floods me at all hours with ever new benefits. Yes, against God, Who has forgiven me by His overflowing Mercy after a vast number of sins.

O my God! I confess that my conduct has been more than diabolical; for I have deserved not one hell, but a thousand. You, O wretched damned spirits, you are not more wretched than I; for I have been more sinful. Indeed you are so unhappy because God was less merciful with you than He has been with me.

Your chances lasted but a moment; mine has lasted many years. You committed a single sin; I have committed countless sins. To you He gave just one grace. He has given me thousands. God condemned you for one sin, and has been willing to pardon me after many, many sins. In spite of all this, I have continued to offend Him. Ought my eyes not turn into a sea of tears and weep all the remaining hours of my life?

(2) Repentance — O my God, Thou dost penetrate all the corners of my heart. My will is to detest, hate, curse sincerely and with all the power of my

soul, all the sins I have committed up to this moment. Ah, would that I could put together within my heart all the acts of sorrow and repentance of all the most contrite penitents, in order to deplore and detest my sins, if not as much as they deserve, then at least as much as is possible for me! In compensation I offer Thee the sorrow, the grief, the agony, which Jesus suffered for my sins, which made Him sweat blood in the garden.

Third Point

The infinite evil of sin is evident on account of the supreme Majesty of God, Whom we offend by sinning. The greater dignity of the person offended, so much the greater and graver is the offense which He receives.

To give a slap to the face of some high public authority for whom the common good requires great respect — would this not be a graver offense against good order than if this were done a hundred times to a criminal? Natural reason teaches this. According to this principle, my soul, evaluate the gravity of sin.

Who is God?

(1) God is One Who is infinitely good — He is a Being Who contains within Himself all possible perfections. He is Infinite Goodness, Infinite Power, Infinite Wisdom, Infinite Generosity, Infinite Mercy. To sum things up, He possesses Infinite Perfections. Now, as He is Supreme Good in Himself, so is He also the origin and source of all good things that there are in creatures.

There is no power, goodness, holiness, beauty, mercy nor generosity in Heaven or on earth, in angels or in men, nor in any other creature, which does not spring from God as the singular, inexhaustible Source that He is. To offend, to disregard, to dishonor, knowingly and deliberately, a God so great — oh, what malice!

(2) God is Infinite Majesty and Greatness — Raise your gaze to Heaven, my soul, and picture the Lord seated there on a throne with thousands of angels about Him, awestricken before the splendor of His Divinity, and who devote themselves to praising and blessing Him to the fullest extent of their powers. Knowing that they cannot honor Him as much as His Greatness deserves, they prostrate themselves humbly before His Face and confess that He ought to receive infinite love and glory — much more than they are capable of giving.

But, now all the while that this is done in Heaven where all blessed spirits vie in holy competition in praising and glorifying the Great Majesty of God, a vile man rises from the ground to do insult to that same Supreme Majesty, heaping that Majesty with reproach and abuse. Oh, what enormous and incomprehensible malice! Oh my soul, it is beyond explanation! Two reflections will be of use to give you some small idea about its enormity.

(1) Imagine that all angels came down from Heaven and took human bodies, and that all men who have lived from the beginning of the world emerged from their graves, and for a thousand year period all did the most rigorous, frightening penance, and that finally all shed their blood for love of God in the most painful martyrdom. With all this could they satisfy for the offense done to God by a single mortal sin? No. It is not possible; for mortal

sin is an infinite evil, and this satisfaction would be limited.

(2) If all the angels of Heaven with all the power of their intelligence were to investigate sin for all eternity, they nevertheless could never fully comprehend the depths of its malice.

Affective Acts

(1) Sincere self-accusation — The light Thou givest me enables me to know, O my God, that my malice has reached a high point. I have offended Thee. . . Who am I? Not a cherub, nor an angel, nor another noble spirit, but a wretched little man, a handful of dust, a worm of the earth. I have offended Thee! Who art Thou? Not a monarch, nor an angel, nor a seraph, but God, Supreme Goodness, Source and Origin of all Good, Supreme Lord of Heaven and earth.

I have offended Thee! And where? Not in secret, nor in Thy absence, but in Thy presence and in the midst of the splendor of Thy Majesty . . . I have offended Thee! With what? With the eyes, the ears, the tongue, the hands, the heart, which Thou gavest me by Pure Mercy. I have offended Thee! But why? Not out of hope to gain a kingdom, nor from fear of being threatened with death, but for a vile satisfaction of the senses, for fear of some slight embarrassment. I have offended Thee!

When? During the very hour in which Thou were engaged in preserving my bodily health, in giving my soul new benefits, in checking the rage of the demon so that he would not drag me with him to hell. O my God! How enormous is my ingratitude, my folly, my madness, my malice! Still in Thy sight my (mortal) sin is something infinitely greater than what

I can know. ("May I know myself, may I know Thee, that I may despise myself and love Thee." - Saint Augustine.)

(2) Repentance — This is how I have lived, O my God! And what has been the way I have offended Thee? And what kind of sorrow and repentance have I had after the offenses? From time to time I have made an act of contrition, I have struck my breast, and then continued living, unworried, as though I were now assured of pardon. How so?

After so many offenses against God, will I be content with a repentance so feeble and so hastily formed? Ought my heart not to be in deep continual grief, and should not my eyes shed continuous tears? I have offended the Supreme, Infinite Good. That fact is enough to let me never cease grieving. Ah! Would that I had never offended Thee! O Being Who art infinitely lovable, why did I not rather sacrifice my body and my life a thousand times?

(3) Resolution — The evil has now been done. I have let myself be deceived by my senses and be overcome and led astray by my evil inclinations. Forgive me, O my God, I beg Thee, by Thy Infinite Mercy and by the merits of the Precious Blood of Thy Son Jesus Christ. I turn to Thee with all my heart and in Thy presence resolve to prefer death rather than ever sin again. O holy resolve! O blessed resolution! But is it sincere? Yes, my Jesus; I sincerely resolve it. Lord, Thou hast mastery over life and death. If Thou foresee that I am to commit another sin, I beg Thee to take me with Thee to Heaven before that sad day arrives. . .

Now pray the Our Father and the Hail Mary and the Concluding Prayers as on page xi.

Meditation 6

The Pains of Hell
In particular, the Pain of Loss

Commentary —With a good sense of order Saint Ignatius puts the meditation on the pains of hell immediately after the one on sin, so that one may the more detest and deplore one's sins if he has unhappily committed any, when he sees the deservingness of punishment which comes about as a necessary consequence. The penalty in the other life must infallibly follow our crime if God does not use His Mercy; because the moment a man sins he incurs a debt — a debt to be paid by eternal damnation — and he becomes like a criminal sentenced to die on a scaffold, who has no way of appealing the sentence.

This is why, after the meditations on sin, Saint Ignatius immediately presents those on hell. It is so that our heart, naturally fearful of punishment, especially eternal punishment, may be withdrawn from committing sin. (". . . Fear Him that can destroy both soul and body in hell" Mt. 10:28.) This is a very right motive for repenting, for grieving over past sin, and for imploring the Divine Mercy (as the Council of Trent infallibly taught.)

Preparatory Prayer as on page x

First Point

Quoting Saint Ignatius: "First preamble, composition of place — with the eyes of the imagination observe the length, width and depth of hell.

"*The second* preamble (the appeal for something that I wish) will here be to beg a deep appreciation of the pains which the damned suffer, so that if, through my faults, I become forgetful of the Eternal Father's love, at least the fear of punishment will keep me from sin.

"The first point will be to see with the eye of the imagination the great fires, and souls appearing as in fiery bodies.

"The second will be to hear the frightful cries, wails, blasphemies against Christ our Lord and against His saints.

"The third will be to smell the smoke, the rock, the sulphur, the filth and putridness.

"The fourth considers the sense of touch — a fire which touches and burns souls."

Explanation — God is just in His awards. He rewards the upright with the glory of Heaven and punishes the wicked with the eternal pains of hell. We have seen how man was created to love and serve God. Now when he sins, he does not love nor serve God, but despises Him (Isaias 1:2), and thus he comes under sentence of eternal punishment in hell. This punishment will be in proportion to the malice of his sins and their number. In sin there are found five evils of malice.

The *first* evil is the contempt with which the sinner treats God. On this account he deserves to be punished with the pain of loss, the loss of what he has made light of or disdained; hence he suffers the deprivation of the sight of God. The *second* evil is his act of rebellion or independence from God, amounting to an abuse of liberty. Thus he deserves to be punished by losing his liberty and suffering slavery and subjection to satan; for God says, "Because thou didst not serve the Lord Thy God with joy . . . therefore in hunger and thirst, in nakedness and in want of all things," you will serve thy enemy. (Deut. 28: 47-48)

The *third* evil is the over-fondness for a created object for which one sinned. Thus a created object, which is fire, will cause torment, and this is called a pain of sense. The *fourth* evil is a sensual or spiritual satisfaction that the sinner finds in sin; thus he deserves to be tormented with a corresponding dissatisfaction, as God commands — *"As much as she hath glorified herself, and lived in delicacies, so much torment and sorrow give ye to her . . ."* (Apoc. 18:7). The *fifth* evil is pride, which consists in man wanting to be happy of himself, independent of God. In hell he thus finds humiliation, confusion, and every pain. Finally, as a sinner in hell is found obstinate in his evil disposition like a rock in a well, the duration of his suffering is rightfully eternal.

Let us begin with the pain of loss: — Picture to yourself, Christian soul, a man whose lot is one of total misfortune, without anything good. Now a Christian who is damned to hell loses God, the Supreme Good, and eternal happiness. To lose God is a misfortune that goes beyond all that the imagination can grasp. It is just as impossible to grasp it, as it is impossible to grasp and comprehend the Infinite Good one gains who possesses God. Yet we can conceive a vague idea of it. Enter into yourself, O my soul, and seriously weigh what it means to lose God.

(1) One who is damned loses the enjoyment of God — At the moment a soul enters Heaven, God

gives it so clear an enlightenment that it can know perfectly — as far as a creature can — all the depths of His Infinite Nature, and inflames the soul with such a burning desire to enjoy God, that any delay, even a moment's delay, would cause it infinite pain.

But because it so ardently desires this Good and at the same time perfectly enjoys It with the infallible certainty that it will eternally enjoy It, the soul experiences such a flood of joy that all other delights of paradise can be counted as nothing by comparison . . . in hell just the opposite happens.

When the soul enters hell, God sheds over it so vivid a light that it can know to the limits of its capacity, the greatness of His Infinite and Divine Essence. This enkindles in it so impatient a desire to enjoy God, that the delay of even a single instant causes infinite pangs.

As it craves with such ardor to possess this tremendous Good and at the same time sees itself violently separated, with the certainty that it will never for all eternity enjoy God, such a painful sadness arises from this that compared to it, all other torments of hell are considered as nothing. . . To sum up, as the happiness of a soul in paradise is beyond all measure because it possesses God so the grief of a soul in hell is boundless due to its loss of God.

(2) One who is damned loses God's devoted, special Providence which cared for him —As long as a man is alive, he is under the care of God, Who enlightens his mind with exalted lights and encourages and fortifies him in his sufferings. But a soul which has entered the eternal abyss must hope for none of this.

71

God no longer cares about it and regards that soul as something which no longer belongs to Him. And so for all eternity God will never again enlighten its mind, will not arouse its will toward the good, nor awaken a pious desire in its heart. That soul will become incapable of any good.

There will be no more than very horrifying specters appearing to the imagination. Only the most distressing thoughts will prevail in the mind. The will shall be forever stirred up with rage, madness and despair. The memory will perceive itself always grieved with very painful recollections. Wherever that soul may turn, it will find confusion and bitterness.

(3) When a soul is condemned, by losing God it ceases to be loved any more by creatures — The Blessed Virgin, one's Guardian Angel, all the saints, love a man as long as he lives on earth. But once he is condemned by God, then God's friends agree in God's judgment and condemnation.

For all eternity they will not have a kind thought for this wretch. Rather they will be satisfied to see him in the flames as a victim of God's justice. ("The just shall rejoice when he shall see the revenge . . ." Psalm 57:11) They will abhor him. A mother will look from paradise upon her own condemned son without being moved, as though she had never known him.

What is worse, is that in all the immense throng of persons damned in hell, not one will fail to increase the torments of his companions, partly due to the horror one causes another, partly due to the anger with which they rage against one another, and also due to the heat, the stench and the closeness.

(4) After losing God and with Him all things, a condemned person also falls under the devil's power — God does not then care about him and delivers him entirely up to the enemy's will. And alas! what will the devil not do with this soul? As the devil is tremendously clever and powerful, has great hatred for men, is full of rage, with an ability to torment him according to the number and gravity of sins a man has committed and for which he is damned, then what will he not do?

He can twist into the form of a serpent, enter the body, and torment him cruelly with his teeth. As a poisonous snake he can enter the mouth and bite and gnaw and destroy lungs, liver, heart and all the bowels. He can make his victim swallow molten metal and feed him poisonous toads. He can torment him practically as he wishes at his own pleasure, for God has withdrawn and the man is left under the fiendish demon's despotic control.

Affective Acts

(1) Confession — O Jesus, how frightening are Thy judgments! How strict is Thy Justice! Oh, what a great evil sin is and how bitter are its effects! To be shut out of paradise for all eternity, to be forever cursed by the elect, to be always tormented and oppressed by the devil's tyranny — this is the reward of sin. Up to now have I believed these truths?

Ah, indeed — that is just what increases my guilt! I have believed that a single sin is enough to make me lose God and with God all happiness forever; and yet I have sinned. I have done this without caring, without alarm. I do not think I know which is greater, my blindness or my malice. O Jesus! Do not take Thy Mercy from me.

(2) Resolution — What will I do? What is it that I will resolve upon? Ah! By all means I want to be able to behold Thee in Thy glory. O Supreme Good, and my last End! Though this would cost me a thousand lives, with all determination I must reach Heaven to embrace Thee there, my Jesus, my beloved Redeemer.

Even if it be only through the cruelest torments, I must yet see Thee, O my dearest Mother, and you, O dear friends of God in paradise, even though it cost me all the blood in my veins. . . This is my resolution — to rather die a thousand times than commit a single sin. Ye angelic spirits, be witnesses to the sincerity of my heart. I prefer a thousand deaths to ever sinning again. I will confess with repentance the sins I have committed up to now.

Second Point

One who is condemned in hell finds God to be as a supreme evil. It is true. One who loses God as his Supreme Good, finds Him to be like a supreme evil. Now how can it be possible that God, Who is a man's Supreme Good and Blessedness, change into that same man's supreme misery? Listen with attention, my soul, to what God does with those who are damned, and you will clearly know this truth.

(1) Within the reprobate, God places and preserves a very vivid knowledge of the Divine Beauty, with a very ardent desire to enjoy it — If the soul in hell did not have a knowledge far greater than it has in this life, then it would be spared its greatest torment.

But because this knowledge is very clear in the (damned) soul and presents very vividly to it the immense happiness and blessedness which it could have enjoyed in God, from this a bitterness comes which is inconceivable, inasmuch as every moment it is driven toward God with a burning desire, and also realizes at each instant that it is cast off by the Lord.

What would be the torment of a thirsty man, tied hand and foot a thousand years where he would see ever before him a large drinking vessel containing a very delicious drink, and could not reach with his lips nor taste a drop of it?

(2) Within the damned person God preserves the sight of the Divine Countenance outraged (by his sin) — Before the eyes of a damned soul, God is never presented in any other aspect than as a Lord supremely outraged, always armed for vengeance and ever engaged in tormenting it and pursuing it. The soul may try with all its might to withdraw from such a painful sight, to flee God's presence and escape His wrath.

But the more it tries, the more closely God approaches it to make it suffer the weight of His hand and all the bitterness of His anger. It will not be hard to estimate the horribleness of this pain. Just as the bare sight of God's loving face is enough to fill all the elect with a boundless joy, likewise the sight of God's angry Countenance is enough to strike infinite terror and an infinite pain into all the damned.

(3) God keeps alive the person who is damned — The strongest desire of a damned soul in hell is to die. (". . . Men shall seek death and shall not find it.

And they shall desire to die, and death shall fly from them." Apoc. 9:6.) For knowing it can never appease God's anger against it, it desires death as the only means of escape. But it will desire this in vain, for the damned person will live as long as God will live. Just as God forever preserves the saints in Heaven to delight them with new pleasures, so He will preserve forever the damned in hell, to always torment them with new sufferings.

(4) God remains angry toward the condemned — The damned wretch will curse his sins a thousand times over again, but will yet be obstinate in them. He will roar with very pitiful moans, capable of moving stones to compassion. He will shed enough tears to flood the earth. A time will come when one could say that he has suffered in these flames a thousand million years for every mortal sin. In spite of this, he will not calm God's anger, nor ever move Him to pity.

The Lord will continue to show wrath toward him and will never cease hating him for all eternity. As the reprobate knows this, he will surrender to a complete despair, will go into a fury, will fill his heart with rage, and in an extreme spite will gnaw his own flesh.

Not satisfied with this, he will conceive an eternal hatred for God; he will become, so to speak, a devil vomiting out continuous curses and blasphemies against God, and will have such a spitefulness against Him that he would engineer God's complete destruction if it were possible.

Affective Acts

(1) Fear — Oh, what a happy affair it is to be at

peace with God, and how bitter it is to have Him angry with us. How sweet it is to find God rewarding us; how painful to find Him an avenger. How fortunate to be plunged into a torrent of delights such as God lavishes upon His elect! How dreadful to find oneself planted in hell, suffering all the evils which God will cause to fall like rain upon the damned. How sweet it is to enjoy God for all eternity, and how bitter to lose Him forever!

What will I do to escape from this infinite evil? Ah, my soul! After sin there is no other remedy but a deep hatred of sin and a sincere confession. — I now have access to this remedy, and turning to Thee, my God, weeping in all earnestness with the most contrite remorse . . . I tell Thee that I am sorry for my sins and I give Thee my word that I will go to Confession.

(2) Repentance — O my God, with all my heart I detest and curse all the sins that I have committed until now. I know what evil I have done. In reference to Thee, sin is the supreme evil, because it is an offense committed against Thy Infinite Goodness and Mercy. It is also the greatest of evils in reference to me, because it is the ruin of my soul, which is immortal. And so I detest it and I curse it with all my heart. . . Oh, would that I had never sinned, my Jesus!

Oh, would that I had never offended Thee, my Sovereign Good! But the evil is done. I have lost Thee, O my last End and only happiness, and I can never again rejoice with Thee except by means of penance and tears. O my heart, repent and do not be satisfied with a half-hearted sorrow, but enlarge, expand, as much as possible, to squeeze into yourself an immense sorrow.

Be witness to this, O my Jesus, that if I had a thousand lives, I would want to spend all of them in pain and torments if in this way I could undo my sins. . . Thus I want to repent and indeed do repent of my sins, O my God! It is my intention to renew this will and repentance in Thy presence as many times as there are drops of water in all rivers and seas. O my Jesus, supply what is lacking in me; and offer to Thy Eternal Father, in place of my sorrow and repentance, that sorrow which Thou had in the garden for my sins.

(3) Resolution — But how will I conduct myself in the future? I will sin no more. If I cannot avoid sin except by dying, I will gladly choose death, even the most cruel death, rather than sin. If I can avoid sin only by bearing insult and contempt, I will gladly suffer being despised and abused by everybody rather than sin.

I want to die rather than sin. Therefore, with this aim I will use all my days and all my hours and moments in loving my Supreme Good and keeping closely united with Him. O my Jesus, engrave deeply in my heart these resolutions; keep them there so that I will never forget to practise them.

Now pray the Our Father and the Hail Mary and the Concluding Prayers as on page xi.

Meditation 7

The Pains of Hell, in Particular the Pain of Sense and its Duration

Preparatory Prayer as on page x

Words of Saint Ignatius — "With the eyes of the imagination observe the length, width and depth of hell. . .

"Beg a deep appreciation of the pains which the damned suffer, so that if, through my fault, I become forgetful of the Eternal Father's love, at least the fear of punishment will help keep me from sin."

Jesus Christ's words according to Saint Luke's Gospel (16:19-31) — "There was a certain rich man, who was clothed in purple and fine linen; and feasted sumptuously every day. And there was a certain beggar, named Lazarus, who lay at his gate, full of sores, desiring to be filled with the crumbs that fell from the rich man's table, and no one did give him; moreover the dogs came, and licked his sores.

"And it came to pass, that the beggar died, and was carried by the angels into Abraham's bosom. And the rich man also died: and he was buried in hell. And lifting up his eyes when he was in torments, he saw Abraham afar off, and Lazarus in his bosom: And he cried, and said: Father Abraham, have mercy on me, and send Lazarus, that he may dip the tip of his finger in water, to cool my tongue: for I am tormented in this flame.

"And Abraham said to him: son, remember that thou didst receive good things in thy lifetime, and likewise Lazarus evil things, but now he is com-

79

forted; and thou art tormented. And besides all this, between us and you, there is fixed a great chasm: so that they who would pass from hence to you, cannot, nor from thence come hither.

And he said: Then, Father, I beseech thee, that thou wouldst send him to my father's house, for I have five brethren, that he may testify unto them, lest they also come into this place of torments. And Abraham said to him: They have Moses and the prophets; let them hear them. But he said: No, Father Abraham: but if one went to them from the dead, they will do penance. And he said to him: If they hear not Moses and the prophets, neither will they believe, if one rise again from the dead." (Luke 16:19-31)

The house of the rich glutton is the world. His father is the devil. His five brothers are sensual people — those whose lives are dominated by the five senses. Woe to one who would not believe he would be damned! (Cf. Mark 16:16) Do you want the testimony of someone who has died? Here you have one who tells you: "Remember my judgment: for thine also shall be so: yesterday for me, and today for thee." (Eccles. 38:23).

First Point

The pain of sense in hell is essentially very dreadful. Picture yourself, my soul, on a dark night on the summit of a high mountain. Beneath you is a deep valley, and the earth opens so that with your gaze you can see hell in the cavity of it. Picture it as a prison situated in the center of the earth, many leagues down, all full of fire, hemmed in so impenetrably that for all eternity not even the smoke can escape. In this prison the damned are sprawled out and packed so tightly one on the other like bricks in a kiln . . . Consider the quality of the fire in which they burn.

(1) The fire is all-extensive and tortures the whole body and the whole soul — A damned person lies in hell forever in the same spot which he was assigned by Divine Justice, without being able to move, as a prisoner in chains.

The fire in which he is totally enveloped, as a fish in water, burns around him, on his left, his right, above and below. His head, his breast, his shoulders, his arms, his hands, and his feet are all penetrated with fire, so that he completely resembles a glowing hot piece of iron which has just been withdrawn from an oven.

The roof beneath which the damned person dwells is fire; the food he takes is fire; the drink he tastes is fire; the air he breathes is fire; whatever he sees and touches is all fire. . . But this fire is not merely outside him; it also passes within the condemned person. It penetrates his brain, his teeth, his tongue, his throat, his liver, his lungs, his bowels, his belly, his heart, his veins, his nerves, his bones, even to the marrow, and even his blood.

"In hell," according to Saint Gregory the Great, "there will be a fire that cannot be put out, a worm which cannot die, a stench one cannot bear, a darkness one can feel, a scourging by savage hands, with those present despairing of anything good."

A most dreadful fact is that by the Divine Power this fire goes so far as to work on the very faculties of the soul, burning them and tormenting them. Suppose I were to find myself placed at the furnace of a blacksmith so that my whole body was in the open air but for one arm placed in the fire, and that God were to preserve my life for a thousand years in this position. Would this not be an unbearable torture? What, then, would it be like to be completely penetrated and surrounded by fire, which would affect, not just an arm, but even all the faculties of the soul?

(2) This fire is far more dreadful than man can imagine — The natural fire that we see during this life has great power to burn and torment. Yet this is not even a shadow of the fire of hell. There are two reasons why the fire of hell is more dreadful beyond all comparison than the fire of this life.

The *first* reason is the Justice of God, which the fire serves as an instrument in order to punish the infinite wrong done to His Supreme Majesty, which has been despised by a creature. Therefore justice supplies this element with a burning power which almost reaches the infinite. . . The *second* reason is the malice of sin. As God knows that the fire of this world is not enough to punish sin as it deserves, He has given the fire of hell a power so strong that it can never be comprehended by any human mind.

Now, how powerfully does this fire burn? It burns so powerfully, O my soul, that, according to the ascetical masters, if a mere spark of it fell on a millstone, it would reduce it in a moment to powder. If it fell on a ball of bronze, it would melt it in an instant as if it were wax. If it landed on a frozen lake, it would make it boil in an instant.

(3) Pause here briefly, my soul, and answer a few questions. First, I ask you — If a special furnace were fired up as was customarily done to torment the holy martyrs, and then men placed before you all

kinds of good things that the human heart might want, and added the offer of a prosperous kingdom — if all this were promised you on condition that for just a half-hour you enclose yourself within the furnace, what would you choose?

"Ah!" you would say, "If you offered me a hundred kingdoms I would never be so foolish as to accept your brutal terms, regardless of how grand your offer might be, even if I were sure that God would preserve my life during those moments of suffering."

Second, I ask you — If you already had possession of a great kingdom and were swimming in a sea of wealth so that nothing was wanting to you, and then you were attacked by an enemy, were imprisoned and put in chains and obliged to either renounce your kingdom or else spend a half-hour in a hot furnace, what would you choose? "Ah!" you would say, "I would prefer to spend my whole life in extreme poverty and submit to any other hardship and misfortune, than suffer such great torment!"

Now turn your thoughts from the temporal to the eternal. To avoid the torment of a hot furnace, which would last but a half-hour, you would forgo all your property, even things you are most fond of, you would suffer any other temporal loss, however burdensome.

Then why do you not think the same way when you are dealing with eternal torments? God threatens you not just with a half-hour in a furnace, but with a prison of eternal fire. To escape it, should you not forgo whatever He has forbidden, no matter how pleasant it can be for you, and gladly embrace whatever He commands, even if it be extremely unpleasant?

Affective Acts

(1) *Fear* — All these truths were already made known to me and I have believed them, O my God! But how have I been living? Oh, what a painful question this is to me! I have sinned and deserved hell. And why? Did someone offer me a kingdom if I would sin, or threaten me with death if I would not sin? Ah, no! I know and Thou knowest the reason for which I sinned, and I blush with shame.

I sinned for a very worthless reason and deserved hell — so great was my blindness and my foolishness, so cruel was I to myself! But I hope Thou hast forgiven me now for my past, O my most merciful God! What fills me with fear and dread is the future. I can sin again; I can die in sin and be damned!

Many evil inclinations in me have not yet died which at other times have made me fall. The mortification I have done is very little, and Divine Justice

Note — What delights us is momentary; what would torment us is eternal. Jesus Christ will say: ". . . Depart from Me, you cursed, into everlasting fire, which was prepared for the devil and his angels!" (Mt. 25:41). And then: "And these shall go into everlasting punishment: but the just, into life everlasting." (Mt. 25:46).

"Where their worm dieth not, and the fire is not extinguished." (Mark 9:47).

"They spend their days in wealth, and in a moment they go down to hell." (Job 21:13).

"As much as she hath glorified herself, and lived in delicacies, so much torment and sorrow give ye to her. . ." (Apoc. 18:7).

". . . Which of you can dwell with devouring fire? Which of you shall dwell with everlasting burnings?" (Isaias 33:14).

"Everyone suffers for what he has done; the crime prosecutes the perpetrator, and the evildoer suffers oppression from his own example." (Seneca the poet).

"Easy is the descent into the lower regions of Avernus: but to retrace that step, to come out into the upper air — that is a task, a toil." (Virgil).

Remember the maxim: The delight passes in a moment, and what will torment you will last forever.

is not entirely satisfied. I cannot yet flatter myself that I have fully met the terms of God's kindness. My fervor is very weak. Alas! It is all too certain that I can die in sin and can be damned!

(2) Humble prayer to obtain grace — O my God, in this uncertainty about my salvation, I know of nothing else to do but raise my eyes, my heart and my hands to Thee, and with sighs I beg Thy Mercy. O my Jesus, my God, my Redeemer, my All! Remember those wounds which Thou let men inflict upon Thee for my sake, those pains Thou didst suffer for me, that precious Blood which Thou didst shed for me.

Remember the patience with which Thou hast put up with my sins for so long. Remember that mercy that in a fatherly way has called me to repentance. Remember that kindness with which Thou hast so graciously forgiven me. Remember that goodness with which Thou, preferring me to thousands of souls, have called me to these holy Spiritual Exercises, and be mindful of that long suffering with which Thou hast borne up with my unworthy behavior until now.

Remember that love with which Thou called me again to perfection after I had abused so many graces. Ah! Is it possible that all this becomes wasted, as far as I am concerned? Yes, O Jesus, it will all be lost if Thou have no mercy on me. . . Ah! Turn, then, Thy Fatherly Eyes toward me, O Jesus, and save me. Perhaps Heaven will have no greater reason to bless Thy Mercy if Thou grant this to me after so many sins.

Second Point

The pain of sense in hell is dreadful in its duration — A most terrible thing about hell is its duration. The condemned person loses God and loses Him for all eternity. Now, what is eternity? O my soul, up to now there has not been any angel who has been able to comprehend what eternity is. So how can you comprehend it? Yet, to form some idea of it, consider the following truths:

(1) Eternity never ends — This is the truth that has made even the greatest saints tremble. The final judgment will come, the world will be destroyed, the earth will swallow up those who are damned, and they will be cast into hell.

Then, with His Almighty hand, God will shut them up in that most unhappy prison. From then on, as many years will pass as there are leaves on the trees and plants on all the earth, as many thousands of years as there are drops of water in all seas and rivers, as many thousands of years as there are atoms in the air, as there are grains of sand on all the shores of all seas.

Then, after the passage of this countless number of years, what will eternity be? Up to then there will not even have been half of it, not even a hundredth part, nor a thousandth — nothing. It then begins again and will last as long again, even after this has been repeated a thousand times, and a thousand million times again.

And then, after so long a period, not even a half will have passed, not even a hundredth part nor a thousandth, not even any part of eternity. For all this time there is no interruption in the burnings of those who are damned, and it begins all over again. Oh, a deep mystery indeed! A terror above all terrors! O eternity! Who can comprehend thee?

Suppose that, in the case of unhappy Cain, weeping in hell, he shed in every thousand years just one tear. Now, O my soul, recollect your thoughts and suppose this case: For six thousand years, at least, Cain has been in hell and has shed only six tears, which God miraculously preserves. How many years would pass for his tears to fill all the valleys of the earth and flood all the cities, for all these tears to fill towns and villages and cover all the mountains so as to flood the whole earth?

We understand the distance from the earth to the sun is thirty-four million leagues. How many years would be necessary for Cain's tears to fill that immense space? From the earth to the firmament is, let us suppose, a distance of a hundred and sixty million leagues. And even this is not half the space to Heaven (according to certain traditions), where the blessed are. O God!

What number of years might one imagine to be sufficient to fill these tears this immense space between earth and Heaven? And yet — O truth so incomprehensible, yet as sure as it is that God cannot lie — a time will arrive in which these tears of Cain would be sufficient to flood the world, to reach even the sun, to touch the firmament, and fill all the space between earth and the highest Heaven.

But that is not all. If God dried up all these tears to the last drop and Cain began again to weep, he would again fill the same entire space with them and fill it again a thousand times a million times in succession, and after all those countless years, not even half of eternity would have passed, not even a fraction. After all that time burning in hell, Cain's sufferings will be just beginning.

(2) This eternity is without interruption and without relief — It would indeed be a small consolation and of little benefit for the condemned persons to be able to receive a brief respite once every thousand years.

Picture in hell a place where there are three reprobates. The *first* is plunged in a lake of sulphuric fire, the *second* is chained to a large rock and is being tormented by two devils, one of whom continually pours molten lead down his throat while the other spills it all over his body, covering him from head to toe. The *third* reprobate is being tortured by two serpents, one of which wraps around the man's body and cruelly gnaws on it, while the other enters within the body and attacks the heart.

Suppose God is moved to pity and grants a short respite. The *first* man, after the passage of a thousand years is drawn from the lake and receives the relief of a drink of cool water, and at the end of an hour is cast again into the lake.

The *second*, after a thousand years, is released from his place and allowed to rest; but after an hour is again returned to the same torment. The *third*, after a thousand years, is delivered from the serpents; but after an hour of relief, is again abused and tormented by them.

Ah, how little this consolation would be — to suffer a thousand years and to rest only for one hour. But there is not even that in hell. One burns always in those dreadful flames and never receives any relief for all eternity. He is forever gnawed and stricken with remorse, and will never have any rest for all eternity.

He will suffer always a very ardent thirst and never receive the refreshment of a sip of water for all eternity. He will see himself always abhorred by God and will never enjoy a single tender glance from Him for all eternity. He will find himself forever cursed by Heaven and hell, and will never receive a single gesture of friendship.

It is an essential misfortune of hell that everything be without relief, without remedy, without interruption, without end, eternal, eternal.

Affective Acts

(1) Thanksgiving — Now I understand in part, O my God, what hell is. It is a place of extreme pain, a place of extreme despair. It is where I deserve to be for my sins, where I would have been confined for some years already if Thy Immense Mercy had not delivered me. I will keep repeating a thousand times: The Heart of Jesus has loved me, or else I would now be in hell! The Mercy of Jesus has pitied me; for otherwise I would be in hell!

The Blood of Jesus has reconciled me with the Heavenly Father, or my dwelling place would be hell. This shall be the hymn that I want to sing to Thee, my God, for all eternity. Yes, from now on my intention is to repeat these words as many times as there are moments that have passed since that unhappy hour in which I first offended Thee.

(2) Repentance —What has been my gratitude to God for this kind mercy that He showed me? He

delivered me from hell. O Immense Charity! O Infinite Goodness! After a benefit so great, should I not have given Him my whole heart and loved Him with the love of the most ardent Seraphim? Should I not have directed all my actions to Him, and in everything sought only His Divine pleasure, accepting all contradictions with joy, in order to return to Him my love? Could I do less than that after a kindness that was so great? And yet, what is it that I have done?

Oh, ingratitude worthy of another hell! I cast Thee aside, O my God! I reacted to Thy Mercy by committing new sins and offenses. I know that I have done evil, O my God, and I repent with my whole heart. Ah, would that I could shed a sea of tears for such outrageous ingratitude! O Jesus, have mercy on me; for I now resolve to rather suffer a thousand deaths than offend Thee again.

Now pray the Our Father and the Hail Mary and the Concluding Prayers as on page xi.

Meditation 8

The Parable of the Prodigal Son

Commentary — Before the final meditation of the first section, which is on the purgative way, we judged it fitting to present the meditation on the parable which Jesus told concerning the prodigal son. This parable offers the sinner a wonderful encouragement to avoid despairing of pardon, no matter how many and how great his sins are. It teaches him at the right time to go to a confessor — who stands in God's place — so that the confessor may hear his confession and absolve him, and thus clothe him in the sacred garment of grace.

The parable as St. Luke tells it in chapter 15 (vv. 11-24) — "A certain man had two sons. The younger of them said to his father: Father, give me the portion of substance that falleth to me. And he divided unto them his substance. And not many days after, the younger son, gathering all together, went abroad into a far country: and there wasted his substance, living riotously. And after he had spent all, there came a mighty famine in that country: and he began to be in want. And he went and cleaved to one of the citizens of that country. And he sent him into his farm to feed swine. And he would fain have filled his belly with the husks the swine did eat: and no man gave unto him.

And returning to himself, he said: How many hired servants in my father's house abound with bread, and I here perish with hunger? I will arise and will go to my father and say to him: Father, I have sinned against Heaven and before thee. I am not worthy to be called thy son: make me as one of thy hired servants. And rising up, he came to his father. And when he was yet a great way off, his father saw him and was moved with compassion and running to him fell upon his neck and kissed him. And the son said to him: Father, I have sinned against Heaven and before thee. I am not worthy to be called thy son. And the father said to his servants: Bring forth quickly the finest robe and put it on him, and put a ring on his hand, and shoes on his feet. And bring hither the fatted calf, and kill it, and let us eat and make merry: Because this my son was dead and is come to life again, was lost and is found."

Preparatory Prayer as on page x

Composition of Place — Imagine you see a young man who is sad and worried, reddened by the sun, wearing tattered clothes, seated on a rock beneath a holm oak, surrounded by a herd of swine. Pressed by hunger, he takes from the ground some of the husks that these dirty animals have drivelled and tread upon, which he eats, as they grunt and stink all around him. He deplores his misfortune, saying: "Oh, what a miserable life this is, as I compare it with what I was!"

Prayer of Petition — My God and Lord, grant me light and grace to understand this parable well; and I beg Thee to grant that, as I imitated the prodigal son in separating myself from Thee, I may now imitate him in returning to ask Thy forgiveness.

First Point

In this parable the Father is a reminder of Our Lord. The elder son, so humble, obedient and good, represents a good Christian who keeps God's law always in every way; and the prodigal son is a very vivid reminder of the sinner.

Youth brings on its own calamities when a young man lets himself be carried away by delusions — by a love for pleasure, for gambling, for going places. He makes companions and friends of those who have his likes and dislikes. He is anxious to see and be seen and to always appear elegantly dressed.

As is the way with young men, he lets himself be drawn by his passions, in particular by impurity. Instead of resisting temptation, he stirs up these passions by the conversations he has with companions and friends. He is always looking for and remaining in occasions of impurity, so that if he did not fall into sin, it would be a greater miracle than that of the three young men who were cast into the fiery furnace in Babylon and walked about in the flames without being burned (Dan. 3:50). But there is a great difference between those three youths and that one. They did not thrust themselves into the furnace, but others cast them in, and because of that God preserved them with a miracle. But the prodigal son voluntarily entered into, and remained in the occasion of sin, and for this reason, he was lost so miserably.

According to the way of young men, he craved independence and wanted to be rid of parental authority, even though it was something suitable and profitable for him. He was even rash and bold enough to ask his father to give him the portion of the inheritance that fell to him. What ingratitude! What bad will!

Affective Acts

(1) Self-knowledge — My soul, you have here a picture of what you have done. You have surrendered to pleasure and fun. You have placed yourself into the midst of the fires of passion, and have let yourself become so inflamed that through all your faculties and senses you have spurted forth sparks of impurity so as to scandalize others and inflame them. Your very eyes have appeared full of adultery, as Saint Peter says of certain sinners. Your mouth has had the rottenness of an open sepulcher, from which evil words come forth and dirty stories, dirty jokes, evil songs, by which you blacken the pure silver of chastity in everyone who has the misfortune to listen to you. Your actions, your bodily movements, and your clothing and manners reveal what you are. Impurity leads you to desire and to gain an independence from God and from your parents and superiors, so that you become fully a person of loose morals. You have the boldness to ask God, your Father, for what you think is your due according to nature. No, you do not ask for it; you snatch it and abuse your whole patrimony. You abuse your faculties and your senses, all your natural graces, such as health, good looks, wealth, and all the rest — which belong not to you, but to God. For what do you have which you have not received?

(2) Repentance — Alas! What a terrible thing I have done! What ingratitude! What injustice!

Second Point

The prodigal son, with the patrimony that he received from his father, went away from his homeland and squandered all he had. A great famine came, and he hired himself out to an employer who made him take care of swine. Here in this parable, O Christian, you have a discourse by Christ Himself about what has happened to you. By sin you separated from God your Father. You wasted everything by a discarded life. You found yourself stripped of grace like another Adam and Eve. A great spiritual famine has stricken you. You lack the bread of God's grace, the Eucharistic Bread, for you do not receive Holy Communion. You lack the nourishment that comes from reading good books and the Word of God. Deprived of these holy foods by which the just man lives, from which you have voluntarily cut yourself off, you are afflicted and hungry. Just as the body cannot live without eating, and if it cannot eat one thing, it will eat something else, so likewise the soul will act. If it is not nourished with virtues, it will feed on vice.

The prodigal son hired himself out to an employer who had him keep swine. And you, O Christian, what have you been doing? Alas! You have hired yourself out — or we will do better to say that you have enslaved yourself — to satan, who makes you keep the unclean swine of vice and sin, such as pride, covetousness, anger, lust, gluttony, sloth, unbelief, indifference, irreligion, impiety.

All of these vices are keeping you company as the swine were company to the prodigal son. Just as he fed himself with the food of the swine he tended, so you feed on vice. You have an employer so tyrannical and cruel that he does not feed you with a satisfactory diet. He does not provide you with enough to meet your needs, nor does he even permit you to fill your stomach with unclean husks. How often you crave riches which you cannot obtain, or thirst for honors which you cannot acquire, or want to get revenge on someone when you cannot, or you want some delicious food and drink that you cannot get! Perhaps you struggle after some elegant clothes, some indecent fun and amusement, and even get it. But is it a diet that satisfies you? You are always left hungry. What a pitiful state!

With the prodigal son, it was his hunger that led him to comprehend the situation. He said, "I am perishing here with hunger. What, then, shall I do? Ah, I know what I will do. I will arise and go to my father and say to him, 'Father, I have sinned against Heaven and against you. I am not worthy to be called your son. But at least admit me to be one of your least servants.' "

You see, Christian soul, the decision which the prodigal son soon made? You, too, should make such a decision. Do you not now perceive that vice is a diet insufficient for nourishing you? Vices can be engaging and fascinating, but they cannot meet your needs and satisfy you. Remember what you were before. Reflect on what you are, and how things go with those who are serving God faithfully. They go about clothed with the garment of grace, virtue, and merit. They feed on the bread of life and understanding, are sustained by a good conscience and by trust in God. They are content, joyful and satisfied. For once, then, decide to arise and go see your Father.

Affective Acts

(1) Determination — I do not want to tend the

unclean animals of vice, guilt and sin. I do not want to give any further service to such a cruel tyrant as satan, who, after enslaving me and degrading me, and making me undergo so many miseries, would give me eternal damnation as my reward. I want to go back to my Father. Now I perceive what I have lost. — Alas! My Father! How evil I have been! How heedless! I have offended Thee. Oh, what a wretched thing to do! What an outrageous thing to do! I have done wrong to myself. I have made no progress. I have gained nothing but discredit, displeasure, hardship, and damnation.

(2) Resolution — My Lord and Father, I am resolved to return to Thee. I know well that I am unworthy to be accepted as Thy son. But at least receive me as the least of Thy servants. Though I have failed as Thy son because of my foolishness and malice, Thou hast not disowned me. Thou hast always been and are my good Father. Thou wilt forgive me. Yes, my Father, Thou wilt accept me. I know Thy generous, kind heart. Thou wilt pardon me.

Third Point

The prodigal son set about his undertaking. At once difficulties appeared. He would have to overcome certain human fears. He would have to overlook the things that might be said by people in his home, by his friends, relatives and neighbors. Doubtless he would say to himself: Alas! Everybody will look. Everybody will talk. Everyone will remember what you were before, what you said and did. And now, when they see you this way, what will they say?

But fearlessly he conquers and overcomes everything. He presents himself at his home. His father receives him with all tenderness, love and joy. As for all those obstacles and difficulties which before had appeared overwhelming, he saw them vanish like smoke.

Yes, Christian soul, make up your mind for once. Then carry out that mind. Go, hasten to your Father. Do not be afraid. Do not let satan deceive you. He will make obstacles appear unconquerable. He will make your conversion appear scarcely less than impossible. He will construct a great barrier by suggesting that God will not pardon such great and numerous sins, that your confessor, who holds God's place, will not welcome you, that he will gruffly send you away. Satan will tell you that there is no longer any remedy, that you cannot get rid of your evil ways, that it is impossible for you to always stay away from certain fun-seeking, from certain sinful pleasures. Also he will bring before you the things that worldly people say. Put no stock in satan. See to it that your change is a genuine one. Make a good confession of all your sins, and you will see that all these difficulties vanish like smoke.

The Father confessor will listen to you with all sweetness and charity. He does not show alarm at the numerous and great sins of a penitent. What gives him pain — and very much pain — is if he sees that the sinner comes without the disposition, without the willingness to correct himself. That is what grieves his zealous heart. But if he sees that a sinner comes with a converted and humble heart, then he is unable — nor would he know how — to have contempt for him. Just the opposite is true. He receives the soul with open arms, and from his heart welcomes him. A tenderness and affection rather incline him to tears. He thanks the Lord as he witnesses this great mercy which is showered on the sinner before him. With joy he admires the sinner's courage and determination in conquering himself and conquering satan and all human respect. Oh, what gladness he experiences! And what joy the sinner feels when the Father confessor, having heard the confession, gives absolution. In the midst of his sobs of emotion he says these words of Saint Augustine: "Those tears that I shed out of sorrow for sin are sweeter than all the delights and pleasures of the theater and worldly amusements." Oh, what gladness does his heart not experience when he finds himself clothed again in sanctifying grace by means of the sacrament of penance! The greatest joy comes when he sees himself admitted to Holy Communion. Oh, what gladness! It seems to him that the whole Heavenly court comes to make festival in his heart.

Affective Acts

(1) Resolution —I am now resolved. I will go to Confession today. I will not delay any longer. I will tell all my sins to the father confessor. I hope to receive pardon for them all. O my Heavenly Father, how sorry I am for my sins! I will always, always avoid sin, my Father, with the help of Thy Divine Grace.

(2) Prayer of Petition — O Mary, my most loving Mother, Advocate of poor sinners who want to amend. I truly wish to amend my ways. I want to make a good confession of all my sins. By Your holy sorrows obtain for me a great sorrow for my sins. Oh, how grieved I am, my Mother, for having sinned! for having offended my God and Thee! For

having again crucified Thy Holy Son, Jesus, by my sins!

O my Jesus! I come to Thee full of sorrow for my sins. I am ashamed and distressed at seeing how I have put Thee on that Cross by my sins. But I am encouraged as I remember that Thou prayed from the Cross for the very ones who crucified Thee. Thy Most Precious Blood does not plead for vengeance like the blood of Abel, but It begs for pity, mercy, pardon. And so, filled with confidence, I pray:

Soul of Christ, sanctify me;

Body of Christ, save me;

Blood of Christ, inebriate me;

Water from the side of Christ, wash me;

Passion of Christ, strengthen me;

O Good Jesus, listen to me;

Within Thy wounds, hide me;

Never let me be parted from Thee;

From the malignant foe, guard me;

At the hour of my death, call me;

and bid me come to Thee

that with Thy saints I may praise Thee forever.

Amen.

Now pray the Our Father and the Hail Mary and the Concluding Prayers as on page xi.

SECTION II

Meditation 9

Fruits One should gain from the Preceding Meditations

Preparatory Prayer as on page x

Composition of Place — Imagine you see Jesus nailed on the Cross and that He says to you: See how much I have done and have suffered, in order to deliver you from hell and save you. And you — will you not do what you should for yourself?

Prayer of Petition — O my Jesus! I do not want to be damned . . . I wish to be saved . . . no matter what it may cost . . . My Savior, grant me the help and grace I need in order to gain my eternal salvation. *Amen.*

We have now considered, my soul, the terrible calamities which a soul must suffer who loses its last End. But of what profit is this knowledge if souls do not set about their duty, using all means necessary to avoid falling into those calamities, and to make sure that they will gain their last End? I will explain to you here what one must do; and you, my soul, collect your thoughts and weigh my words with attention in the presence of Jesus Crucified.

First Point

The first fruit the soul should gain from all the preceding meditations is a sincere repentance and a perfect contrition of all the sins committed. . . Tell me, my soul, in what state is your conscience at present? If an angel came down from Heaven at this moment and told you, "Prepare yourself; for you will die within an hour." What would your heart tell you? Would you feel peaceful about dying in the state you are in at present? Have your confessions been such that you can have good grounds for relying on them and you can confidently trust that your sins will prove to have been pardoned? Would you be content to die at this hour and in the state you are now in? Make an answer, but let your answer be before Jesus Crucified Who knows your heart. Realize, my soul, that the first step in going to God, the first rung for mounting to holiness, the first means for gaining interior peace, is that one's heart, by means of sincere repentance, become in such condition that it is ready to die at any moment, even by sudden death, and appear before the Divine Judge. In order for the soul to enter into this very happy condition, the two following resolves are necessary:

(1) Resolution — During the time of the retreat make a general confession of your whole life, or for the period since the last general confession, with an exact examination, with such earnestness, such repeated acts of contrition, such sincerity in the admission of your sins, as to enable your conscience to always tell you: I have done as much as God requires in order for Him to pardon my sins; now I can appear before His tribunal without fear. O my soul, what sweet consolation, what well-founded interior peace, what sure hope of eternal life one gains by this kind of confession!

(2) Resolution — After you have reasonably satisfied yourself in this way (as far as possible in this life) of your present state of grace and future glory, make your confessions in the future with such a

correct examination of conscience, with such deep contrition, with such sincerity, as you would if you knew with certainty that it was the last confession of your life.

Second Point

The second fruit the soul should gain from the preceding meditations, is to give God all the satisfaction possible for the sins you have committed. . .

Return, my soul, to the reflection on the prison of hell and ponder the following thoughts: Suppose that at this moment a ray of Divine Mercy penetrated that dark dwelling and a Divine Voice echoed there, which said, "Cain, come forth! Thou hast been here now six thousand years burning in these flames. I choose to make use of My Mercy with thee, but on condition that you are to suffer in silence all pains, all ailments, all contempt, all insults, all crosses and reverses, for love of Me, and in this way I will pardon thee thy sins and will save thee."

Oh, what a joyful voice that would be for the heart of Cain!

"Oh, Immense Mercy! I am glad to suffer cheerfully for a thousand years as much as a man could ever suffer, if I can in this way finally gain mercy and escape the eternal pains of hell and can come to behold Thee in Thy glory . . ."

Ah! Tell me, my soul, have you not deserved to be cast into hell as much as Cain? Now this grace which God has given you, of granting you a period for repentance — is it not equal to what God would have given you if He had drawn you out of hell?

Then why do you not apply yourself to doing genuine penance and making up to God for the wrongs done Him through your sins? Why do you not practise forbearance in your troubles?

The two following rules are for achieving this purpose:

First rule — Practise with extraordinary care and earnestness the means which God has ordained to satisfy for sin. The principal ones are: 1) the holy Sacrament of Penance, 2) the holy Sacrifice of the Mass, 3) holy Indulgences, 4) frequent acts of true contrition, made as earnestly as one can, 5) works of penance and mortification.

Second rule — Bear in silence for love of God all the harassments which your state of life carries with it, and all the troubles coming to you from Divine Providence. In all the sufferings you meet, let this be the sigh of your heart: "O my good God, Who art so merciful, what I have deserved is the everlasting horrible pain of hell, and what I suffer here is a cross rather light and short-lived."

Third Point

The third fruit which the soul should adopt from these meditations is to avoid all venial sins, especially those which pave the way for grave sin. It is not enough, my soul, to have a firm resolve to suffer death rather than consent to any grave sin. It is necessary to have a like resolution to venial sin. He who does not find in himself this will, cannot have security. There is nothing which can give us such a certain security of eternal salvation as an uninterrupted cautiousness to avoid even the lightest venial sin, and a notable, all-extensive earnestness reaching to all practices of the spiritual life — earnestness in prayer, and in dealing with God; earnestness in mortification and self-denial; earnestness in being humble and in accepting contempt; earnestness in obeying and renouncing one's own self-will; earnest love of God and neighbor. He who wants to gain this earnestness and keep it, must necessarily have the resolve to always avoid especially the following venial sins:

(1) The sin of giving entrance into your heart to any unreasonable suspicion or unfair judgment against your neighbor.

(2) The sin of introducing talk about another's defects or offending charity in any other way, even lightly.

(3) The sin of omitting out of laziness our spiritual practices or of performing them with voluntary neglect.

(4) The sin of having a disordered affection for somebody.

(5) The sin of having a vain esteem for oneself, or of taking vain satisfaction in things pertaining to us.

(6) The sin of receiving the holy Sacraments in a careless way, with distractions and other irreverences, and without a serious preparation.

(7) Impatience, resentment, any failure to accept disappointments as coming from God's Hand; for this puts obstacles in the way of the decrees and dispositions of Divine Providence concerning us.

(8) The sin of giving ourselves an occasion that can even remotely blemish a spotless condition of holy purity.

(9) The fault of advertently hiding from those who ought to learn them, one's bad inclinations, weaknesses, and mortifications, seeking to pursue the road of virtue not under the direction of obedience, but under the guidance of one's own whims.*

My soul, if you do not resolve to quit these venial sins, you will not draw the least fruit from these spiritual exercises, you will never set foot on even the lowest rung of perfection, you will never come to have any communing with God nor interior peace and quiet of heart, nor a condition wherein one can look forward to death without fear. But if you do resolve to avoid these sins, then present your resolves in the following form, while on your knees with crucifix in hand:

O my God, O my crucified Love, my Jesus! Thou hast enlightened me enough by Thy Infinite Mercy. Now I know what it is to possess Thee forever and what it means to lose Thee eternally... How blessed I am if I come to possess Thee! But woe to me if I come to lose Thee! I know quite well that I cannot expect to ever possess Thee and must always fear the prospect of losing Thee, as long as I do not entrust myself entirely into Thy Hands, avoiding all sins, even the smallest, and begin to serve Thee with care and earnestness...

Indeed I do resolve upon this, and with the deepest affection of my heart I love Thee and embrace Thee, O my Jesus! Thou art my Sovereign Good, worthy to be loved above all things, more than all angels and men, more than my soul and my life. Oh, blessed be Jesus Christ!

Now pray the Our Father and the Hail Mary and the Concluding Prayers as on page xi.

---

*Note — This speaks of times when we might have worthy direction if we seek it, but we prefer to follow our own dim lights.

Meditation 10

Our Duty to separate from Occasions and Dangers of Sinning

Commentary — Up to this point our meditations have been of the first section, the goal of which is genuine repentance of all sins committed and a good confession of them with the firm resolve not to commit them again. This resolve of not sinning again is precisely the goal of the meditations in the second section. The first of these meditations is about separating from the occasions and dangers of falling. These are the traps of which satan makes use to catch people who are not cautious. God tells us that he who separates from the snares will be secure.

Preparatory Prayer as on page x

First Prelude

Composition of Place — Imagine you see yourself in this world as in the midst of a great field with traps laid everywhere in it, like the vision seen by Saint Anthony; or, as Saint Bernard says, with robbers lying in ambush who wish to rob us of our rich treasures of grace and virtue.

Second Prelude

Prayer of Petition — My Lord Jesus Christ, give me the wings of a dove so that I may fly and quickly escape the dangers of sin and take refuge in Thy Most Holy Wounds.

First Point

My soul, you must consider how important it is to shun the occasions of sin and to know this for the following reasons: One maxim agreed among philosophers is this: Remove the cause and you remove its effect. Thus, with fire put out, the heat is gone. If the spring dries up, the stream stops flowing. If the cause is not removed, in vain are efforts to stop the effect. When a wise and experienced physician wants to cure a sickness, he endeavors to find the cause that produced it and remove the cause; otherwise he would be wasting his time. So too, a man who is trying to correct himself would spend his time in vain, if he does not remove the occasions and dangers of sin. Moreover, in the spiritual warfare against vice, and in particular against impurity, he who is the most careful to flee, conquers more gloriously. God Himself declares that ". . . He that loveth danger shall perish in it. . ." (Ecclus. 3:27); "He that toucheth pitch, shall be defiled with it." (Ecclus. 13:1); and he who touches fire will feel its burning. Thus one who voluntarily puts himself in a proximate occasion, sins already, and he remains defiled and stained; for he loves the danger, and by that fact perishes in it. The occasion makes the thief, according to the proverb, and it is so true, as experience has shown concerning many people who, not having any intention of sinning, the occasion in which they found themselves hurled them down, as they did not know how to flee, like chaste Joseph (Gen. 39:12), nor cry out, like chaste Susanna (Dan. 13:24).*

* Joseph, "leaving the garment in her hand, fled" from his master's wife. Susanna, approached by the wicked elders, "cried out with a loud voice."

Affective Acts

(1) Repentance — O my God, now I know that if I have sinned, it has been because I did not flee, as Joseph did, nor cry out, as did chaste Susanna. Alas! I have been not only neglectful, but I have been rash, like Sampson, David, and Solomon, who fell because they put themselves in the occasion of sin.

(2) Resolution — O Lord, I resolve to sin no more, and to achieve this I will separate myself from the dangers and occasions of falling into sin. I will be mindful of that maxim of Saint Philip Neri, which says, "In the warfare of sensuality, the cowards who flee are the winners."

Second Point

Consider, my soul, that our chief enemy, satan, never stops laying traps, as he seeks every chance that presents itself to carry out his aim. He makes people incautious when they frequently go about with persons of the other sex. At the outset he sees to it that their association is upright. Then he proceeds to mix in some silly behavior, then he keeps going further until finally they fall miserably into sin. The same happens to them as happens to the moth which hovers about the flame, singes its wings, and falls to its doom. Ah, how many souls were once chaste, but because they proceeded like the moth to the flame of that danger, the flame of that occasion, they were singed, were burned, and perished forever! Oh, how many of both sexes have miserably fallen because repeatedly they frequented dances, theaters, and engaged in love-affairs and the like! The same thing happens to many as happens to a pitcher of cold water which, when placed next to a fire, proceeds imperceptibly to receive heat until finally it comes to a boil and boils over. Many begin friendships and courtships, go out to certain entertainments without the least precaution, and little by little, almost without knowing how, they find themselves caught by passion, in which they simmer and boil over. Just as there is no more effective remedy for stopping the pitcher from overflowing and cooling it down, than to move it away from the fire, likewise the most effective remedy is keeping away from dangers and occasions of sin.

Affective Acts

(1) Fear — Alas! I am alarmed about myself. I am astonished that I have not sinned more, considering the danger in which I have been. I find myself like one who has been asleep, and upon awaking discovers he is on the edge of a cliff, or notices that he has at his side a poisonous snake. Oh, what fear seizes him! How promptly he moves away!

(2) Resolution — I will move away from sin and the occasions of sin as from the sight of a serpent.

"Flee from sins as from the face of a serpent," says Ecclus. (21:2-4), "for if thou comest near them, they will take hold of thee. The teeth thereof are the teeth of a lion, killing the souls of men. All iniquity is like a two-edged sword. . ."

I do not wish to do as Eve did, who, being idle and engaging in conversation with the serpent, fell miserably into sin. I will strive to be always worthily occupied and stay away from all occasions of offending my Lord and God.

Third Point

Consider the means you must resort to in order to not put yourself in danger of sinning. The first will be to reflect that you have at your side your guardian angel who, like a protector and guide, counsels you with the words of the psalm: "Turn away from evil and do good: seek after peace and pursue it." (Psalm 33:15).

The second will be that if anything in the course of time becomes an occasion of sin, leave it, or uproot it and cast it far from you, as your Master and Redeemer teaches you and commands you. Even if it be something as necessary as the eyes of your face, uproot it; though it be a person as useful to you as your hands or feet, cut it away and put it far from you (cf. Mt. 5:29, 30).

The third means will be the holy fear of God. God truly sees you. God hears you. God perceives all your thoughts and inclinations. This God Who watches you, Who hears you and Who knows all things, has power not only to take the life from your body, but He also has power to cast body and soul into hell. Thus He is One you must fear, as He teaches you in the holy Gospel (Mt. 10:28).

Get away from dangers and occasions of sin not only because of the holy fear of God, but also understand that you are being wise; as the Holy Ghost declares that the fool is over-daring and over-confident and therefore falls; while the wise man walks with fear and thus escapes evil. ("A wise man feareth and declineth from evil: the fool leapeth over and is confident." Prov. 14:16). Indeed, one who puts himself in danger shows his foolishness. He lets you see that he does not even know himself; for if he knew himself and that he is so fragile, and more so than glassware, that he is more flammable than gunpowder, he would not proceed as he does to put himself in danger of offending God. Gunpowder is not ignited by itself. All the harm comes from without; so that if glass or gunpowder is well protected, even if quite fragile or flammable, it lasts for ages. But a man, in addition to facing external hazards, has internal ones which he cannot so easily avoid, but which makes him all the more obliged to avoid external danger. Ah, Christian soul! Is it true that you do not know that you live in a body which breeds a destructive element and that in that body is the root of your ruin! Oh, if you were wise, how surely you would save your soul! Oh, if you knew yourself, how surely you would move away from danger! Fear God, and you will be wise; fear God, and you will be saved.

Affective Acts

(1) Prayer of Petition — Lord, grant that I may know what I am and what Thou art . . . Ah, if I knew myself I surely would not be so overconfident in myself, nor would I put myself in occasions of sin. The soldier who knows that gunpowder easily ignites, does not proceed to turn over hot coals with a cartridge; for he knows and understands well that the powder would explode and injure him. If I knew well how easily I am excited with the fire of passion, I would not be so foolish or rash about putting myself in the occasion of sin. Oh, if I knew Thee better, my God, I would respect Thee, I would love Thee, and I would fear Thee with a filial fear, and thus I would never sin again.

(2) Resolution — I am resolved to separate always and promptly from the persons, places and things which I know can be an occasion of sin. If any occasions present themselves to me which would catch me by surprise and would make me fall, I will say to Thee, my God, the prayer of the Prophet, "O God, come to my assistance; O Lord, make haste to help me" (Ps. 69:2). And I will address Thee, my Jesus, as the Apostles did, ". . .Save us! We perish!" (Mt. 8:25). And Thee, O Most Holy Virgin, I beg and will beg, that You pray to God for me now and always and at the hour of my death. And you, O ye angels and saints, I remind you of the charges that you have from my Heavenly Father, to guard me in all my ways so that I may not fall into sin and may happily arrive at my fatherland in Heaven.

Now pray the Our Father and the Hail Mary and the Concluding Prayers as on page xi.

Meditation 11

Venial Sin

Preparatory Prayer as on page x

First Prelude

Composition of Place — Imagine you see a soul living the life of grace, but because of venial sin it resembles Job on the dunghill amid crawling worms and filth, in a dying condition, now almost at the point of falling into mortal sin and undergoing a death of grave guilt. For God Himself says that one who makes light of small faults, little by little comes to fall into grave sins. (". . . He that despises small things, shall fall by little and little." Ecclus. 19:1).

Second Prelude

Prayer of Petition — Grant me, my Lord, a horror for light faults so that I may never fall into them, and a great sorrow for those I have committed up to now, so that I will not have to pay for them in purgatory.

First Point

Consider, my soul, what venial sin is, and why it is called venial. It is an offense, though a light one, which a creature does to the Creator. It is called a light fault not in itself absolutely, but by reference to mortal sin, in comparison to which a venial sin, though enormous in its mischief, is called a small evil; just as the earth, vast in itself, is called small in comparison with the whole universe. Or it is like the Mediterranean Sea, which is itself immense, but compared to the ocean is small.

Venial sin is an offense done to God, and this offense contains in itself so much malice that one should not commit it, not even if thereby he could save a man's life, not even if he could save all the inhabitants of the world. If, for example, by a small lie one could draw all the damned out of hell and convert them into saints and save everyone, one could not tell that lie, because it is an offense against God.

Saint Camillus de Lellis used to say that he would let himself be cut into a thousand tiny pieces rather than commit a single venial sin advertently . . . Venial sin is more terrible than the pains of hell. Convinced of this truth, Saint Anselm said that if on one hand he saw hell opened up and he saw that on the other hand he would be obliged to commit a deliberate venial sin advertently, then rather than commit it, he would choose to fall into hell. I ought to do the same in such circumstances; for hell is an evil of suffering, and venial sin is an evil of guilt.*

*Note — While this is true doctrine, it is not the wise approach for the priest while hearing confessions, according to Saint Alphonsus de Liguori, who teaches that to receive forgiveness, our sorrow indeed must be supreme — supreme in our rational appreciation of things (summus appreciative) — so that we detest nothing more "than sin and would rather undergo all the evils of this world than mortally sin against God; yet there is no need, and in fact it is not expedient (for the confessor) to make particular comparisons — for example, 'I prefer to undergo this or that evil rather than sin mortally'; for this is dangerous. . . It is even less expedient to imagine our choice of hell. Since hell in God's present Providence is destined for those who have become fixed in sin (at death) with an eternal hatred for God, a man acts incongruously who, to avoid sin, would choose hell, in which he could not remain without sin." (Theol. Mor., vi, 433).

The same saint says: "Something that often discourages many on their way to God, is worrying about the painfulness of having to proceed until death with much strictness, always resisting selfish impulses. The best means to conquer this temptation is to imagine that you only need live for that day. If one knew he had but one day to live, would he not take care to do everything well and perfectly?. . . But souls that are strong and fervent in Divine Love do not need to shun thoughts of the hardships ahead; for they are glad to and thirsty to suffer in order to please God." (Vera Sposa, vii, sec. 4, n. 16) And he adds: "Holy souls . . . live always with a firm resolve to suffer death rather than sin with eyes open, even venially." (Ibid., v, 3.)

Suffering — as suffering, is not an offense against God; so no matter how horrible a suffering may be, it is a lesser evil than sin, even if it were the destruction of the whole world, the exile of all angels and saints from Heaven, and the condemnation of all souls to the fires of hell. The reason is that all these evils, great as they are, touch limited creatures, whereas sin, even light sin, touches and offends God, Who is Infinite and most deserving of all honor and glory, Who ought to be loved above all things and yet is disregarded for a trifle. God is a lovable God, a loving God. He has created us for Heaven. He preserves us. He gives us every kind of natural, supernatural, visible and invisible benefit. And we fail to love Him! We offend Him! Oh, what ingratitude!

If the malice of venial sin is frightening, its frequency is more horrifying. Alas! Scarcely a day passes that you do not commit many venial sins, either out of malice or from frailty, or by not paying due attention to what you do. These sins may be vain, useless thoughts, a dislike for neighbors, disordered affections, or words that are idle, proud, loose, sarcastic, untruthful, or actions or omissions. They may occur in our eating, our drinking, in our retiring or our rising, by acts of laziness. They may happen in public streets, at home, in church, in the way we walk or look about, or otherwise behave. And even in undertakings which are good, how many faults do you not commit, by being too hurried, or by carelessness or laziness, by voluntary distractions, by unfaithfulness to God's inspirations! So many are the faults you commit that one may say they outnumber the hairs of your head.

Affective Acts

(1) Admiration — O my God, I am full of wonder and alarm! Yes, my Jesus, I am frightened as I consider the malice of venial sin and the great number I have committed. I can say that from the soles of my feet to the crown of my head I have nothing but the bruises of sin. I am also alarmed, my Jesus, at Thy patience in bearing the many faults by which I have offended Thee. I cannot bear a fly that harasses me, but am quick to chase it away. I cannot endure it if a dog snaps at me, and for a long time Thou hast borne it when by my venial sins I have harassed Thee and snapped at Thee!

(2) Repentance — O my Jesus, pardon me. My will is to sin no more. I know now the malice and numerousness of the venial sins I have committed. Note: Saint Alphonsus de Liguori writes: "Because our nature is infected by sin, we carry within us such an inclination to evil as to make it impossible, without a very special grace (such as was granted [for example] to the Mother of God), to avoid all venial faults throughout life, even those committed without full awareness... As for deliberate, fully voluntary venial sins, with Divine help these can all be avoided, just as holy souls indeed avoid them who always live with the firm resolution to rather suffer death than commit a venial sin with eyes opened." (Vera Sposa, V, nn. 1-3). And the saint adds: "in confession one's purpose of amendment must be universal ... This is meant to refer to all thoughts, words, deeds that could take away God's friendship ... More spiritual persons, furthermore, ought to be resolved to avoid all

deliberate venial sins. As for unintentional ones, since it is impossible to avoid them all, it is enough to resolve to guard against them as much as one can."*

I repent, and I declare with the Prophet: Cleanse me, Lord, of all my sins, grave and light, known and unknown, and I ask pardon for the sins that I did not commit myself, but caused others to commit." ("Who can understand sins? From my secret ones cleanse me . . . and from those of others spare Thy servant." Ps. 18:13-14.)

Second Point

Consider, my soul, the effects which a venial sin causes. It does in a soul what sickness does in a body. There are two ill effects which sickness causes in a body: a present one, which is weakness, fatigue, pallor, and the like; and as for the future, it hastens death. Likewise venial sin, which is a sickness of the soul, at the present time does not eliminate the life and beauty of grace, but does remove that special bright splendor which would be enough to move the Divine Eyes to tender, devoted satisfaction. It is true that it does not deprive the soul of God's friendship, but it does deprive us of many special favors. Alas! Venial sin makes a soul unworthy of God's generous gifts, it prevents many particular, extraordinary graces. It deprives it of a large part of the fruit of the holy Sacraments, especially Holy Communion, as it hinders that very intimate union which the Lord would want. As heavy fluids in the body hinder movement and perception, venial sins do the same thing and worse in the soul. They weaken the will;

*(Ibid., XVIII, sac. 1, n.7).

118

they make devout exercises distasteful and boring; they make a soul dislike to do works of charity; they cool down its fervor, and leave it miserable.

The soul in venial sin is like a sick person with a stomach obstruction, who eats without relish, sleeps without resting, laughs without joy, is so wearied in everything and so fully bored that he drags himself rather than walks. Such is the soul with venial sins. They make a soul captive of bad habits and inclinations, which leaves it with a kind of obstruction to all good works, so that many are omitted, and the few that are performed are done without devotion and with distaste and reluctance. Prayers and penances are omitted, or if they are done they are without fervor, few in number and small in merit.

Because of venial sins the soul proceeds to grow weaker, graces continue to withdraw, and finally it comes to the point where it falls into mortal sin. A seriously wicked act of grumbling into which one lapses, a secret hatred which rages in the heart, an impulse for revenge which is not yet put down, a depraved desire to which one consents — these succeed in extinguishing and putting out that dying flicker of God's grace. The Holy Scriptures are full of examples of this truth. There is the example of David: From a curious look came desire; from desire came acts of adultery and murder. With Judas it was from a disordered love of wealth. In the beginning this was a light fault; but in time it grew so much that he even sold Jesus Christ, his Divine Master. The Jews began with a light sin of jealousy and envy at the miracles and wonders which Jesus Christ performed. But on seeing everyone follow Him, the envy in their hearts grew to such size that they did not stop until they did away with Him by crucifixion. Who should not be horrified at the effects of venial sin!

Affective Acts

(1) Admiration — Ah, my God, how much the tubercular patient arouses our sympathies when he is too helpless to do anything! Now if one sickness puts a body in such bad condition, in what condition is my soul, with as many sicknesses as there are venial sins that I have committed? For every venial sin is a cancer which gnaws into the soul; it is a leprosy which loads it with filth; it is a palsy which weakens it from doing good; it is a dropsy which gives it a thirst for the goods of the world; it is a gout which will not let it march promptly ahead; it is an asthma which hinders it from sighing for Heaven; it is a deafness which will not let it hear God's voice; it is a blindness which will not let it see the way of perfection.

(2) Supplication — O my Jesus, Son of David, have pity on me as Thou pitied the blind man on the road to Jericho. Grant that I may see! Cleanse me, O Lord, as Thou cleansed the leper! O my Jesus and my Redeemer, O true Samaritan! Pour the oil of Thy Mercy and the wine of Divine Grace upon my wounds and bruises caused by the thieves which are venial sins, into whose hands I have fallen. See, Lord, how they have robbed me of virtues and merit and have left me half dead along the way.

Third Point

To perceive the malice of venial sin, a suitable way is to observe the sufferings with which God has punished it, taking into account that He Who punishes is a wise God, Who does nothing from ignorance; that He is a just God Who does not let Himself be carried away by passion; that He is a merciful God Who is on His part more inclined to forgive than to punish; that He is a kind God Who does not punish except when constrained to do so; and yet He punishes venial sin in a soul which is in grace, which is His friend and an heir to Heaven. Yes, He punishes it nevertheless.

Oh, how great must be the evil of venial sin!

Numberless examples are in the Holy Scriptures. Because Mary, sister of Moses, had murmured venially against her brother, the Lord suddenly punished her with the unclean disease of leprosy (Num. 12). God punished Lot's wife and turned her into a pillar of salt because she had venially sinned by turning her eyes out of curiosity toward the city, against the Lord's command (Gen. 19). For a small mistrustfulness into which Moses and Aaron lapsed, they did not enter the Promised Land (Num. 20). The deaths of Nadab and Abiu (Lev. 10:2), sons of Aaron, the deaths of Oza (2 Kings 6:7), of Ananias and Saphira (Acts 5:5), and of many others, resulted from venial sins. Who will not fear? Who will not walk with care to avoid such faults? Not only does God punish those faults with these penalties, but He also punishes them with other greater sufferings in purgatory. For a light lie, for an indecent smile, for an improper word, for grumbling, etc., etc., souls there suffer a pain of loss from being denied the sight of God, and a pain of sense in very dreadful fires for a longer time than people think, and their suffering is more than all the pains that can be witnessed or experienced in this world. What conception would you have, my soul, of those light sins which you easily commit, if you were now in Purgatory amid the sufferings you deserve for them? Would you call them slight faults which keep you from an Infinite Good, which is the sight of God and the possession of glory in Heaven? Would you count as trifles, and dismiss as scruples, the faults that earn a most dreadful confinement with the most painful afflictions? Suppose you saw some distinguished person dragged from his home or palace and carried off to prison, and that there, in the middle of the courtyard, they set a fire and thrust that person into its great blaze. Suppose then, when you asked what crime he had committed, the person in charge answers that he was punished this way for having told a lie, for a little grumbling, or another venial fault. Would you then say that a venial sin is nothing? Realize, then, my soul, that in Purgatory venial sins are punished by very painful confinement and torment.

Affective Acts

(1) Repentance — O my God, now I know something of how great is the evil of venial sin! Ah, if I had understood it before, I would not have sinned as I did! Up to now I have treated it as a joke. But I give Thee my word, my God, that from now on, with the help of Thy grace, I will avoid sinning again. Forgive me, my Father, because Thou art Who Thou art, Infinite Goodness, and I promise Thee I will yield worthy fruits of repentance.

(2) Resolution — My Father, I give Thee my word that from now on I will make use of the means I know to be best suited to keep me from ever falling again

into venial sins. Therefore I promise, my God, that every morning I will make a firm resolve not to sin venially that day, and at night I will examine myself and make an act of repentance if at any time I have sinned. I will avoid the occasions of falling down; I will proceed with more caution in my conversations, and I will keep my passions and senses mortified. I will in particular keep my eyes modest and recollected, and will take greater care to guard my tongue. I will keep silent, and when I have to speak, I will proceed with great caution so that my words will not be lacking in the truth, in charity, in humility, or in chastity. I will reflect that I am in Thy Divine Presence, and that on Judgment Day Thou must pass judgment on everything, even an idle word. (Matt. 12:36) and even things that are just. (". . . I will judge justices." [Ps. 74:3], says the Lord.)

Now pray the Our Father and the Hail Mary and the Concluding Prayers as on page xi.

Meditation 12
Death

Commentary — There is nothing that restrains man from sinning so much as the thought of death. It was the thought of death that God appealed to in order that our first parents, Adam and Eve, might observe the command that He had given them. In fact, they did not break the command, nor did they sin, until satan led them to make light of the thought of holy fear of death. "You will not die the death. Do not be foolish; do not be silly," he said to Eve; "you will not die."

Alas! When that restraint was removed, she fell miserably into sin. Let us then think continually on death; and thus we will never sin.

Preparatory Prayer as on page x

Composition of Place — Imagine that you see yourself sick in bed, and that you have been advised to confess your sins to the priest and receive Holy Viaticum and Extreme Unction. Then imagine that you are dying, that the prayers for the recommendation of your soul are being said, and that you are losing your senses, and finally die.

Prayer of Petition — O my Jesus! By Thy most holy death I beg Thee to grant me the grace never to lose sight of my death and that I may always be well prepared to die. May I firmly and constantly withdraw myself from evil and keep myself aloof from sin, and always practise virtue; for virtue will be the only thing that will render my death happy.

First Point

What is it to die? It is to suffer the separation of the soul from the body. Death is also an eternal separation from all the things of earth. It is a separation from your money, from all your worldly interests and all your possessions. It is a loss of all titles of nobility and of all earthly pleasures and diversions. To die is to take leave of one's father, mother, children, husband, wife, brothers, sisters, friends and acquaintances without the hope of ever seeing them again on earth until the day of the Last Judgment.

Death means taking out of your home that body of yours and taking it to the cemetery, where it will remain alone day and night, surrounded by skulls and bones of the other dead. To die is to leave your body alone, a lifeless corpse, to be eaten by worms. This is what cadaver means; namely, caro data vermibus — flesh given as food to the worms. Cadaver also refers to something as having fallen (Lat. cadere = to fall). Yes, that man, that woman, has fallen like a tree that fell and is abandoned so that it will serve as firewood for whoever wants it. Just look at what happens to that body, once so beautiful and so pampered, now dead. It is now buried; it has fallen. Presently insects will come. Toads, nasty bugs and vermin will taste it and take pleasure in the bad odor that it will yield and in the rottenness that develops. Rats also will come and perforate its clothes or shroud. They will entangle themselves in the hair, enter the mouth and begin to eat the tongue. Then they will come out and they will explore the whole body between the flesh and the clothes.

In the meantime the rotting process has built up.

We can see a great number of worms multiplying to eat the flesh of the stomach, the face and the whole body. Then their feast is over. The worms die of hunger, leaving bones that are dark and bare, which in due time will calcinate and convert into dust. Remember, O man, that as far as your body is concerned, thou art dust, and unto dust thou shalt return; for you are a man of slime or earth.

Affective Acts

(1) Act of Candor — Are you not disillusioned, my soul, at the sight of a dead body? Its fate will come to your body, too, which you pamper and idolize so much. Yes, you will die, and experience what others have experienced.

(2) Resolution — In order to pamper the cravings of my body I have many times offended God. But from now on I will mortify my flesh and crucify it with all its vices and concupiscence, as the Apostle Saint Paul admonishes me: "They that are Christ's have crucified their flesh, with its vices and concupiscences." (Gal. 5:24).

Second Point

The death of the just: Death will reach everyone, the good and the bad; but the destiny of each one is quite different. The just man sees himself in this valley of tears as a prisoner, serving a very hard term. He considers himself a slave in this world, suffering an extremely distressing servitude. He regards himself a sailor caught in a horrible storm. And as death means an end of his confinement, an end of his slavery, and is the port of his salvation, he ceases not to cry with David, "Woe is me that my sojourning is prolonged!. . ." (Ps. 119:5). He ceases not to ask with the Apostle, ". . . Who shall deliver me from the body of this death?" (Rom. 7:24)

Thus it is that a just man is not frightened by the sight of death. It is certain that he must leave the things of this world, the goods, the riches, the dignities. But what is all this in the estimate of one who knows his heart is perfectly right with God? A flower which appears fresh at dawn and at night fades; a vapor which vanishes in an instant; a shadow which flees with rapidity without leaving a trace of itself. And will the soul which has this appreciation of this world, feel very pained at leaving these counterfeit goods? The just man knows that he is not made for this world nor this world for him. He knows that its pleasures are misleading and deceitful. He knows that worldly rank and dignitaries are vanity and nothing more. With these lights, what value will he give to those things? And if he does not value them, how can their loss afflict him? If he abhors and detests them, how can it grieve him to have to separate himself from them? Is it not insanity to grieve over goods which must perish? Or for honors which must lose all value? Or for pleasures which carry such bitterness and disgust? No, the just man is not troubled like the wicked Baltasar (Dan. 5:6) on hearing the sentence of his death. Nor does he rave like the proud Nabuchodonosor. (Dan. 4:27-30). Nor does he become spiteful like the impious Antiochus. (2 Mach. 9:4). On the contrary, it is then that he says what the angelic Saint Aloysius Gonzaga said to a fellow religious, "Do you not know the good news that they have brought me, that I must die within eight days? Be so kind as to join me in saying the Te Deum in thanksgiving for this favor that God is granting me." It is then that the just man says with the psalmist, "As the heart panteth after the fountains of water, so my soul panteth after Thee, O God!" (Ps. 41:2). Then it is that the just man takes leave of his companions with joy — of his father and mother, like the little Marquis of Castellon: "O mother," he said, "do not cry for one who is to live with God, as if he were dead. This absence will not be long. We will see each other again and be happy without ever separating again."

Thus they take leave, thus they sigh — the Davids, the Pauls, the Aloysiuses, and all the just, at the moment of death. It is true that the just, also, at that hour feel the pains and afflictions of their illness; but in what sweet peace are their souls! God places them under His Sacred Mantle, and under His Shadow they remain calm and tranquil. How precious is the death of the just! And what renders it so precious? What, other than a holy life?

Yes, a holy life is what leads a man to a happy death. This is as natural as it is for a good tree to produce good fruit. Death is the echo of life. What exquisite pleasure, then, is caused by the memory of the virtues one has practised, of the Sacraments well received, and the works of mercy one has done! What great consolation there is for the soul that loved God with devotedness and served Him faithfully! What sweet joy for the just man at death to have withdrawn from dangers of sin, not to have taken part in sinful amusement, and of having deprived himself of unlawful pleasures! Can you compare this joy with anything else in this world? A man engaged in litigation rejoices at the news of having won a lawsuit of importance. One in exile is happy when his painful banishment ends. A prince is greatly cheered at a victory which assures him of the crown. But what is all this in comparison with the triumph which is declared in favor of a holy soul at the hour of death? He wins a victory of infinite importance over his enemy. An exile that is sad, painful and full of dangers ends for him. He obtains a victory which brings to him a pure, perfect and eternal blessedness, a victory which assures him of an unfading, incorruptible crown and of an immense reward. Oh, blessed mortifications! Oh, happy tears! Oh, happy fasting, that give so much joy to the upright soul at the moment of his death! Then he blesses his birth and his parents who gave him existence. Then he blesses the day he received the grace of Baptism and the ministers whom God used to bring all this about. He praises his days spent in the service of God and glorifies His mercies. The past consoles him beyond measure. The present gratifies him because he approaches the end of his labors. The future fills him with content because of his well-founded expectation of eternal happiness. Thus the death of the just is like a foretaste of final bliss.

Affective Acts

(1) Joy — Ah, Lord, "I rejoiced at the things that were said to me," that I would go to the holy house of Thy heavenly glory! (Ps. 121:1). O death, how sweet you are to the soul which desires to go with fervor to see Jesus!

(2) Resolution — I resolve to abstain from every fault, to practise virtue, particularly the love of God,

and to awaken the desire to die like Holy Mary, Saint Paul, and the other saints.

Third Point

It is certain that the sight of his sins can cause the servant of God who had the misfortune of offending Him some fear. But the prayers of the Church encourage him, the protection of the angels and saints comforts him, the favor of the Blessed Virgin inspires him with great confidence, and the consideration that a God was crucified for him gives to a pure and penitent soul an unspeakable security which no temptation nor tribulation that he might experience can take away; no, not even the natural horror of death. It is also true that the devil attacks the dying with greater fury than ever. But he who has prepared himself for death, he who already has wept over his sins, can insult satan with the words of Saint Martin — "What are you doing here, you fiendish beast? I have already confessed all my sins. I have put my affairs in order. You will not find in me anything that you can accuse me of."

No doubt the thought of the judgment which follows upon death, will terrify the sinner; but the just man solves his fears by being ready for death. You will not find anyone who feared more the judgments of God than Saint Jerome. However, with what eagerness finally he desired death! With what fond expressions did he invoke her! "Come," he said; "come my friend, my sister, my spouse. Let me see the God that my soul loves! O death! You are wrapped in darkness, but that darkness unveils for me the inaccessible light in which my God is found. You terrify earthly kings because you take away their splendor and majesty. You are frightful to all who place their hopes in the goods of this world. But for me you are most agreeable, because you deprive me of what I abhor and you lead me to the possession of what I love."

What do you say, my soul, upon hearing this? "Friend, sister, spouse," Saint Jerome calls death. Why? Because it opens to him the door to infinite glory; because it is the end of all his labors and the beginning of his happiness; because it brings him to the eternal possession of the Heavenly Spouse of his soul. Yes, this happy hope consoles the man of upright will at the last moment. Angels and saints surround his bedside. The Gates of Heaven are open wide to him. The Blessed Virgin Mary invites him with mercy. Jesus Christ beckons him with open arms. The Blessed Trinity offers him the mansion of Its glory. Thus the upright person sweetly closes his eyes, surrendering his last breath with the greatest peace. The angels and saints receive his blessed soul. They, together with their loving Queen, present him to Jesus. Jesus gives him the kiss of peace, embraces him fondly, and in the midst of joyful hymns leads him into the region of the blessed. Indeed, the death of the just is precious in the eyes of the Lord.

O my soul, do you want to gain this happiness? You are not asked to fast all your life on bread and water, nor to take continuous bloody disciplines. You are not asked to lock yourself up in a cave forever. All that is asked of you is a fruitful confession and a reform of your life. All that is commanded is that you constantly observe God's sweet plan and law for you and the laws of the Church. With this alone you will die without anguish or distress. The privation of your goods, your relatives and friends, will not torment you. The fear of judgment and eternity will not distress you. Just the contrary. You will be greatly consoled at leaving behind a few worldly goods in exchange for other solid ones, a few earthly friends for Heavenly ones, a life full of labor and fatigue for one full of happiness. Courage, my soul! Take courage! A little labor and fatigue brings you a tranquil life, a happy death, and eternal glory.

Affective Acts

(1) Resolution — I am resolved to employ the necessary means to attain the death of the just. I will make a good general confession of all the sins I have committed until now, and I hope that God in His Goodness and Infinite Mercy will forgive them. Thus I will not need to fear about the past. For the future my will is to observe God's law and that of the Church and accomplish with exactness the obligations of my state, avoiding all sin, not only mortal, but also venial. I will receive frequently and fervently the holy Sacraments of Penance and Communion, and I will practise works of charity, and do all that I know is pleasing to God and for the good of my neighbor.

(2) Prayer of Petition — O Most Holy Virgin and Mother of God, pray for me now so that I may live uprightly and pray for me at the hour of my death. O glorious Saint Joseph, pray for me, assist me and defend me from satan at the hour of my death. *Amen.*

Now pray the Our Father and the Hail Mary and the Concluding Prayers as on page xi.

Meditation 13
The Death of the Sinner

Preparatory Prayer as on page x

Composition of Place — Imagine you see a man who is over-fond of this world, over-anxious for money, whose ambition is to receive high honors, a title before his name, and public distinctions, who gives himself over to gluttony and all kinds of amusement and pleasures of the flesh, who is unmindful of God and His law and of the holy Sacraments. At an hour least expected he is a victim of a mishap, and he hears a voice saying, "Prepare yourself, for tomorrow you will die."

Alas! What panic! He sees himself surrounded by devils. Some are showing him the money he must leave behind. Others show him a picture of the woman he loves, whom he must leave. Others are waiting for him to breathe his last so that they can see him off to his grave and to hell, like the glutton in the Gospel.

As soon as he breathes his last, Jesus appears before him to judge him according to his works. Finally Jesus issues the sentence of condemnation.

Prayer of Petition — O Immaculate Virgin Mary, Holy Mother of God, pray for me now and at the hour of my death. Obtain for me the grace to learn from the bad example of reprobates, so that I will not live like a sinner and so that my death will not be like theirs. *Amen.*

First Point

To die in sin — to die an enemy of God! What a

dreadful disaster! What a terrible calamity! To be at the point of death with a conscience burdened with sin! What terror, O my soul! Oh, the unspeakable distress! The past, the present, and the future will torment the sinner in that moment which decides his eternal fate.

Before him is a very vivid display of all his evil ways in all their ugliness. What a horror to see oneself burdened down with bad habits! What a nightmare to perceive oneself plunged down in a fathomless water hole of sin! His past sacrileges distress him; the hatreds he has entertained now torment him; and the unclean pleasures of his life bring on great despondency as he sees that they have wrecked his soul. The anguish reaches even the marrow of his bones. Then the sinner remembers with unspeakable bitterness the times he has violated Holy Days, the bad confessions he has made, and his unworthy Communions. If he has cheated people by usury, theft, or robbery, these things he remembers. He recalls the times when his sins of grumbling, detraction, lying, have taken away the good reputation of his fellow man. He remembers his blasphemies, his acts of revenge, his impure talk, and all the evil and scandal with which he has ruined many souls. Before his mind is a woman whom he scandalized, the girl that was corrupted, the little boy whom he lured into sins he would not have committed had he not taught him. Before his eyes are the duties he should have fulfilled and did not, the donations he should have made to charitable causes but did not, and the other good works he ought to have done and did not. In a word, at the hour of his death the sinner very plainly sees all the good he should have done and did not do, and all the evil things he did which he was bound to avoid.

What grief! What distress he will experience! What a painful torment the recollection of his past will inflict! "O ye days I have wasted! Ye graces I have forfeited! And the calls, the lights and inspirations from God, which I have disregarded! What great distress you cause me! My life has ended. My fun is over. My pleasures are finished. Other people will enjoy my belongings. Others will live in my house. *The grave alone remains for me*. Of what use now are the lands I bought, the homes I built, the offices I held, if I am going to give them all up with one stroke as I surrender my life? *Therefore I have lost everything* — meaning everything on earth. It is cut off with a bitter death." This is the result that the sinner will achieve at the hour of death. In this way his past will torment him.

Affective Acts

(1) Act of Candor — What does it profit a man to possess everything in the world, to have every dignity and honor, and to give his body over to every pleasure, if in the end he loses his soul? (Mt. 16:26) Alas! For a passing delight one undergoes an eternal punishment! While such a person has life and health, he does not think of death nor does he want to think about it. But the door is not closed by this unmindfulness. That hour, when least expected, arrives. It puts an end to the days of the sinner and confronts him with an eternity of torments.

(2) Exhortation — In all your works be mindful of your death, of the judgment, of hell and of glory; and in this way you will never sin; ("In all thy works,

remember thy last end, and thou shalt never sin."
Ecclus. 7:40) for then you will live an upright life
and will be saved. Otherwise, your death will be an
unhappy one; it will be disastrous; and you will be
damned. Perhaps you will say that you do not believe
these things. Well then, that admission is a telling
argument for your eternal damnation; for Jesus
Christ says that he who does not believe will be
condemned. (Mk. 16:16).

Second Point

And now, alas! the pains are increasing. The dying
man's energies are playing out; his afflictions are
great and he is suffering a mortal anguish. His friends
make their departure. The household servants withdraw. His relatives are taking their leave. His children are weeping and his wife breaks into tears. The
physician can offer no remedy. Nor can all the dying
man's influence in the world alleviate him; even less
can his money help him. Death is at the threshold and
cannot be turned back. He is horrified, terrified, that
he must undergo it. What will the sinner do in this
state? He will gaze over to one side, and the multitude of his sins appear, declaring: "You have made
us; you have not wept over us. Therefore we must
accompany you into eternity in order to provide your
everlasting wages." He will turn his eyes to the other
side, and his frantic gaze will find nothing but frightening specters and horrible demons ready to bury
him in the depths of hell. He will raise his eyes above,
and the wrath of the Supreme Judge will appear,
Who will declare the terrible sentence of condemnation against him. He will look downward, and con-
front a dreadful grave full of filth, corruption and

worms, in which he will remain until the end of the world. O my soul! What will the sinner do in a moment so critical? Can the rich man not escape by paying several thousand gold pieces? No. Can the powerful, influential man not escape by means of some of his resourceful schemes? Can the prince not summon all his army? The army will be of no use. Can the valiant man not engage his valor and out-match the stroke of death? No, no, no.

Affective Acts

(1) Resolution — From now on I choose to put no stock in things that will be of no use at the hour of death, such as riches, honors, pleasures. I will only strive for things which, in that hour, will console me and offer me good company. And these will be good works, alms giving, mortification, partaking in the Sacraments, Mass, and devotions.

(2) Amendment — I know that it has been decreed that a man die only once. (Heb. 9:27). If one could die twice, in preparation for his second death he could amend what was wrong at his first death. But since we cannot do this, what, then, is the remedy? What indeed? It is to correct now what you wish you had corrected before, at the hour of your death, and do now what you would then wish you had done. Reflect well on this. Meditate seriously on it, and carry out the task, saying to yourself: I must die, and I must be judged then and there. Do I believe that this is so? I cannot doubt it. Faith declares it; reason confirms it; and experience makes it obvious. God has given me the being I have and the life which I live. God gives me time in this life minute by minute, in such wise that I cannot rely on having more than

the present minute. Thus I no longer have the time that has passed, and the time that is to come I do not have either, nor do I know if the Lord will give it to me. And if He does not, no time will be left for me and I will die, just as all those who have died up to now. I am convinced that I am to die. This is quite certain — that I am to die and be judged.

But when will I die? I do not know. I do not know what year it will be, nor the month, nor day, nor hour. I only know that I am to die, and I have no idea at what hour. I know that in that hour the Lord will come to judge me, as He tells me in His holy Gospel.

Where will I die? I do not know that either. I know where I was born, but not where I will die. I do not know if it will be indoors or out of doors, nor do I know if it will be at sea or on land. I know nothing about this. I only know that God has jurisdiction and power everywhere and that the life which I enjoy is His property. I know that He can take it from me anywhere, and that He will ask of me a reckoning of how I have spent it.

How will I die? I am likewise ignorant of this. I do not know if it will be a sudden death or a foreseen, well-prepared ebbing away — a natural death, or a violent death. I do not know if I will die from a thunderbolt, or at the hands of a murderer; whether it will be from poison, from a fall, from apoplexy or from some lung disease. I just do not know. I only know with certainty that I am to die, that I am to be judged, that I will be either saved or damned for all eternity. Oh, what an alarming reality! How undeniable this truth is! — How impossible for us to withstand it!

Third Point

What is the sinner to do? Suppose he seeks refuge in some thoughts of the future. The future indeed? He only approaches a future full of pains. Oh, the thought of eternity! It is a frightening thought for a dying sinner. To forsake property, office, amusements, is very painful to a sinner fond of these. To forsake friends, relatives and children is even more painful for one who put all his hope and reliance in flesh and blood. To give up extravagant clothes, a soft bed, pleasures and delights of the body, in order to surrender that body to a horrible burial, to become food for unclean animals, is a very painful thing for a man who had been treating his belly as his god and thought about nothing but pleasing himself. To enter eternity with a conscience burdened with sins is an affliction that has no equal. "Ah! I am dying, and I am dying without having done penance, without having made a good confession. My sins are countless. My conscience is greatly entangled in confusion and difficulties. I have wicked habits and my passions have chained me down to the service of the devil. This infernal dragon, who during my life assured me that salvation would be an easy matter by telling me that God is Infinite Mercy, now tells me that God is Infinitely Just and therefore can do nothing but pass the sentence of my damnation. I want to turn to the protection of the angels and saints, and the devil tells me that there are no angels or saints for one who has despised them, cursed them and blasphemed them by word and deed. I endeavor to turn to the protection of the Blessed Virgin, and the infernal spirit whispers into my ear that Mary is Mother of repentant sinners who turn to

Her kindness at a suitable time, but that She is not a Mother to wicked persons like myself, who have wickedly put things off until there is no remedy. To bring some relief to my afflicted heart I want to find refuge in the Blood of Jesus. But Lucifer closes the door to me, persuading me that I will find no mercy from a Lord Whom I have so much offended and Whose Wounds I have renewed with great impiety. Alas for me!

"I believed the devil and not God's ministers, and now I am receiving my due. The priests used to tell me not to wait until death to reform my life, for I would put my salvation in obvious peril. The devil used to persuade me otherwise, saying that by an act of sorrow at the time of death, everything would be set right. I heeded the devil and not the priests. Now, as just punishment, I find myself in the hands of the wicked dragon, who crushes my spirit with sentiments of despair, anguish and remorse.

"Oh, cursed be the time that I lent my ear to my worst enemy! Oh, cursed be the hour I made light of the warnings from the pulpit! Oh, cursed be the day I rejected God's inspirations and calls! What a comfort it would be to me now if I had cooperated with the graces that were offered me for a genuine conversion! But I did not choose to do so. And now — for me there is no God, no Blessed Virgin, no angels, nor saints, but only room for devils, for panic and despair. Farewell children, property, homeland! Farewell to Heaven, to glory, to that blessed Mount Sion! I am damned and I am damned forever beyond all remedy. Come, O devils, and snatch me from this world. Come, Lucifer, and take possession of my wretched soul. Come, cruel dragon, take this obstinate sinner away as your captive. Quickly torment me, tear me asunder with your claws. Quickly break my bones and bury me in hell, to burn continuously forever!"

In this way, with anguish, agony and frenzy, the sinner ends his miserable days. As soon as his body has been taken to the grave, even his best friends soon forget him, while his heirs enjoy his property. In the meantime he has not a single drop of water with which to relieve his tongue in those burning flames. So ends all the glory of this world, O my soul. So perishes all its vanity and pride. So vanishes all its glitter. So it comes to pass that the sinner's end is a wretched one and his death in every way a disaster.

Affective Acts

(1) Repentance — I know, O Lord, that it is sin that makes one's death a bad one. I now hate my sins and I am sorry for having offended Thee. I appeal to Thee, O my Lord Jesus Christ, true God and true Man, my Creator, Father and Redeemer. Because Thou art what Thou art, Infinite Goodness, I am sorry for having sinned and I resolve, with the help of Thy Divine Grace, to avoid sin in the future; and I promise to go to confession and fulfill the penance which is imposed upon me. I offer Thee my life, my toils and my hardships in satisfaction for all my sins. Even as I make this appeal to you, I trust that Thou will forgive me and grant me grace to amend my ways and to persevere in Thy Grace until the end of my life. Amen.

(2) Prayer of Petition — O Mary, Mother of sinners who choose to reform, pray for me that I will do penance and sin no more.

Now pray the Our Father and the Hail Mary and the Concluding Prayers as on page xi.

Meditation 14

The Last Judgment

Preparatory Prayer as on page x

Composition of Place — Imagine you see Jesus seated on a magnificent throne in order to pass judgment on everyone, and you in particular; and that there, surrounded by the Apostles and saints, in the presence of all the peoples who have existed, now exist, and will exist, He asks you for an accounting of all the good and evil that you have done, all your deeds and omissions, even your idle words.

Prayer of Petition — Lord, I beg Thee to grant me the grace I need to live a good and holy life so that when Thou dost come to judge me Thou wilt not have to condemn me.

First Point

At the approach of Judgment Day everything will be in dreadful turmoil. The sun, the moon and the stars will not give light, and the world will be left in darkness; vegetation and flowers will wither and bear no fruit.*

Sickness and contagion will multiply and become acute, and will leave parents bereaved of children, and children grieving at the loss of parents. Families will lose heirs and cities will be left without inhabitants.

*Note — The 1859 Barcelona text, which appears to be the most authentic, gives this last sentence as follows: "The sun, the moon and the stars will not give light, and the world will be left in darkness; the stars will not have their enlivening influence on trees, vegetation and flowers, and hence they will wither and bear no fruit." The theory of the enlivening influence of stars on plants was fashionable in some learned circles in Saint Claret's day. It is not rejected today by all learned men.

Prolonged and cruel wars will bring desolation on the most flourishing kingdoms. Bloody strife among men will end in frightful public disorder. Famine will wipe out whole families and destitution will bring thousands of the survivors to the grave.

After this, the most cruel tyrant that has ever been seen in the world will come to power. He will be that bloodthirsty beast, the Antichrist, who will spread deceit and terror throughout the world. Oh, the distress! the calamities!

What great panic there will be! Who will want to live during those bitter days? Mortal men will weep, with no one to sympathize. They will be overwhelmed with pain with no one to bring relief. How even speak of relief? Suffering will grow every moment.

Yes, God's wrath, held back for so many centuries, will release the elements so that they will be stirred up to concerted action against the sinner. The air will yield lightning and radiation which will cast buildings to the ground. A terrible hail with rocks from the sky will lay waste the farmlands.

Dreadful crashes of thunder will be heard that will bring panic. The ground will quiver with frightful earthquakes. Great holes will appear which will swallow up entire cities. The richest palaces, the strongest forts, will shake and fall to ruin.

The sea will burst the dikes, and as its raging waters rise up to the clouds, its waters will dash over all the land, will terrify men with frightening roars, and under its waves it will bury great and little, and all who can escape the world-wide disaster, will rush for refuge in the caves of high mountains.

From there they will see a flood of fire come in order to reduce to ashes everyone who has escaped the fury of other elements. What panic there will be! What anguish! Oh, the wailing that will be heard everywhere! Who will escape those immense flames? No one, neither rich nor poor, nor prince nor vassal, nor young nor old.

Everything will burn — kings with their armies, cities with their fortifications, palaces with their tapestries — all will be fodder for those flaming volcanoes. A column of fire will run from east to west. It will mount to the highest and descend to the lowest places. It will track down everything and reduce it to ashes, even gold, silver, precious stones, rational creatures and brutes, fish, birds, the hills, the islands, and the mountains.

Thus the world will end with all its vanities. Is it possible, my soul, that this should be the end of everything created? Oh, what are we to say? Are there still men who thirst after rank and riches? Are there still fools who, unmindful of the last day of the world, surrender their lives to wicked desires?

Affective Acts

(1) Scorn — I do not want anything in this world. In this meditation God teaches me that I must regard all the things in this world as fleeting, as things that serve and belong to what is subject to decay and corruption. Therefore I do not care for them. In due time they will be delivered over to flames. I do not care for them, nor do I value those things that may cause me to burn in the fire of hell.

(2) Resolution — The goods that will not burn in this fire are virtues. Therefore I want to amass these and treasure them. I will cultivate them with every effort and care. Help me, Jesus and Mary.

Second Point

Oh, what weeping there will be when the angel calls all the dead to judgment! Yes, after all the goods of the world are reduced to ashes, the voice of the angel will peal forth and say, "Arise ye dead and come to judgment." This awesome utterance will be heard in all the four corners of the world. It will be heard in Heaven, in Purgatory, and in hell. No one will be able to resist God's summons transmitted by His angel. We will all arise in the same bodies that we had, but not all in the same way.

Holy souls will come down in glory from above and will give a very sweet embrace to their bodies, which will join them forever. The body, clothed again in the four qualities of glory — [The qualities of glory possessed by the bodies of the elect on Judgment Day are: 1- Impossibility, whereby they can no longer suffer; no sickness, no pain, nor any need of food, drink, rest, or anything else. 2- Clarity, whereby they will shine like the sun and other heavenly bodies. 3- Agility, whereby they will be able without effort to pass in a moment from one place to another and from earth to Heaven. 4-Stability, whereby they can pass through any body without hindrance, as Christ did after His Resurrection.] — and the happy and blissful souls will bless one another.

"O happy feet," the soul will say, "which walked along the path of virtue! O blessed hands, which labored well! O blessed tongue, which spoke the truth and sang Divine praises! O all ye senses, which shunned evil and embraced righteousness; now you will receive the reward of mortification and penance.

Now you will enjoy all delights and consolations. Now, my body, enjoy an eternal glory which eye has not seen nor ear heard, nor has any mind been able to comprehend what God has prepared for His chosen ones."

"Bless you, O my soul!" the body will say, "May blessings be upon you, for you ruled and governed me; you taught me the way of holiness, you obliged me to keep the Commandments of God and the Church. Come, my faithful and happy companion! Come, let us together enjoy the reward of virtue. Let us unite to enjoy God forever!" In this way the just will speak.

But how different it will be with those who are condemned! What different greetings these doomed ones will exchange! Body and soul will gaze at one another, and seeing each other filthy, hideous, of frightening appearance, they will curse one another with rage and panic. "O hateful body!" the unhappy soul will say. "O bag of rottenness! Must I enter such a rotten prison? Must I be thrust into this slimy mass of filth? O cursed body! Because I gave you pleasure I see myself doomed! And you want me to keep you company? Go back to the grave, wretch, to be food for worms, and let me go alone to hell!"

"O treacherous soul!" the body will reply; "you are responsible for my ruin. Why did God make me except for you to rule over me? Should you not have mortified my animal appetites? Were you not bound to guide me along the way to Heaven? Then why did you let me run on the path of sin? O you cursed one, get out of my presence! I would rather see the devil than you!" In this way these former companions in sin will curse one another. They will hate to be joined who once loved each other in such a disorderly way. But they will have to unite, even though it grieves them.

This is the way the Resurrection of the Dead will take place. All the just, shining more brightly than the sun, and the condemned, more horrible than monsters, all will swiftly rise, with body and soul re-united, and then await the judgment of God.

Affective Acts

(1) Admiration — Yes, I am to rise again. And how will I rise? Will I be in the number of the just or will I be among those condemned? Look at your works and they will tell you.

(2) Resolution — My Lord and God, I detest and hate all my sins. I will strive from now on to do all the good works that I can; for they are what will help me on that fearful day. They are what will earn for me a victorious and glorious resurrection, in particular good Communions that are frequent and devout. . .

Third Point

Oh, what a dreadful judgment for some! What a consoling judgment for others! The Sovereign Judge will come down from on high with great splendor and majesty. The sight of Him will bring joy to the upright and terror to sinners.

Those who are saved will be placed at His right, and the others at His left. What distress, my soul, it will be for princes and lords of the world to see themselves put to shame and ranked with criminals and the lowest slaves!

What sweet consolation it will be for the poor little

ones of the world to find themselves in the company of holy rulers of the earth and angels of Heaven!

How much do you think the wicked and proud Jezebel would give to see herself at the side of the humble, pious Esther? On that day how much do you think Julian the Apostate would give to be in the company of Ferdinand the Catholic? What would the treacherous Judas not do to be at the right of his Divine Master?

Oh, what panic there will be for the miserable ones who are doomed! What pitiful cries they will make! What will it be like when the consciences of each one are laid bare in the clearest way? What will it be like when the trickery, the cheating, the lies, the thefts, the vice, the murders, all the crimes of sinners are disclosed before all the world?

Ye holy Heavens, what a distressing humiliation it will be! What extreme anguish! Sinners will wail with frenzy; they will beg the mountains to fall upon them and bury them under the wreckage; but it will not help them at all. Much to their distress they will have to undergo the strict accounting God will demand of them.

"Listen, O men! Harken, ye tribes! Give ear, ye nations!!" The Lord will say. "What should I have done for sinners that I did not do? I invited them peacefully. In My Mercy I called them. I delayed the rigors of My Justice; but the wretches remained ever obstinate in their sin.

"I spoke to them through preachers of My Gospel and admonished them through the ministers of penance. I threatened them with punishment. But these sinners disregarded both words of mercy as well as words about justice. I brought them forth from nothingness, preserved their life, redeemed them at the price of My Blood; but these ungrateful people abused these great benefits, outraged My Holy Name, and trampled on My Precious Blood. I held My peace at all this; I bore it all with much patience and for a long time awaited their conversion. But what has been the fruit of this long delay? It has been sin, injustice, vice, hatred, sacrilege, every kind of iniquity. Did you think I would be forever peacefully silent? Now, wielding My power, I will speak and I will make you burn in the deep pit. Go, ye accursed ones, into the eternal fire. Depart from Me forever."

Then, turning with a kind, peaceful look toward those who are saved, He will tell them: "You are My chosen portion, My glory and My crown. Though you were of the same flesh and blood as the doomed ones, you did not live as they did; for you ordered your lives according to My commandments and laws. You will enjoy My eternal reward. Come, ye blessed of My Father, to possess the kingdom which was prepared for you from the beginning of the world."

What different sentences, O my soul! Upon hearing the first sentence, those who are doomed will frantically wail. They will blaspheme against their parents and themselves; they will rave against everything; and while they are spitefully ranting, raving and despairing, they will fall like a thunderbolt into hell.

On hearing the second sentence, the just will pronounce a thousand blessings. They will bless their mortifications and toils; they will bless their faith, their hope, their charity and other virtues; and amid these blessings they will enter rejoicing into the possession of glory. Henceforth this group will be happy forever, whereas the other group will be unhappy forever. This group will enjoy immense favors, whereas the others will suffer infinite evils. This group, the elect, will ceaselessly enjoy all delights. Those who are doomed will experience all kinds of torment without relief.

Affective Acts

(1) Shame — Consider the shame which a person of rank suffers when his secret failings are made public before a great multitude. Now on Judgment Day the faults into which you have fallen in thought, word and deed will be made known to the whole world, unless you have made a good confession of them all; whereas if all your sins have been properly confessed, they remain forgiven, covered up, erased.

(2) Resolution — I resolve to make a good confession of all my sins, without hiding any on account of shame; for if I have this shame now and feel too ashamed to tell my sins to the Father confessor, what will be the shame on that day when the Lord will make public before all the world all my sins that have not been confessed or have been poorly confessed?

My desire, my will, is to sin no more, mortally or venially. I want to be upright and I will be, by the help of God. I will keep myself away from all sin; I will practise virtue; I will observe the holy law; I will follow the counsels of the Gospel; and I will frequently receive the holy Sacraments; I will be devoted to the Blessed Virgin Mary. I will practise the seven Corporal Works of Mercy, which are: To feed the hungry, to give drink to the thirsty, to clothe the naked, to harbor the harborless, to visit the sick, to visit the imprisoned, to bury the dead.

And I will practise the seven Spiritual Works of Mercy, which are: To convert the sinner, to instruct the ignorant, to counsel the doubtful, to comfort the afflicted, to bear wrongs patiently, to forgive injuries, and to pray for the living and the dead.

Now pray the Our Father and the Hail Mary and the Concluding Prayers as on page xi.

Meditation 15

The Glory of Heaven

Preparatory Prayer as on page x

Composition of Place — With the gaze of my imagination I will picture a city of beauty, of joy, of brilliance — the capital of the supreme King, who is seated on a throne of unspeakable majesty, attended by angels and saints.

In spirit I see many of my patron saints who beckon me to become their fellow citizen and a member of God's household. How lovely and peaceful is this city! How lovable, how blessed are its inhabitants! How fortunate I will be if I finally arrive in their company!

Prayer of Petition — My Lord and God, grant me light to see and know the great value of heavenly glory, and give me grace to be one of the just on earth throughout my life, so that hereafter I may be one of the saints in Heaven.

First Point

If somewhere in the world there were a city where squares, streets and buildings were made of precious stone, of silver and of purest gold; if all its inhabitants were very rich and noble, very kind, agreeable and courteous; if, furthermore, this city were governed by a king who was a man of peace and of virtue, fond of doing good and who truly brought happiness to all who wanted to go live in his fellowship — how quick would men not be to journey to that blessed city?

Would they not be hastening from the farthest parts

of the world to enroll under his banner? Knowing he would become rich, honored, and well-blessed, would anyone hold back so as not to suffer the little trouble of travel?

My soul, with a little trouble during this life, you can become a citizen of the city of God, the city of heavenly glory. You can dwell in endless peace amid all that is good. You can live with a King Who is infinitely kind, peace-loving, rich, and mighty, Who has the power, the will and the means to bring happiness to whoever chooses to live in His company.

Ah! What has God failed to provide in Heaven for those who dwell there? If on earth He has made such beautiful things, what would He not provide in the heavenly Jerusalem for His citizen-subjects?

If I were to say that this eternal city is paved with finest silver and purest gold, I would be saying nothing. If I said that this blessed Sion were constructed with diamonds, rubies and emeralds, I would say nothing. If I said that in that blessed country rivers flowed with milk and honey, that it has the most delightful flowers and gardens, that one finds tasty and rich fruits of every kind, I would say nothing.

Oh, paradise! You are the masterpiece of things produced by the magnificence of an all-powerful God. You are the price of the Blood of an infinitely kind and generous Savior. You have the best of all good things, to the exclusion of all that is bad. Oh paradise, in you is found a river of delights into which the person who has been saved is plunged.

In you is found light, glory, gleaming splendor that causes darkness to flee. Oh, my sweet homeland! My heart is wonderfully gladdened as I think of you. My soul feels inexpressible joy as I reflect on your sacred courts. O divine tabernacles! When will I come to possess you? O Heaven! When will I leave this valley of tears to enjoy your delights?

My ears, my eyes, all my senses and faculties direct themselves to thee, assured as I am that in possessing thee, I would find the fulfillment of all my desires. Might I be deceived? No. Faith and reason assure us that God made man to be perfectly happy. As he does not find this perfect happiness on earth, faith, and reason as well, teach me that Heaven is the place assigned by God to fill every void of the human heart.

Affective Acts

(1) Hope — O Heaven, my homeland! When will I possess you? There I have my Father, Who is God; my Mother, who is the Blessed Virgin Mary; my brethren, who are the saints. I hope to go there soon. Yes Lord, indeed snatch me soon from this world. Bring my exile to an end. Open the gates of Heaven to me.

(2) Prayer of Petition — O Mary, my Mother! Just as a little child always cries for his mother, I will always weep until I see You, until I see You in glory. Take me soon, O Mother. You well know that I cannot live without You and that "I pine away because I die not." I wish to die so that I can go to Heaven and be with You for all eternity.

Second Point

Yes, in heavenly bliss man finds the fulfillment of all his desires. Once his body is dressed anew with the four glorious properties which all who are saved will receive at the time of the General Judgment, he will have a brilliance greater than that of the sun and stars, he will enjoy an agility and power of penetration like that of an angel; he will be impassable, incorruptible, and eternally blessed.

His eyes will enjoy the sight of the beauties of paradise. His ears will be delighted at the melodious music of heavenly spirits, and he will perceive the exquisite fragrance of that blessed place. O home of infinite delights! Here, the blessed, the redeemed, will taste the sweetest savor and enjoy the happiest companionship.

Ah! If association on earth with a very prudent, wise, agreeable and affectionate person brings great consolation, what will it not be to associate in Heaven with angels and saints, all of whom have the highest degree of prudence, wisdom, virtue, lovableness and affection?

What sweetness will one not experience in talking to, in seeing, in hearing creatures that possess such great beauty, knowledge and virtue? What pleasure will there not be in hearing, speaking to, and seeing the choirs of the fairest virgins, of the charming confessors and martyrs, of gloriously brilliant apostles, prophets and patriarchs?

What will it not be like to behold, to hear, to talk with angels, Cherubim and Seraphim, who are afire with love for God? My soul pines away as it considers the delights of glory. My heart desires to depart from my breast in order to go forth to enjoy such great happiness.

There in paradise, all are immensely rich crowned princes. There all virtues reach a heroic degree, all holiness is genuine, all charity is overflowing, all love is sincere. There peace prevails as well as concord, and all awards are perfectly just. One finds abundance, magnificence and grandeur. Not a thing there is faulty or blemished. Sin gains no entry and death holds no sway.

But where will my talking this way lead to? Is there yet more one might say? How does one tell it?

Our Blessed Mother Mary is the charm of the saints. Jesus Christ is the joy of the elect, as likewise He is the immense and sovereign God wherein the angels and saints find their rest and satisfaction. But is Blessed Mary not a portion of the inheritance of the just? Yes. Indeed, what will the joy not be of seeing Her fair face, Her gracious eyes, Her lovely person? What a delight it will be to behold the Queen of Heaven and earth, endowed with every grace, adorned with every perfection?

What a joy the just man will experience from being in his Mother's company, in partaking of Her gifts, in witnessing Her devotedness. Even if there were nothing else among the created enjoyments and glories of Heaven besides enjoying seeing the sweet and Blessed Virgin Mary, the hermits would consider their penances well worth it; the martyrs, their torments; and the confessors and virgins would remain satisfied for all their privations and toils.

And what shall I say about the happiness which the saints will experience from seeing and possessing Jesus Christ? This sweetest Savior appears in Heaven with all the splendor of His glory. One is allowed to see His Holy Humanity in all the pefection that the Hand of the Almighty gave It. One sees His Sacred Head crowned with resplendent stars.

The locks of His golden hair well suit the purple of a great King. His eyes are brighter than a thousand suns. His face, more handsome than any other sons of men, will shine with the glory of God.

From His feet and hands rich rivers of grace gush forth. That loving breast is an immense sea of treasures and blessings. O most holy Humanity of Jesus! When will I see Thee at the right hand of the Father? O Infinite God! When shall I enjoy Thy presence? When will my eyes see Thee face to face? When will my soul, once it is free of the chains that shackle it on earth, become free and active in Heaven?

Affective Acts

(1) Resolution — I resolve to sin no more, not even venially; for I know that nothing defiled can enter Heaven. I will do penance for my sins, even those that have been pardoned in Confession, so that I will not be detained in Purgatory.

(2) Prayer of Petition — I will perform all my works in grace so that they will have merit for Heaven. Indeed, I will direct everything to God's greater glory. I will suffer with great patience every pain and ordeal that I must endure in this world, keeping mindful of the great glory that awaits me. I will remember that great rewards are not gained except with great labors.

I will continually do battle against the enemies of my soul — the world, the devil, and the flesh — and be ever mindful that one will not be crowned unless he has lawfully fought.

Third Point

The blessed see God with unblurred vision and

love Him without any reserve or holding back. They see the Creator of the universe and cherish Him whole-heartedly. They behold His Infinite Being and are engulfed in His immense love. They have a clear knowledge of the mysteries of the Trinity, the Incarnation, the Eucharist, and the rest.

They comprehend the good use which the just have made of their graces and the little account which the reprobates have made of theirs. In the Divinity as in a clear mirror, the blessed soul sees whatever has happened in the world.

It knows the power of the elements, the course of the stars, and the influence of the planets. It understands all sciences and arts. In a word, the mind sees all things in a clear and simple vision and it does not want to know more.

And the will? The will, now enjoying an immense Good, does not and cannot crave anything else for all eternity. One loves as much as one is capable. One possesses as much as one can possess. One enjoys as much as one can enjoy, for what it enjoys is God Himself. One lives in the love of God and is plunged in God.

Indeed, in God the blessed soul finds everything. It finds immense treasures and riches. It finds inexpressible sweetness and delight. For this soul God is a lovable Father, a fond and sweet Spouse, a faithful Friend whom one can never lose. And what makes the blessedness of the just soul complete is this: They live in Heaven without fear of losing it for all eternity. O Heaven! Oh, Heavenly home! O mansion of the blessed!

How is it that I am not seeking thee in all earnestness? How is it that I do not run, panting for breath, in pursuit of you? The Queen of Sheba, on hearing many wonderful things related to her about Solomon, hastened to see for herself. When she saw his magnificent palaces, his exquisite gardens, his immense treasures, and perceived his great wisdom and the good order that prevailed in his service, while deeply moved and beside herself she exclaimed: "Blessed be the Lord thy God Whom thou hast pleased! Blessed are they who have the good fortune to hear thy words! And blessed are all who serve thee and stand in thy company!"

Ah, my soul! How much greater will be the good fortune of those who are in the company of the Creator, enjoying His immense delights, hearing His Infinite Wisdom, seeing His lovely palaces! What a tremendous good fortune to behold Him in the midst of pure virgins, glorious martyrs, resplendent patriarchs and crowned princes! What a glorious experience to see the Queen of them all leaning on Her beloved Son? Ah, I count the remaining days of exile and tears of my life on earth. After that, I have the hope of being joined forever with the Good that my heart adores. This hope eases all my pains, tempers all my afflictions, and sweetens all my labors.

The worldling has no further reward for his fatigue than a bit of the world. Heaven is forever, and is the reward for the upright Christian. He labors for things that are solid and everlasting; the worldling toils for things that are miserable and perishable, which of necessity he is going to lose. What a difference between the hope of one and the hope of the other — the reward of the one and the reward of the other! Ah, my soul! Let us run in pursuit of that great reward. The labor is short-lasting. The happy gain is everlasting. Have a bit of patience; for soon indeed the sinner's merriment will change into tears, and the just man's tears will change into merriment. A little patience, my soul; for presently an infinite and eternal glory will come which no one can take from you.

You will then bless your toils and tears and be forever glad of your good fortune. You will then bless the Lord and all who stand in His presence, and with more reason than the Queen of Sheba had for blessing Solomon and his attendants. Have courage, my soul, for soon you will rest in the possession of the Good which you desire and sigh for.

Affective Acts

(1) Prayer of Petition — O Jesus my Savior, save me! O Divine Jesus, lead me into the Land of Heavenly Promise. Deliver me soon from this exile on earth.

O Heavenly Father, by the merits of Jesus Christ, Thy Son and my Brother, grant me the glory of Heaven.

O Holy Spirit, sanctify me and take me soon into glory!

O holy Virgin, pray to God for me, now and at the hour of my death.

And hasten, so that I may soon go to Heaven.

O ye angels and saints, pray to God for me, that I may soon go to Heaven and sing with you the Lord's eternal mercies.

(2) Resolution — When things are distasteful and difficult, I will say: Oh, how little for something so great! Oh, what a little bit you have to do and suffer!

Oh, how great is the repayment that awaits you!*

I will hear the voice of Blessed Mary, who keeps speaking to me the very words which that mother of the Machabees spoke to her son: *"I beseech thee, my son, look upon Heaven . . ."* (2 Mach. 7:28).

I will say the words of Saint Ignatius: *"Ah! How distasteful the world is when I look at Heaven!"*

Now pray the Our Father and the Hail Mary and the Concluding Prayers as on page xi.

---

*NOTE — ". . . The sufferings of this time," says Saint Paul, "are not worthy to be compared with the glory to come that shall be revealed in us." (Romans 8:18)

SECTION III

Meditation 16

The Reign of Jesus Christ

Commentary — In the First Section we have meditated on the things that separate us from our End, and they are sins. Thus we (presumably) have repented of them and have confessed them.

In the Second Section we had more deeply renewed and confirmed our repentance and our firm purpose of not sinning again.

In the Third Section, which is the present one, the retreatant is taken as cleansed of all sin and as having a firm purpose of sinning no more, and we are to see how to advance on the road of virtue and perfection and how to love God with all our heart and with all our strength in order to gain thereby our Last End.

We have become almost blind precisely because of the sin of our first parents and our own sins; and thus we are to turn to Jesus Christ that He may enable us to see, as He enabled the blind man on the way to Jericho to see. We are to beg Him to enlighten us with His Divine Grace — He Who is the true Light that enlighteneth every man who cometh into this world (John 1:9). Lastly, we are to follow Him and imitate Him; indeed, for this reason the Eternal Father gave Him to us, and Jesus Christ Himself tells us, "I am the way, the truth and the life. No man cometh to the Father but by Me." (John 14:6). The meditations, then, of this Third Section will be on the life of our Lord Jesus Christ, on the imitation of His example and the practice of His virtues. In order that these meditations may produce happier results, one will keep a rigorous silence. He will speak only with Jesus, about steps he considers taking, or with Mary most Holy, or other persons connected with the mystery.

During the meditations of the Third Section, in free time one will read the holy Gospel or Thomas a Kempis, or the lives of the saints that relate to one's state in life, or Granada, or whatever the director will propose.

Preparatory Prayer as on page x

Composition of Place — Place before your mind the synagogues, villages and towns where Christ Our Lord preached.

Prayer of Petition — I beg Thee, my Lord, for the grace I need to not be deaf to Thy sacred calls and to promptly perform and carefully follow Thy most Holy Will.

Words of Saint Ignatius — "The first point is to put before my mind a human king, chosen by God Our Lord Himself, to Whom all princes and all Christians pay reverence and obedience.

"Secondly, I will consider how this king speaks to all his subjects, saying, 'It is my will to conquer all infidel lands. Therefore, whoever wishes to come with me must be content to eat as I eat, drink as I drink, dress as I dress, etc. He must also be willing to work with me by day and watch with me by night. Thus he will share my victory as he has shared my toils.'

"Thirdly, I will consider what the reply of worthy subjects should be to this generous and noble king, and will reflect how anyone, if he would refuse the request of this king, would deserve to be despised by all and considered an unworthy knight."

The second part of this exercise is the application of the example of this earthly king to Christ the Lord, and conforms to the three previously mentioned points.

Regarding the first point, if we respond to such a call of an earthly king to his subjects, how much more worthy of consideration is a call from Christ Our Lord, Whom we see as the Eternal King, when we see before Him all mankind, to whom, and to each man in particular, Christ calls and says, 'My Will is to conquer the whole world and all My enemies and thus enter into My Father's glory. Whoever wishes to come with Me must labor with Me, so that by following Me in suffering, he may follow Me also in glory.'

In reference to the second point, I will consider that everyone who has judgment and reason will offer themselves completely for this work.

Concerning the third point, persons wanting to show the greatest affection and distinguish themselves in every service rendered their Eternal King and Universal Lord, will not only offer themselves completely for the work, but by laboring against their own sensuality and carnal and worldly affection, will make offerings of greater value and importance, saying:

"O Eternal Lord of all, I make this offering with Thy Grace and aid in the presence of Thy Infinite Goodness, and in the presence of Thy glorious Mother and all the saints of Thy Heavenly court: namely, it is my will and desire and my deliberate choice — provided only that it be for Thy greater service and praise — to imitate Thee in bearing all injuries, all evils, and all poverty, both physical and spiritual, if Thy Sacred Majesty should will to choose me for such a life and state."

First Point

Explanation — The following of Jesus Christ is something very just and it is something we owe Him. There are two reasons that show clearly how the following of Christ is called for from us. Apply yourself, O my soul, to consider them well.

The first reason is the end for which Jesus Christ came into the world. Ah! What a misfortune it would have been if Jesus had not come! Our first parents had fallen and had been deprived not only for themselves, but for us, of the right to glory. Of the thousands of millions of men who have been born from the beginning of the world and who will be born until the end of the world, none would have been able to enter Heaven nor enjoy God for all eternity. Can you imagine a state of affairs more deplorable for the human race? Likewise, just as none of these thousands of millions of men would ever have been able to enter Heaven nor enjoy God, none of them would be able to forever praise Him. Oh! How much less would be the honor paid to God!

But now that Christ has come into the world, we can all enter paradise. Its gates are not shut to us, provided we are willing to follow Christ. In Heaven there are whole choirs of saints who praise and bless the Holy name of God for all eternity. Tell me, what more noble, what more sublime end, could there ever be than the eternal glory of God and the eternal blessedness of man?

The second reason is the conditions with which Christ invites us to follow Him. Kings of the earth, when they are to start some undertaking of great toil or some hazardous venture, do not generally go in person, but send lowly servants in their place. Jesus Christ does the opposite. "I do not ask," He says, "that they who follow Me, clothe or feed themselves more poorly than I, nor in their eating and drinking do they have to observe greater poverty than My poverty. Nor do I want them to weary themselves more, nor be the first to set about the task; because I will go before them. Truly, the only thing I want from them is that they follow Me."

This is something very noteworthy. Jesus is innocent; I, am loaded with sin. Jesus is Supreme Lord; I am a heap of dirt. Heaven belongs to Jesus; whereas hell is the more suitable place for me. Yet He does not ask of me that I weary myself nor labor more than He, but simply that I follow Him.

Affective Acts

(1) Thanksgiving — O my Jesus, if Thou had no other end in inviting me to follow Thee except the glory of Thy Heavenly Father, I would be obliged to obey Thee. He is the Supreme Good and my Supreme Master and Lord; on Whom I totally depend. For this reason I have always been bound to even shed my blood for His Glory. But Thou hast not considered only the honor and glory of Thy Eternal Father, but have considered also my salvation and the eternal happiness of my soul. Thou hast invited me to follow Thee in order to make me share together with Thee, the same joys and delights, the same blessedness, that belongs to Thee. Ah! What praise, blessing and thanksgiving do I not owe Thee!

(2) Resolution — Because, O my Jesus, on this

following of Thee depends the glory of Thy Most Holy Name and the salvation of my soul, I resolve to follow Thee unreservedly and with as much perfection as possible - let nature resist as much as it will, cost what it may to conquer myself; I am a creature loaded with sins, a creature whom you drew out of nothing, a creature who has deserved hell. How will I be able to be excused from doing and suffering what Thou hast done and suffered, Who are by nature innocence and holiness, Supreme Lord of Heaven and earth, my God, my Creator, my Redeemer? No, my Jesus, I will never do this: Thy life henceforth is to be the rule for mine; observing Thy footsteps, I will follow Thee; the way that Thou didst walk, I will walk, with Thy help.

Second Point

The following of Jesus Christ is something easy and light — Two facts make it easy to follow Jesus Christ. Let us consider them with attention. The first is the interior peace, joy and satisfaction with which Jesus, even in this world, rewards those who follow Him. The life of Christ in this world indeed had its delights.

At His birth men obliged Him to occupy a stable, but angels came down from Heaven to announce His Glory to the world. In the desert He was tried by the demon; but angels refreshed Him. At the time of His preaching He was blasphemed and outraged; but He was transfigured on Mount Tabor.

If Christ's life had its delights, yours will too; for He places this express condition: "I am not willing that they suffer more than I." Yes, indeed, my soul, the greater the perfection with which you follow

Jesus Christ, the greater will be the consolations which the Heavenly Father will heap upon you.

Listen to His own words, which cannot fail: "My yoke is sweet and My burden light." To be near Jesus brings sweetness even in the midst of troubles. To be far from Jesus always is something bitter, even in the midst of pleasure. Be certain that if no more than one drop of the consolations of Heaven were to fall to earth, it would fall on the heart that faithfully follows Jesus Christ.

The second fact that makes it easy to follow Jesus is the infinite glory and blessedness with which Jesus Christ rewards in the next world those who have followed Him. Ah! A few years from now and I will be in paradise! What a consoling thought! Oh how this joyful thought lightens our troubles!

O my soul, imagine that the Divine Redeemer appears to you with a heavy cross on His shoulders and that He attentively gazes at you with kind and fond eyes, and that at the same time Heaven opens and you are allowed to see a high throne, placed above many millions of souls in Heaven — a throne of such extraordinary beauty that its like has never been seen. Suppose that then, turning to you, Jesus Christ says: "Do you see? This throne is yours and you will possess it forever, if you follow Me for a few years."

Ah! My soul, would you not resolve to follow Jesus Christ joyfully? And would not this promise of Jesus Christ provide a special tonic in all your fatigues and troubles? Now why can faith not do for you what this vision would do? Faith teaches that if you follow Jesus Christ, a heavenly kingdom awaits you, an eternal kingdom, a kingdom of infinite joy.

Affective Acts

(1) Hope — My Jesus, I believe this, and I see that one must admit that Thy yoke is sweet and Thy burden light. Thy lips have pronounced these words, Thy lips which cannot deceive. All it can cost me to follow Thee, is to give up my self-love and my cowardice. If in a short time I would learn to conquer myself and follow Thy footsteps, I would quickly understand well by experience how true are Thy words.

Oh, how miserable have the lives not seemed of those people of both sexes of all states and conditions, who in times past lived buried in deserts or in dark caves in the mountains! Yet it was these persons into whose hearts Heaven shed streams of delight.

How depressing in appearance has been the lives of those persons who ended their days undergoing persecution and oppression amid insults and disgrace, with crosses and trials. Yet they have been the ones with whom the Divine Redeemer has shared the closest familiarity and whom He has enriched with the best graces!

Will I be the only one whom Jesus will abandon in the midst of pain if I follow Him? The only one whom He will not let share any consolation? Will I be the only one to whom He will never give any relief? Will He fail to let me, alone, experience His sweetness? Ah, no! Thou will not act thus, my Jesus. I await this blessing and I promise it to myself on Thy Mercy.

This is something that will make it sweet to follow Thee. With this confidence I earnestly turn to Thee and promise to follow Thee in everything and through everything that may come.

Third Point

To follow Jesus Christ is something necessary —
I am persuaded, my soul, that you have a firm resolve
to be perfect. If we assume this, it is absolutely
necessary that you follow Jesus Christ in everything
as much as you can. "If thou wilt be perfect," said the
Divine Redeemer to the young man, "come and follow Me." Do you realize that all this is true? Ah! It
is not that there is lack of knowledge. But what
frightens me is that I see Jesus trodding such a rough
road.

But this is the way it must be; because, first, Jesus
Christ is Infinite Wisdom and Goodness. He came
down from Heaven to earth in order to show you, my
soul, the way that leads to Holiness. Is this not so?
Then if there were another smoother, surer way than
the one He showed us, we would have to say either
that He is not Infinite Wisdom on account of His
ignorance of that way, or that He is not Infinite Truth,
since He has not taught it to us. But who could think
such a thing without blasphemy?

Second, Jesus Christ is Infinite Love and Kindness. He is not fond of making us suffer without a
reason, and He takes no pleasure in such things.
What follows from this? It follows that if He had
known that a smooth, pleasant way were available
to lead us to Holiness and to our last End just the
same as a rough, painful way, then the love that He
bears us would not permit Him to lay it upon us to
take the rough way. Ah, how well this God saw that
by taking the smooth way of pleasure, we could not
expect anything but eternal damnation. Therefore
He set before us the bitter way in preference to the

pleasant way, and He Himself chose to walk that way. And now He invites us to follow Him on it.

Pause here a moment, my soul, and ponder within yourself. In this world there are two ends that we can reach. One is infinite unhappiness, which is hell. The other is infinitely happy, which is Heaven. Two roads, no more, lead to these ends. The broad, pleasant way along which such a great number of men go, leads to hell. The narrow, rough way which Jesus Christ takes with His small following of worthy souls, leads to Heaven.

Oh, what a supremely important truth! Only the road along which Jesus Christ walks, leads to Heaven! This is a truth pronounced by Jesus Christ Himself: "No one comes to the Father but by Me." It is as though He said: No one reaches the Father, no one arrives at Heaven, unless he walks the way that I have walked. What, then, am I to do? Which of the two roads will I choose?

Affective Acts

(1) Repentance — O my Jesus! I do not find anything that can truly console me if I reflect on my past life. I have adored Thee until now as my God and Redeemer, but I have not followed Thee as my Captain and Guide. The virtues that Thou callest a yoke that is sweet and a burden that is light — these are some things I have always regarded as a very heavy load, one not suited to my powers.

I have not considered that this somehow was a blasphemy against Thy Wisdom, as though that Wisdom knew not how to measure my powers; or a blasphemy against Thy Goodness, as though Thou wanted to overburden me. O my God and Redeemer, my Master and Guide! I confess my error, my blame-worthiness, and I regret it with all my heart. Oh, how fortunate I would be now if I had always lived according to Thy spirit and had always walked along the way Thou didst walk!

(2) Consecration — How long will I persist in this error? Thou art the Way, the Truth and the Life, O my Jesus! I dedicate myself to Thee at this moment with all my heart and without reserve. I choose to follow Thy footsteps and take the same way that Thou took.

Go before me, my Jesus, and be my Captain. Let me suffer humiliation or insult, expose me to persecution and slander; I will follow Thee. Afflict me with pain and misfortune; I will yet walk after Thee. Place me in humble subjection to others where I must completely give up my own wishes; and I will continue to follow Thee. Where Thou art, O Jesus, my life, I wish to be also. What Thou sufferest, I want to suffer. One thing only I beg, and I know Thou will not refuse it. It is Thy help, Thy assistance, Thy powerful Grace, O my Jesus.

Now pray the Our Father and the Hail Mary and the Concluding Prayers as on page xi.

Meditation 17

The Incarnation and Birth of Jesus Christ His Wonderful Humility

Preparatory Prayer as on page x

Composition of Place — Picture the house at Nazareth and all it contained. Then consider the road going from Nazareth to Bethlehem, at times broad, at times narrow, sloping now upward, now downward, and all the other circumstances. Finally, entering into the cave of Bethlehem, consider what sort of place it is — what persons and things you see.

Petition — Grant me the grace, my Jesus, to know the deep humility Thou art teaching me and the great love Thou art showing me. I wish to be humble and fervent in Thy holy service.

Text of the Holy Gospel according to St. Luke* — "God sent the angel Gabriel to a city of Galilee called Nazareth, where a Virgin dwelt . . . The angel said, Hail, Full of Grace, the Lord is with Thee; Blessed art Thou among women . . . And Mary said, Behold the Handmaid of the Lord; let it be done to Me according to thy word . . .

"Joseph, being of David's clan and family, came up from the town of Nazareth, in Galilee, to David's city in Judea, the city called Bethlehem, to register his name there. With him was his espoused wife Mary, Who was with Child; and it was while they were still there that the time came for Her delivery. She brought forth a Son, Her First-Born, Whom She wrapped in swaddling clothes, and laid in a manger,

* Luke (1:26 - 2:7)

because there was no room for Them in the inn."*

First Point

Explanation — In His Incarnation and Birth, Jesus Christ has humbled Himself to a point beyond measure. Oh, in how many instances and in what wonderful instances, we may consider this mystery of His humiliation! Let us now consider just a few of them.

The *first way* He humbled Himself was in taking on human nature. Even if you had an enlightened vision of the facts, you could never sufficiently appreciate this Mystery. Let us express it with a simile. Picture, O my soul, a king of a vast empire, of great power and riches, endowed with wisdom and all those talents and gifts that are suitable for a ruler. The nobility, the army, and the people love him as a father. Nothing that can be imagined is lacking to make him happy.

This great monarch secretly lays aside his purple, abandons his dominions, dresses himself in poor, tattered garments, and wandering away to a strange country, engages himself as a farm hand. He continues to live in this way, unknown and engaged in this lowly occupation until death.

What man could sufficiently appreciate this example of humbling oneself? O my soul, awaken your Faith and tell me: Who is that lovable Infant Whom you see in the stable at Bethlehem? It is the only begotten Son of the Eternal Father, the Lord of hosts, the Most High God. This Lord, disregarding His greatness and His exalted standing, came down from Heaven where He was adored and praised by all the choirs of angels, and chose to dwell on the earth.

He became a poor man, and in a lowly human form He remained here unknown until His death. Can a greater self-effacement ever be conceived by the human mind?

The *second way* Christ humbled Himself was in taking on human nature in the condition of an infant. Does anything arouse compassion more than that condition does? An infant cannot stand on its feet, much less walk. It always has to be carried. It cannot feed itself nor provide for any of its needs. It requires the hands of others. It cannot speak, and if anything troubles it, it cannot show it except by crying.

We pass over in silence many other handicaps to which they are subject, which are known to all. You and I were able to bear these hardships easily, since we were deprived of the use of reason at that time. But Jesus Christ, endowed with the fullness of wisdom, experienced the full weight of this humiliation. He could have come into the world as a fully developed man; but to humble Himself more perfectly, He did not choose that, but chose the condition of an infant.

The *third way* Christ humbled Himself was His taking on human nature in such wise as to hide all the divine and human perfection with which He was endowed. I ask no more, my soul, but that you glance at that little Babe in the manger. Behold, here lies that Almighty God Who created Heaven and earth out of nothing; and yet He cannot take a step nor stand on His feet.

Here lies that God of Infinite Power Who, though He could move all the immense machinery of the world by a mere nod, has reduced Himself to a condition of such helplessness that He needs to be carried in the arms of His Mother. Here lies the Wisdom of the Father, rendered incapable of uttering a word. Here lies that God of Infinite Riches Whom the most respected, the most fearful rulers, must turn to for aid. Yet He has nowhere to rest except in an unclean stable. Oh, what self-effacement! Oh, what an example of humility is my Redeemer!

Affective Acts

(1) Shame — O Jesus, most humble Jesus! How different are the desires of my heart from those of Thy Heart! Thou, from Thy love for humility, humbled Thyself by coming down from Heaven to earth; whereas I venture to praise myself, to extol myself to the skies. Thou didst lower Thyself to the condition of a little child; I puff up with continual ambition for higher rank and honor in the eyes of men.

Thou hidest all Thy Infinite Perfection to escape praise and honor; I put in the sight of all whatever good I seem to have, in order to gain esteem and praise. Thus all Thy thoughts are directed to humbling and lowering Thyself and all my thoughts strive toward my exaltation. Alas! I see that I must confess, O my Jesus, that I do not yet have any of Thy Spirit and that my thoughts are as far from Thine as Heaven is from earth!

(2) Repentance — I know well, O my Jesus, how much I have deceived myself! This is not the road that Thou hast walked. But from this moment I repent of all the desires and vain satisfactions to which I have consented, of all the words of vainglory I have uttered, of all the works I have performed for vanity's sake. It is right for Thee alone to have honor and glory, and to Thee alone will I pay it; for Thou

art Source and Fount of everything good. Henceforth I will not look at anything else but Thy self-effacement and humility, to love it and embrace it with all my heart according to the rule of Thy doctrine and Thy example.

Second Point

In His Incarnation, in His Birth, and all His life, Jesus of His own choice consented to self-effacement and to being despised by others. Thus consider first how Jesus Christ was received into the world at His Birth. Can there ever be a greater affront done a man than to be cast out by his fellow citizens so that he does not find anyone in his own country who grants him lodging, even for a night?

Now this is just what happened to Jesus Christ in Bethlehem. There were lodgings for everyone else, old and young, men and women, nobles and peasants. Only Jesus, with His Mother, seem to have been cast off by everyone; and it was necessary for Him to be born in a stable.

Now how did Jesus Christ bear this strange treatment? He bore it with such cheerfulness that He even made it possible for it to happen. For otherwise, if He had not been willing, He could have sent ahead armies of angels to announce His coming. In this way He would have been able at His coming to move His fellow citizens to venerate and respectfully adore His Majesty. He did none of this, and this was simply in order to have an occasion for suffering insults.

How was Jesus treated by the world after His Birth? Even far worse than at His Birth. A new star appeared in the sky. Kings from the East went to Judea and told of the Birth of the Savior of the world.

Now surely all Jerusalem would come to adore the Child Jesus. Oh, the ingratitude of these people!

Of so many thousands of men there was not even one who took a step to go see and adore Jesus. Rather, they reasoned among themselves to find a way to do away with Him promptly. His death was decreed and the day was appointed for His impious execution. In order to escape it, Jesus Christ found Himself obliged to flee from His homeland.

What idea did the world have of Jesus Christ when He was grown up? No more favorable than what they formed of Him at His Birth. Jesus lived in Nazareth with His good Mother. His occupation at home and away from it was hard work and fatigue to earn a living by the sweat of His brow.

Who would have ever thought that under the appearance of a humble laborer, a God was hiding Who had become man? His Eternal Father wanted to keep this mystery hidden and would not let it become apparent that this was His Beloved Son. Mary and Joseph also kept it secret, and Jesus always hid the treasures of His Divinity and humanity from the view of men.

So it happened that everyone believed He was a young son of a carpenter Who was called Jesus, that He submitted faithfully to His Mother and to the one who took the part of father, and that His employment was that of an artisan. This, my soul, is all the praise that this God Who had become Man obtained from the world during the space of thirty full years. That is to say, the Lord Who made Heaven and earth was a hard-working carpenter.

Affective Acts

(1) Contempt of self — Ah, what a loathsome thing in Thy sight, O my God, is the honor and esteem of men! And how greatly contempt is valued in Thy sight! By any chance did Thou lack means to obtain honor, if Thou hadst wanted it? In just a single hour Thou couldst have filled the world with miracles and thus drawn all the admiring gazes of men. But Thou didst not want to do this. Thou wanted to hide all the treasures of Thy Perfection under Thy humble condition as a workman so that in this way Thou might escape esteem and honor.

Oh, how bitter this truth is for me! Thou dost flee honor, and I flee contempt! Thou dost love to live unknown, and I strive to make myself known. Thou dost rejoice in receiving affronts and I rejoice in receiving honors. O my Jesus! Alas for me! What a wretched state I am in! If Thy Spirit is the way of holiness, my spirit is that of damnation. If Thy humility is the key to Heaven, my pride is the key to hell.

(2) Desire for humility — What shows me my pride most clearly is that I see myself honored much more than Thou were, and even so I am not satisfied. My status is respected, and because of it I am treated with respect. But who treated Thee with respect when Thou didst present only the status of a poor artisan? Alas for me! I want to be esteemed more than my Redeemer was.

I know this well, O my Jesus! And I do not know what to do. Deeply rooted in me is this desire, so loathsome to Thee, for honor, and this horror that I have for contempt, a horror which is abominable to

Thee. Everything must yield to my wayward self —
even Thy honor, the good pleasure of Thy Eternal
Father. Yes, true progress in virtue must yield; the
sanctity of my soul must yield. This is a wound that
Thou alone can cure, O my Jesus!

Third Point

Reflections on the Humility of Jesus Christ

Here you have, my soul, one of the most important
points of the spiritual life. Ask God for light and
reflect on it well.

First reflection — Nothing can be found in a soul
so beneficial for it before God as the experience of
contempt and humiliation. Let us suppose that we
were here in the world before the Birth of Jesus
Christ, and that the Eternal Father, to let us know our
pride, asks us what way He should send His Son into
the world. What answer would we have given?

Doubtless we would have said: The suitable thing
is that His foster father should be a great monarch,
His Mother a great queen, His dwelling a magnificent palace; that He send squadrons of angels to
announce His coming; and that they instruct people
to go promptly to pay profound adoration to the
New-Born God. The suitable thing, too, would be for
Him to sit upon a lofty throne and display His
Majesty and Wisdom and rule the world with supreme authority.

That is what you would have thought. But what
does the Eternal Father do? The Mother of My
Beloved and Only-Begotten Son — He says — is to
be a poor maiden. His lodging is to be a stable. His
bed, a little straw. He is not to rule, but to obey. He
is to be hidden from view and to engage in a humble

occupation. He is to live and die as a victim of discredit and contempt.

Alas, my soul! We are so blind! The thing we cherish most among ourselves is honor and worldly praise and glory, and the Heavenly Father cherishes only those who despise and humble themselves before men. Turn your eyes to Jesus. What do you see in Him except a victim of humiliation, discredit, and ill treatment?

It was just that sacrifice — such an exalted one! — in which the Eternal Father took so much satisfaction and for the sake of which He worked out the salvation of the world.

Second reflection — There is nothing more loathsome to God than fondness for worldly glory. The less a soul resembles Jesus Christ, the more loathsome it is to His Heavenly Father. Now what resemblance can a soul ever have to Jesus Christ if it is fond of praise, honor, and worldly glory?

Jesus' thoughts were all of humiliation and self-effacement. Jesus' desires were directed to nothing but to be a victim of contempt. Jesus' joy and satisfaction were all founded on much suffering for His Father's glory. Jesus' life began and ended amid insults. In their midst He was silent. Now you, O my soul, place yourself alongside Jesus and see if you resemble Him.

Affective Acts

(1) Self-accusation and repentance — It were better that I weep than utter a word, O my Jesus. I would almost say that my heart has as much resemblance to Thine as a fallen angel has to one of the holy ones. Thy Heart fosters a supreme loathing for

all praise, honor, and human glory, and has a burning desire for contempt and affronts in order to give glory to Thy Father; whereas my heart feels a loathing for these things and has a fondness for all that is the opposite. But what increases my bad condition is that I convert medicine into poison.

The most effective means to uproot my pride would be to undergo insult, belittlement, and mockery. But, alas! I love my sickness and hate the remedy for it. I defend my pride and cast humility far from me. Will there be any other remedy for me, O most humble Jesus? Ah! Thanks to Thy Mercy, I should know, at least now, my deplorable condition and hate it.

Indeed, O my Jesus, I do hate and curse all vain thoughts, vain feelings, and vain desires, all the vain satisfactions I have taken in receiving praise and honor, and everything I have done for the sake of vainglory. Yes, all this I hate and curse and I desire that it be forever cursed. Thou art the font and source of everything good. To Thee alone is praise, honor and blessing rightly due. I, who am a sinner, deserve only to blush in confusion and to be despised by all.

(2) Resolution and Prayer of Petition — O my Jesus, if in times past I have fervently begged Thee to grant me a grace, I now in a particular way beg Thee for a sincere and deep humility. I am asking for a great favor; because humility is the special quality that belongs to Thy Spirit and to Thy true followers. It is the key for entering into familiarity with Thee and the gate to paradise. A proud soul can never have close friendship with Thee, for it is an object of horror in Thy eyes. To obtain this virtue, any price, no matter how great, should seem little to me.

Two things I resolve upon, my Jesus: *First*, to never deliberately admit any vain satisfaction or vain thought, nor to ever say a word of self-praise, nor to do anything for vainglory. *Second*, to gladly accept and bear in silence the contempt that befalls me from any quarter. But, O my Jesus, how easy it is to make a promise, and how hard it is to constantly keep these resolves. Thou alone, O my Jesus, can help me. Thou alone are my hope, my helper, my strength. To Thee I cling, O my beloved One, so humble, so despised, so down-trodden!

Now pray the Our Father and the Hail Mary and the Concluding Prayers as on page xi.

Meditation 18

Jesus Christ's Hidden Life and His Admirable Obedience

Preparatory Prayer as on page x

Composition of Place — Imagine that you see Jesus toiling in a carpenter shop, obeying the holy Virgin, His Mother, and St. Joseph.

Prayer of Petition — O Jesus, I know that all the evils in the individual and in society come from disobedience, and on the contrary, all blessings come from obedience. Therefore Thou hast taught and urged it with such earnestness and have practised it unto death with such heroism, even to the death of the Cross. Grant me grace to imitate Thee, Lord, and to be obedient unto death.

First Point

My soul, before you, Jesus Christ saw all the difficulties which perfect obedience brings with it, and He overcame them all out of love for His Eternal Father and for you. To live one's life through to death according to the judgment and will of another, is something subject to many great difficulties. What would you do, O my soul? All these difficulties are an effect of Divine Providence, and Jesus Christ encountered them all before you did, and for your sake.

Let us reflect — The first difficulty which obedience presents is the burdens and duties which are assigned to us according to the responsibilities and state in which we live. Let us imagine, if you please, that a task has been allotted us which is too lowly to suit our taste. We are persuaded that persons who have been preferred to us have less talent than we. We flatter ourselves that we have enough talent to fulfill any role.

Now, what do I hear, O my soul? That this assignment is too lowly for you? Cast a glance at Christ. Who is this Man? He is King of kings, God of hosts, Supreme Ruler of the universe. What are His talents? He has so much Wisdom that doubtless with no difficulty He could convey the knowledge of His Divinity to all men. He possesses the power to fill the world with miracles. He has enough eloquence to be able to move all hearts to love Him, enough virtue and resourcefulness to be able with no effort to convert everyone.

Yet what is the assignment this great Lord is filling? Oh, wonder above all wonders! For a period of about thirty years He is employed in a workshop in the status of carpenter's helper, and in this lowly employment He obeyed His foster-father in everything. Turn, then, your eyes to this workshop. Observe the Divine Workman there; and after that, complain of your occupation, if shame does not hinder you.

The second difficulty which obedience presents, arises from the superiors who direct us. It is quite certain that in the period of a lifetime, either in our home or at work or in social life, we will have superiors whose directions seem troublesome. One superior will lack the discernment needed to know the abilities of his subjects, and he will not know how to manage things rightly. Another superior will lack the charity to sympathize, the kindness to show due concern about others. One superior will not be meek nor use politeness and kindness to win the hearts of others and sweeten the yoke of obedience to him. Another superior will not be impartial with everyone.

One who wants to practise true obedience must raise his heart above all these weaknesses. For this, our model is Jesus Christ. See Him standing before Pilate's tribunal. Pilate pronounces the sentence and condemns Him to die. What could it have cost Christ to escape this sentence? He could have overwhelmed everyone with full proof of the injustice of this sentence. He could have hurled Pilate from the tribunal into hell. As He did on other occasions, He could have made Himself invisible and so escape His captors. (Cf. Lk. 4:30 and John 8:59). But Jesus does not avail Himself of any of these ways.

He accepts the sentence of death from Pilate's lips as coming from the lips of His Eternal Father. He promptly obeys, and obeys to the point of suffering death, even the death of the Cross. Now who then, should have it in him to complain about superiors, after Christ offered such heroic obedience to the most unjust judges in the world?

The third difficulty that obedience presents arises from the nature of obedience. In the home and elsewhere many things are commanded which do not agree with our opinions and which seem to us neither useful nor necessary nor wise. Things are commanded for which we feel a natural dislike.

Many things will be commanded, probably, which completely oppose our taste and which are in themselves difficult, especially if they are to last a long time, or for the rest of our life. But tell me, my soul, how Jesus acts in His role as your model and for love of you? Do you think it was easy for Him to spend thirty years in a workshop and obey every suggestion of a carpenter? Do you think it was not wearying for Him to travel three years, walking from place to place amid continuous mockery and much other ill-treatment and persecution, while people were continually seeking to put Him to death?

Was it something agreeable for Christ to hear the sentence of death, a sentence to die in disgrace on the Cross? In all these things He obeyed, and obeyed without contradicting, without delaying, without resentment, and with perfect compliance... Ah! What is our obedience compared with that of Jesus Christ?

Affective Acts

(1) Humiliation — From whatever aspect I look at my soul, I cannot find it resembling Thee at all, Who are the Model of Holiness. My duty is to rid myself completely of self-will. I should look on my superiors with a lively faith, O my Divine Guide, and lean on all their directions, and not only should I avoid taking with ill feelings what they order, but I must carry out orders well, even with joy. That is the way I must obey; for my state as son in a household, or as a citizen in a community requires it, just as the glorious example of Christ presented to me requires it of me. But have I behaved this way?

O my Jesus, Thou knowest how many sins I have committed in this matter. I know not how to count them — how many sins from a stubborn mind, how many instances of a rebellious will, how many faults of grumbling and other such faults from selfish interests, and how many times, when I did manage to obey, I fulfilled things badly. Would these sins alone not be enough? Yet have I not others that will come before Thy tribunal?

(2) Repentance — Now I know my unfaithfulness, O my Jesus, and I repent of it with all my heart. Oh, how tragic in Thy sight have been the sins which have seemed trivial to me up to now! In the authority of my parents and superiors I should have recognized an authority that was not mere men's, but Thine. Therefore it is not a man whom I have offended by my disobedience, but Thy Supreme Majesty. As many times as I preferred my judgment to my parents' and superiors', I have likewise made light of Thy Infinite Wisdom.

As often as I have, inwardly or outwardly, criticized my parents' or superiors' orders, I have cheaply regarded the provisions and wishes of Thy Infinite Goodness and Love. "He that heareth you, heareth Me; and he that despiseth you, despiseth Me. . ." (Lk. 10:16). These are Thy words, O my Jesus, and by them I realize the evil I have done. Oh, how blind I have been! How little notice I have taken of these sins! Now I know them and repent of them with all my heart, my Jesus.

Second Point

God wills obedience — God demanded this virtue of our first parents in paradise. He demands this virtue of obedience of all children, that they show it toward their parents, who stand in the place of God. He sets this requirement before soldiers, that they show obedience to their officers. It is for subjects to practise toward civil powers, for all the faithful to practise it toward the Church. When obedience is practised perfectly, all runs in good order, everything is peaceful and happy. But if it is lacking, all is disorder, confusion, anarchy and ruin.

By word and example Jesus Christ has chosen to teach this virtue of obedience. Oh, what wonderful advantages a soul has which acts with obedience in everything! An exception would be what opposes God's Law; for that is sinful, and one who commands sin does not represent God,* but satan.

*Note — As St. Peter said, "We ought to obey God rather than man. (Acts 5:29) Thus, we must not obey civil authorities if they command us to do something that is against the law of God. For example, many Nazi officers were rightly condemned to punishment at the Nuremberg trials after World War II, even though these officers claimed that they were merely "obeying" the orders of their superiors. No one may transgress the law of God, claiming obedience to human superiors.

What is true in the civil order also holds true within the Church. A Catholic has the duty to resist orders from ecclesiastical superiors, even from the highest authorities, if they command anything contrary to the traditional teaching and practice of the Church.

In Sacred Scripture, Paul "upbraided Peter (the first Pope) to his face because he walketh not in truth." (Gal. 2:11-20). St. Thomas Aquinas, basing himself on this scriptural passage, speaks of the duty for an "inferior" to resist and correct a superior who commands anything contrary to the law of Christ. (See *Summa theologiae*, II. II, q. 33, a.4., and *Super Epistulas S. Pauli, Ad Galatas*, 2, 11-14, lec. III, n. 77 & nn. 83f).

Likewise, the great theologian, Cardinal Juan de Torquemada (1388-1468), citing the doctrine of Pope Innocent III, says that even if the Pope should command something that is incompatible with the law of Christ, then that Pope must not be blindly obeyed:

Torquemada writes, "By disobedience, the Pope can separate himself from Christ despite the fact that he is head of the Church, for above all, the unity of the Church is dependent on its relationship with Christ. The Pope can separate himself from Christ either by disobeying the law of Christ, or by commanding something that is against the divine or natural law. By doing so, the Pope separates himself from the body of the Church because the body is itself linked to Christ by obedience. In this way the Pope could, without doubt, fall into schism . . . Especially is this true with regard to the divine liturgy as for example, if he did not wish personally to follow the universal customs and rites of the Church. . . . Thus it is that Pope Innocent III states (*De Consuetudine*) that, it is necessary to obey the Pope in all things as long as he, himself does not go against the universal customs of the Church, but should he go against the universal customs of the Church, "he need not be followed . . ."

Many other saints and theologians, including St. Robert Bellarmine (see *De Romano Pontifice*, lib. II, chap. 29, in Opera omnia) teach the same important distinction in regard to true obedience.

You have seen, O my soul, the obedience of Jesus Christ. Consider now the blessings that this virtue brings with it.

First Blessing — An obedient soul is sure of doing God's Will at every moment. Suppose that by a special Divine Decree your Guardian Angel (who otherwise would assist you invisibly) accompanies you visibly day and night, and in all circumstances informs you what God wants of you, and what God does not want of you. Could there be a better fortune than this? O my soul, is your faith alive? Then realize that by wisely obeying,* you are always and at every moment sure of doing God's Will. This is as sure as it would be if an angel who was accompanying you in visible form, assured you of it. It is as sure that you would be doing God's Will, as it is that Christ did it at Nazareth. You can be as sure of this as the Apostles were who received their orders from the lips of Jesus Christ.

Second Blessing — An obedient soul elevates his works, making them have an immense value before God. Nothing in the world has a value equal to obedience. Every work, even the least, that is done from obedience, becomes very great before God; whereas those works, no matter how great, that are done against obedience, lose all value before God.

To eat and drink moderately out of obedience is something so precious in God's sight, that thereby one gains a merit beyond all calculation. Fasting on bread and water undertaken against the will of one who rules us, though it lasted a whole year, does not earn the Divine pleasure; rather God regards it with contempt. It is a little thing to wash a dish, to sweep a floor, and quite great thing to travel over the world preaching the Gospel.

Yet God values highly that washing, that sweeping, when done from obedience, and counts that preaching as nothing if done against obedience. The only rule for measuring the excellence of a deed is God's Will. Whenever God Wills something, though it be no more than weaving baskets like the anchorites of old, it is a deed so great that no man on earth and no angel in Heaven can do anything greater.

Look again, my soul, at Saint Joseph's workshop. See Jesus Christ there, and you should know that the lowly office He performs there is so noble that one cannot speak of anything nobler. Why is this? It is because He does the Will of His Eternal Father.

Third Blessing — Infallibly and in a short time an obedient soul obtains perfect holiness for two reasons: The first is that obedience is the very essence of holiness and perfection. For if holiness means nothing else than fulfilling God's Will in the way God wishes, an obedient soul, as one who does only what God Wills, when he sleeps or works, meditates or does anything else, by occupying in this way every moment of the day and night in fulfillment of the Divine Good Pleasure, he must necessarily reach a perfect holiness and reach it in a very short time.

The second reason is that the Lord has so ordered things. Because God loves an obedient soul, He carries it in the bosom of His Providence as a mother carries her tender baby, nourishes it, coaxes it, and takes special care of all that pertains to it. Thus even all hell and all the world can be roused up against it, even its superiors can, of set purpose, strive to op-press it; and all their efforts will be absolutely in vain; for this soul enjoys the protection of a God of Wisdom, Power, and Infinite Love, Who will infallibly lead it in this life to that degree of holiness which He wants it to reach, and in the next life will raise it to that throne of glory which He has destined for it from Eternity.

Affective Acts

(1) Faith — It is true that superiors** do not rule us except in the name of Jesus Christ. I ought to gladly accept the orders they give me, not because it is their will, but because it is the Will of Jesus Christ. The Lord's words are very clear, and one who does not put complete trust in them treats Jesus Christ as a liar. "He who hears you, hears Me; he who despises you, despises Me." (Lk. 10:16) I submit my mind to this, Thy word, O my Jesus. I believe that the will of my superiors is Thy will. I believe that what they order, Thou dost order. I believe that I cannot withdraw myself from their bidding without separating from Thy Providence.*** This I believe, my Jesus, and I believe it on Thy word.

(2) Hope and Confidence — As alive as my faith

**Note — Since obedience is the tool used by enemies infiltrated into the Church to destroy her from within, it must be noted that superiors have limited jurisdiction. So if a superior commands something beyond his jurisdiction, even if it is not sinful in itself — one does not sin by refusing the order even if it is against the wishes or "orders" of the person who is one's superior in other matters.

In this matter, since he does not have jurisdiction, he is not a superior. This is clearly the teaching of the Church. By promulgating the Code of Canon Law wherein the limits of jurisdiction are spelled out — the Church clearly teaches who has authority — in what matters.

***Moralists would further point out that some disobedience is not always a Mortal Sin.

is, O my Jesus, so great is my trust. I have promised obedience, and I have perpetually and entirely surrendered my will and liberty. Thou — so I hope — hast accepted this sacrifice and have chosen and promised to rule and guide me by the voice of my superiors. I surrender myself, then, to the bosom of Thy Providence and am living on in safety. Thou art Infinite Wisdom and know what my superiors' directions are, and that they are the most suitable for me. Thou art Infinite Goodness, and will take care that my superiors always provide what is more profitable for me. I hope and trust in Thee, my Jesus. Thou will arrange things so that my superiors always do what is more serviceable toward my last End, and so that, thanks to Thy Providence, I may attain that degree of glory in paradise which Thou hast prepared for me from eternity.

3. Let us make the Act of Oblation which Saint Ignatius made: Lord, receive all my freedom. Take the whole of my memory, understanding and will. Whatever I have or hold, Thou hast given me. I give it all back to Thee and surrender it completely to the guidance of Thy Will. With Thy love and with Thy Grace I am rich enough. Give me but that and I ask for nothing more. *Amen.*

Now pray the Our Father and the Hail Mary and the Concluding Prayers as on page xi.

Meditation 19

The Public Life of Jesus Christ His Admirable Charity and Meekness towards His Neighbor

Preparatory Prayer as on page x

Composition of Place — Imagine you see Jesus Christ in the company of His Apostles, journeying about Palestine, teaching His heavenly doctrine, arousing all to the practice of virtue.

Prayer of Petition — Grant me, my Jesus, light to understand Thy heavenly teaching and grace to imitate Thy example.

First Point

Before we have had to bear them, Jesus Christ had borne all those annoyances which make the practice of charity and meekness toward our neighbor so burdensome and bitter. My soul, let us try to consider a virtue which, just as it is most essential to holiness, is likewise the most subject to annoyances and difficulties. Reflect on the example which Jesus Christ gave us, and resolve to suffer what He suffered before you and for love of you.

The first annoyance is the necessity of dealing with people for whom one is wasting his efforts and all his toil. Ah, my soul! How much did Jesus not weary Himself in order to convert the Hebrews! For three years He journeyed from one city to another, one village to another; He preached to them; He was bountiful in bestowing benefits on them; He moved them with miracles; and like a loving Father He invited all to the bosom of His Mercy. And what fruit came of it? Some belittled Him, calling Him son of a carpenter. Others ridiculed His heavenly doctrine. Pharisees mocked Him as a man who lived a bad life and broke the law. The high priests publicly condemned Him for false doctrine, and took every care that the people not let themselves be taught by His Words; and they went so far as to expel from the synagogue those who would follow Him.

Thus it came about that of the many who heard Him, only a few were converted, the others remaining obstinate and rendering His labors fruitless. Must it not have been rather a hard thing for the Heart of Jesus to love that kind of people? Not even the tenderest, most affectionate father can look upon his son with favorable eyes who, disregarding all his admonitions, continually offers him new occasions of displeasure.

The second annoyance is to have to deal with persons who, out of hatred and envy, interpret everything in an unfavorable way. During the whole time of His preaching Jesus met this harassment. Frequently on the Sabbath day He would cure some sick person out of compassion for his ailments, and people of ill will would attribute it to the devils, because Jesus (they said) was not keeping the Sabbath.

He sat at table with public sinners to draw them to repentance by sweetness and charity, and people criticized Him as being a glutton who wanted to satisfy His hunger at other people's expense. He worked miracles to lead men to a knowledge of His Divinity, and they said this came not from His power, but from that of the devil, who was working them through Him. In brief, there was nothing which they would not interpret unfairly and unfavorably.

The third annoyance is having to deal with persons who show no appreciation for acts of charity extended to them and return evil for good . . . Jesus went to Nazareth. He preached in the synagogue. He showed the most refined and sincere charity to His countrymen. What thanks did He receive from all this? Just what could be expected from a person who returns evil for good? They took Him to the edge of a cliff in order to throw Him over. "But Jesus," according to St. Luke (4:30), "passing through the midst of them, went His way."

He also preached in Jerusalem. He said that He was the Son of God and the promised Messiah Whom they had long awaited. But in return for the truth which He preached to them, they took Him to be a blasphemer. They took up rocks in order to stone Him on the spot.

The fourth annoyance is living in the midst of insincere, hypocritical people. Jesus knew what was in Judas' heart and all the bad will that he possessed, that he was the one who would sell Him one day for a few pieces of silver and deliver Him over to death.

The fifth annoyance is having to deal with persons whose extreme hatred is recognized. For quite some time in advance the high priests and scribes had condemned Jesus to death in a secret council. It had been publicly declared that all who adhered to His doctrine were cut off from the synagogue. It had been decreed that He was to be arrested as a seducer and put into their custody; and they had plotted other similar evils against Him.

See, then, my soul, the number and kind of harassments which Jesus' Charity had to outmatch to enable Him to love this kind of people, who deserved

God's eternal hatred rather than His Fatherly love. But in the midst of such great provocation, how did Jesus conduct Himself? You will hear it shortly. For the present I will only tell you this: that with all these harassments, He loved them and loved them very tenderly.

Affective Acts

(1) Shame — O my Jesus, how ardent, how solid is Thy love! And how weak and cold mine is! Thou had to deal with persons who outraged Thee and vomited out injury and insult into Thy Face; persons who, using a veil of friendship, sought a way to deliver Thee over into the hands of Thy enemies; persons who, in effect, had resolutely determined not to rest until they had put Thee on the Cross. Oh, the intolerable outrages! But all this could not extinguish Thy love. Thou didst love them even to the Cross, even to death.

Alas! How little of the meekness and charity of Jesus Christ there is in me! An unfriendly look from someone, a slighting word, a refusal, a trivial offense, is enough to extinguish my love and change my meekness into anger and indignation . . . This is as far as I have advanced, O my Jesus, after so many graces that Thou hast granted me; and after Thou hast supplied me with so many means of advancement, this is the progress that I have made. What a showing I will make one day before Thy divine tribunal, with my scarcity of virtue!

(2) Resolution — Will it always be this way, O my Jesus? Will this heart of mine always remain so hard and cold? Will I always surrender myself to a pampered life? Will a time not come when I will

have the consolation of possessing true love and true meekness? Oh, what ruin it would be for me if that time were never to come! Thou hast called me, O my Jesus, to Thy school, and as my teacher Thou tell me that I should learn from Thee, that Thou art meek and humble of Heart. How will I appear before Thy Judgment, when I find myself so poor in this virtue? What account shall I render Thee for all the graces I have received and used so poorly? Ah! My Jesus! I turn to Thee with my whole heart. . .

Second Point

Consider the admirable qualities of the love with which Jesus loved men — Endeavor now, my soul, to penetrate the interior of Jesus' Heart and learn how to love.

(1) First Property — The charity and meekness of Jesus' Heart was always affectionate and ardent. Jesus, with His Infinite Powers, daily saw thousands of persons who hated Him, who considered Him to be a seducer, a blasphemer, and a sorcerer. He saw many others who were tearing His reputation apart with lies against Him, with insulting and over-critical remarks, and who would mock Him. He saw thousands of others who were anxiously seeking to crucify Him. All this was quite evident to Him; for nothing could be hidden from Him. But yet He was never resentful nor did He hold back in His supremely earnest love for all. How would your heart be disposed if there were a hundred persons who considered you a villain, who defamed you everywhere with calumnies and false charges and even endeavored to put you to death?

(2) Second Property — The charity and meekness

of Jesus Christ showed itself always to be affable, sweet and resourceful, in His words as well as in His manners and actions, in spite of all the outrages. Recall again the case of Judas, my soul. Jesus knew his soul well, and knew that in the end Judas would betray Him . . . Yet this was not enough to hinder His charity toward the man. For three full years He always had him at His side. He treated Judas with the same affection as He did the other Apostles.

He bestowed on Judas along with the others the gift of performing miracles; also He washed Judas' feet along with the feet of the others. Thus even at the Last Supper the Apostles were not able to learn Judas' wicked design. And when Judas delivered Jesus into the hands of His enemies Jesus called him His friend and gave him a kiss. Is it possible that Jesus treated His beloved Apostle John more affectionately?

(3) Third Property — The charity and meekness of Jesus Christ was always generous and benevolent, returning good for evil to those who treated Him the worst. Every day among the ungrateful Jews, a fury and rage against Jesus was growing; and a magnanimity on Jesus' part toward them would appear the most liberal at every turn. Each day He directed ardent sighs to His Eternal Father for their salvation.

Every day He multiplied more His miracles so that they would recognize His Divinity. Daily He loaded them with new favors to soften their stony hearts. Not content with that, He showed them a favor the very moment they outrageously wronged Him. Was not Malchus a very perverse man? He was one of those who went to seize Jesus in the garden; and in the instant in which He is carrying this out, Jesus stretches out His Divine hand, and restoring the man's ear, cures it perfectly.

Affective Acts

(1) Repentance — Now I know what it is to love, O my Jesus. To love those by whom we are loved, those who are very fond of us and who do good to us — that is, to love in the way the Jews and pagans do. To love those who do not love us, who murmur against us and wrong us — is to love in the way Thou hast loved. How, then, have I loved until now? Alas! My heart has within it so much corruption! How defective is my love! I have generally loved as the Jews loved.

Rarely have I loved as Jesus loved. . . I have gone astray then. I have erred in that virtue which makes up the essence of Christianity, which is the substance of a true disciple of Jesus Christ, which is the core of holiness and perfection. . . I recognize my mistake and I repent. O my Jesus, I detest with all my heart all that I have done contrary to this virtue which is so pleasing to Thee. By the merits of Thy Precious Blood I humbly beg forgiveness.

(2) Act of Love — Henceforth my greatest endeavor, my most conscientious concern, will be to love God with my whole heart and above all things, and my neighbor as myself for the love of God. These are the two chief Commandments which Thou hast taught us in Thy discourse and have shown us by example. I humbly submit myself to both. From this very moment my will is to carry them out.

I love Thee; I embrace Thee, O my Jesus, with all my heart, preferring Thee above all creatures of Heaven and earth. With so much love and earnestness do I love Thee that I stand ready now to give my life and shed my blood for Thee. And as I love Thee for Thyself, so do I love all men, because Thou command me to love them all. Therefore I love them and love them as myself. I beseech Thee, O my Jesus, to have pity on them all, granting each one all the temporal and eternal benefits that I desire for myself.

(3) Resolution — This affection I have expressed is indeed holy. To prevent it from remaining within the limits of my heart, it must show itself; for love must operate and cannot be idle. Otherwise it would not be love. How, then, shall I deal with my neighbor? I will do for him what I wish done for me. I want everyone to have a good opinion of me. Therefore I will never admit into my mind a suspicion or judgment which could mean disesteem or contempt for my neighbor. I want everyone to be kind and agreeable with me.

I, too, will be that way with everyone and will endeavor not to say or do anything that can cause my neighbor unhappiness or bitterness. I want everyone to patiently bear with my defects and weaknesses, and I desire that no one speak ill of me. I will do this, too; I will pleasantly bear with the faults of others. I will never talk about another's defects*. . . I want others to do me favors according to charity; I will do the same for them.

O Jesus, Who art True Love in its Essence, grant me so much grace that henceforth I may love Thee as Thou hast loved me . . .

Now pray the Our Father and the Hail Mary and the Concluding Prayers as on page xi.

---

*Note — Unless this law of God requests it for the common good.

Meditation 20

Conclusion of Meditations in the Third Section and the Practice of the Virtues Contained Therein

Preparatory Prayer as on page x

Composition of Place — Imagine you see Jesus crucified on Calvary, the Model of all virtues, and that you hear the Heavenly Father's voice saying: See, and do according to the example that has been put before you on Mount Calvary. (Cf. Ex. 25:40)

Prayer of Petition — O my Jesus, with Thy Grace I can do all things. Without it I can do nothing. Therefore I beg Thee to help me in order that I may follow and imitate Thee.

First Point

Having thus far considered, O my soul, the exalted virtues and example of Jesus Christ, let us now see in what way we should and can imitate this Model.

(1) The more one has of the Spirit of Jesus Christ, the more one realizes virtue and perfection. If you want to know, my soul, what progress you have made in perfection, you can easily estimate it by how much or how little you have of the spirit of Jesus Christ. If in you there is little of this spirit, then little would be your perfection. If there is much, then there will likewise be in you much genuine sanctity. If all that is in you agrees with the spirit of Jesus Christ, you will have reached true and perfect sanctity. He is the highest sanctity and is the Model of all holi-

ness. The more you become like that Model, the more perfect and the more holy you will be.

(2) The more one possesses His humility, obedience, meekness and charity, the more one possesses the Spirit of Jesus Christ. There are no virtues, certainly, that failed to shine forth with supreme perfection in Jesus Christ. It is likewise certain that He exemplified no virtues more gloriously than the four just named. He has urged two of these on us with as much zeal and resourcefulness as if they contained the whole substance of His Spirit and the most sublime element of His Holiness. "Learn of Me," He said, "for I am Meek and Humble of Heart."

(3) One will discover the reason why there are so few who arrive at sanctity, in this observation: The majority of rather devout people are content with those practices that present no great opposition to corrupt nature. They give themselves to meditation and prayer; with a good intention they carry out the tasks entrusted to them; and they fulfill the duties of their state. They perform works of penance, submit to other restraints which their director assigns them.

But as for renouncing their own will, as for being receptive with holy indifference to the bidding of superiors, as for uprooting every tender sprig of vainglory, willingly accepting contempt, vigorously suppressing their anger and dealing in a friendly and sincerely affectionate way with those who oppose them, returning good for evil and laying aside all selfishness — these are the practices that few have the will to undertake. Only those do it who have a heroic heart. And because of this (ungenerous) behavior, the heart never becomes free of its disordered inclinations nor adorned with those virtues that are so acceptable to God.

It then follows that God never shares Himself much with these persons, and He lets them live and die in their mediocrity.

Therefore, my soul, if you desire in all sincerity to attain perfection and union with God, and do not want to rest until you reach this, it is absolutely necessary to follow in the footsteps which Jesus Christ has left imprinted for us and to imitate His virtues.

I will now explain briefly the practice or way of doing this. (We will speak first of obedience, then of humility, and last of meekness and charity.)

Obedience (1) In God's presence let one put himself in a complete indifference regarding all that superiors may dispose, without desiring or seeking or rejecting anything.

(2) Continually see God in the superiors in all circumstances, firmly believing that their legitimate orders express God's Will.

(3) Receive all orders with reverence and fulfill them with care.

Second Point

Humility (1) Surrender before God every desire for honor and worldly glory so that one does not admit within himself any vain self-esteem or vain satisfaction with himself, and so that in his outward conduct he says not a word and does nothing, on the prompting of vainglory.

(2) Let one put his honor and reputation in God's Hands in such wise that the soul is ready to suffer

contempt at every quarter of an hour if this should please God.

(3) Accept in good spirit every contempt and humiliation from wherever these things may come, and bear them cheerfully with a truly light regard for self.

Third Point

Meekness and Charity (1) Have a heart so affectionate toward all that one never advertently and deliberately admits any suspicion, judgment, contempt, anger or resentment that is uncharitable to his neighbor.

(2) In outward conduct in all circumstances deal with all in a friendly way and with sincere affection.

(3) Bear in silence any offense our neighbor does us, and if we can, return good for evil.

These are the points, my soul, that embrace the whole spirit of Jesus Christ and the true imitation of His virtues. Are you now willing to follow this Model and become a living likeness of Jesus Christ? If you are, kneel at His feet, consecrating yourself to Him and say the following:

Affective Acts

Colloquy with Jesus — What does this spirit of Thine, my Jesus, consist in? Does it not consist in shrinking from honor and loving contempt, in renouncing self-will, in obedience to another, in treating everyone with love, and silently bearing all weakness and offenses, in loving everyone wholeheartedly and in returning good for evil?

Indeed, my Jesus, this is certainly Thy spirit. Thy conduct was just that, and mine ought to be likewise, if I want to live according to Thy spirit. And not only is this Thy spirit, but it is the only road that leads to Thy love and union with Thee. Thou art Holiness itself, and Thou dost not take Thy pleasure in dwelling in a heart uncleansed of all bad inclinations and not adorned with Thy virtues.

Thanksgiving — Oh, what ardent love, what intimate familiarity, what close union I would be having with Thee, my Jesus, during these hours if I had been willing to die to selfishness and live according to Thy spirit! Alas! What immense benefits I have deprived myself of! But may thanks and infinite praise and blessing be given Thee, O my Jesus, my Supreme Good! For all is not yet lost.

Now, thanks to Thy loving kindness and mercy, I know Thy spirit and the way that leads to Thee. . . There is yet time to purify my heart of all the uncleanness of my disorderly affections; I can still come to have an inner familiarity with Thee and experience other effects of Holy love. I can still come to the possession of an intimate union with Thee.

O my Jesus! Oh, sweet is the hope that I can yet reach an intimate union with Thee! Yes, I, O my Jesus — I who have offended Thee so many times, I who for so many years have closed my ears to Thy loving invitations! Oh what kindness! What Mercy! May it, then, be so. I come to Thee, O my Jesus. I want to practise those virtues. So be it.

Now pray the Our Father and the Hail Mary and the Concluding Prayers as on page xi.

206

SECTION IV

Meditation 21

The Two Standards
— One of Christ Our Lord,
the Sovereign Commander;
The Other — of Lucifer, Mortal
Enemy of Our Human Nature

Preparatory Prayer as on page x

First Prelude

Consider how Christ Our Lord calls us, and wants everyone under His Standard; and Lucifer, on the other hand, would have everyone under his.

Second Prelude

Composition of Place — With your imagination see a vast plain extending over the whole region of Jerusalem, where the Commander-in-Chief of upright souls is Christ Our Lord. See another plain in the region of Babylon, where the enemy's chieftain is Lucifer.

Prayer of Petition — O my Lord and my God, I ask Thee for knowledge of the snares of the evil chieftain and for the valor to escape them. I beg Thee to acquaint me in good time with the upright and holy life which our Commander-in-Chief and true Captain teaches us with His doctrine and example.

Words of Saint Ignatius — "The first point is to picture the chieftain of all the enemy forces in that great plain of Babylon seated on a great throne of fire and smoke — a horrible, frightening sight.

"The second point is to consider how he issues a summons to innumerable demons, and how he scatters them, some into such and such a city and others to another, and thus throughout the world, not missing a province, a place, a class, nor a single person.

"The third point is to consider the discourse he makes to them, how he admonishes them to have their snares and chains ready. They are to first present the temptation for a greed of riches — according to their usual practice — so that more easily men will taste the empty esteem of the world and then reach greater pride. From these three steps he lures everyone to the other vices.

"Then picture the true Commander-in-Chief, Who is Christ Our Lord.

"**First,** consider how Christ Our Lord takes His stand in a great plain in the Jerusalem region, assuming His humble, beautiful, gracious manner.

"**Second,** consider how this Lord of all the world chooses so many persons as Apostles, so many as Disciples, etc., and sends them throughout the world, spreading His holy teaching among all kinds and classes of persons.

"**Third,** consider the discourse which Christ Our Lord gives to all His servants and friends whom He sends on this errand, charging them to seek to help all. They should thus encourage men to embrace the highest poverty of spirit, and in cases where it pleases His Divine Majesty to choose men for it, they should also encourage them to embrace actual poverty.

"Secondly, they should encourage men to have a hunger for insult and contempt, because from these two, humility develops. Thus there are to be three steps: first, poverty against riches; second, insult and contempt against worldly honor; third, humility as opposed to pride; and with these three steps let them lead men to all other virtues."

Explanation — This meditation has as its object the following of Jesus Christ, whereby one acts and suffers for love of Him. As one cannot follow Jesus Christ, live according to His Spirit, and practise His Virtues, without encountering very many difficulties, objections and reverses which can be overcome only by a truly generous and magnanimous heart, at this point Saint Ignatius presents us with the example of Jesus Christ in order that we do not refuse to suffer for God what God has suffered for us.

Hence the present meditation aims at bringing it about that we resolve effectively and at all costs, to follow Jesus Christ more closely and live according to His spirit. The saint directs our thoughts to these two leaders, Jesus Christ and Lucifer, noting how each undertakes to draw every man under his standard to become a follower.

First Point

If we have to follow either Jesus Christ or Lucifer, let us realize it so that we may set these two leaders before our minds. What now, is the end each of them has?

The aim of Jesus Christ is to persuade all men to be His followers so that in this way they can come hereafter to praise and bless His Heavenly Father forever and gain the eternal bliss of Heaven. A two-fold love burning in His Heart presses Him on to all this. Of these the first is the very devoted love

He has for the Father. From this comes His desire that we love, honor and praise His Father with all our hearts, just as He loves His Father. The second love is His tender affection for man. From this comes the desire He has to obtain our salvation, so that with Him we can have that eternal happiness with which He Himself is happy.

Lucifer's goal is to enlist all men under his standard so that, by abandoning God, men may dishonor God and plunge themselves into damnation. A twofold hatred burning within him spurs him on to this.

The first is an implacable hatred for God because he was once cast out of paradise by a very just Divine judgment. From that time on he conceived against God a supreme and incomparable hatred which ceaselessly agitates him so that he cannot bear to see God praised, honored and loved by any man.

The second hatred is a furious loathing for men; for, knowing that God has appointed for them that infinite glory and bliss from which he and his whole company have been forever excluded, he is beside himself with rage and undertakes to cause men to lose that happiness and to hurl themselves into damnation with him. . .

Now, my soul, what will you do? Which of these two leaders will you follow, Jesus Christ or Lucifer? When the young Tobias was waiting to learn the way to a far-away country, the Archangel Saint Raphael appeared to him in the form of a young man and offered himself as companion and guide.

Now let us suppose that two young men had appeared before Tobias; the Archangel Saint Raphael disguising himself as the first; and Lucifer as the second, and that both offered to be Tobias' guide. If Tobias, turning his back on the Archangel, had chosen Lucifer as his guide, would he not, by his own act, have plunged himself into the greatest misfortune that can be imagined? O my soul, you are now on a journey to eternity and Jesus Christ and Lucifer are offered as guides. . . To which one will you entrust yourself? Which one do you want to follow? Choose . . .

Affective Acts

Oh! How important this decision is! I am on a journey to eternity. The way is unfamiliar to me and it has many hazards and snares. Two guides are offered — Jesus Christ and Lucifer — Jesus Christ, the Only-Begotten Son of the Eternal Father; Jesus, Holiness by nature; Jesus, Who deeply loves me; Jesus, Who seeks my happiness with all His Heart. Oh, how secure one is in following such a guide! The second is Lucifer — Lucifer, God's greatest enemy; Lucifer, a damned spirit; Lucifer, who regards me with extreme hatred; Lucifer, who seeks nothing else than my eternal ruin. . . What shall I do? Ah! I am ashamed to ask such a question. What, then?

Will I be so utterly lacking in judgment as to want to abandon Jesus and follow Lucifer? Will I hate myself so much as to want to quit the road to Heaven and take the one that leads to hell? Ah, no! Never will I do that! Thou, O my Jesus, art the Way, the Truth and the Life — the Way that leads securely to the Father, the Truth that enables me to discover all snares and deceits, the Life where one finds everlasting blessedness. . . Recruit me under thy standard, O my Jesus. . . I will follow Thee and follow Thee even until death.

Second Point

By the goals to which Jesus and Lucifer lead us, we can know which of the two should be followed. The difference is scarcely less than infinite, first, between the invitations of Jesus and those of Lucifer, and second, between the outcome which Jesus leads one to, and that which Lucifer leads to. Let us ponder them both attentively.

The invitations which Jesus Christ proposes to us for fighting under His standard have as their object some practices that are difficult and bitter to fallen nature. The principal ones are these: voluntary poverty; obedience; the continuous denial of one's selfish inclinations; humility and patience in bearing contempt and wrongs; silence when being tyrannized and persecuted; blessing God in our pains and bitter experiences. This is what the spirit of Jesus Christ is. It is to this that Jesus invited everyone who would follow Him; likewise it is to this that you must adjust yourself, my soul, if you want to fight under His standard.

There is no doubt that a life appears bitter which must adjust and conform to these practices. But, oh how sweet and desirable afterward is the outcome to which this leads! And what is this outcome? I will tell you briefly — but, my soul, reflect upon it continually as long as you live. The outcome, the end to which Jesus Christ leads, is the deliverance from an infinite evil, that is, from hell; and it is the obtaining of an Infinite Good, that is, Heaven; and both last forever!

All the invitations by which Lucifer calls us to follow beneath his standard, present things that are pleasing to fallen nature.

He promises his followers temporal goods, riches, honors, worldly glory, the esteem of men, comforts, pleasures of the senses, an easy life, one that gets rid of restraints against all the desires of the flesh. This is the spirit of Lucifer. To this he invites all who would follow him. But what is the outcome that this crafty and evil spirit leads one to hereafter with these invitations? Ah, my soul! Do not let yourself be misled. The outcome is the loss of an Infinite Good, namely, Heaven, and the incurring of an infinite evil, namely, hell; and both outcomes last forever.

Pause here a little, my soul, and turn your gaze upward. Picture the Heavens opening up. See Jesus Christ seated there at the right hand of His Eternal Father, and at His side a multitude of elect in immense glory and splendor. . . Now who are they that are so close to Jesus Christ?

They are the Apostles, men who saw themselves obliged to flee from one city to another, who were dragged from prison and persecuted everywhere. . . They are monks, hermits, apostolic men who, amid a thousand persecutions, insults and scoffing, promoted God's Glory. They are virgins who, for love of Jesus Christ, silently and patiently suffered temptations, injuries and similar troubles. . . All of them, because in this life they stayed close to Jesus in suffering, are now close to Jesus in Glory. . .

Continuing your reflection, my soul, take a look downward. Picture the earth opening up before you. See Lucifer there in the midst of a deep pool of fire, surrounded by a multitude of people who are damned and are suffering unspeakable torment and pain. . .

Who are they that are so close to Lucifer? O my soul, how different are things of this world from those of the next!. . . These people are most influential lords and ladies who during life came barely short of being adored. Their great share of riches and temporal goods has hurled them into this fire. . . They are lords and ladies who in this world enjoyed splendor and greatness. Their high position has condemned them to these flames. . . They are men and women who, unwilling to contradict in certain things the cravings of the flesh for comfort and pleasure, have come to find themselves in this state. On earth they were next to Lucifer in joy, and now they are next to him in hell. . .

Affective Acts

O my Jesus, the more I look at Thee and contemplate Thee, the more clearly I come to realize that till now I have had little knowledge of truth in my mind, and little love of virtue in my will! In this world Thou didst not prize anything other than poverty and frugality, contempt and injury, pain and fatigue. . . Thou regarded all this as the means best suited to holiness, as the surest signs and safest pledges of an eminent glory in Heaven.

On the other hand, as for temporal goods, riches, worldly honor and splendor, bodily pleasures and comforts — all this Thou despised and regarded as the strongest inducements to cause us to plunge into hell. This is Thy way of judging, O my Jesus, and this is Thy doctrine. This is Thy spirit and it is the attitude of Thy Heart. . . But what are my attitudes and sentiments?

Oh, what good reason I have for blushing with shame! I dare not raise my eyes to look upon the Cross. What Thou dost cherish, I despise. What

Thou cravest, I flee from. What Thou lovest, I abhor. What Thou dost embrace, I push aside. Thy invitations become always distasteful to me. . . Could my heart resemble Thine less if I had made a formal, express resolve to serve not Thee, but Lucifer?

What shall I do, then, O my Jesus? Oh! It is necessary that I go to Thee and look upon Thee as the Model of True Holiness, that I love what Thou hast loved, and that I hate what Thou hast hated.

Third Point

If one must follow Jesus Christ or follow Lucifer, let him make his decision according to the final end for which God created us and called us to the Faith. Turn back a little in your thoughts, my soul, and bring to mind your last End. You are a Christian, a disciple of Christ, Who teaches you that you are to be perfect as your Heavenly Father is perfect. You ought to serve and love God in this world with perfection in order to enjoy Him eternally in the other world with an eminent glory. But how would this be possible without imitating Jesus Christ faithfully? In order to make plainly evident the impossibility of any other alternative, reflect attentively on the following truths:

First truth — Perfection is a precious, most particular gift of God. God is Infinite Power, Infinite Wisdom, and the Inexhaustible Source of All Good. But even though He has all these perfections, He cannot give me a more sublime and precious gift than perfect love and union with Himself. This is the gift of all gifts, the grand total of all mercies and the most precious jewel of all His treasures. Once a soul has reached perfection, it finds itself in a state so outstanding that not only do all monarchs of the world lose importance by comparison, but, by eternal values, many thousands of millions of men of any and all times, rank together as less important.

Second truth — No one can obtain grace except by those means that God has appointed. That a soul rise to perfection is a pure mercy of God. He is no more obliged to grant it such a grace than a king is to pick a poor laborer's daughter for his bride and have her sit on a throne at his side. Therefore it is quite legitimate for God to prescribe for you some conditions that you must fulfill, certain means which you must put into practice, if you want to obtain such a grace.

Third truth — These means consist in one thing — in the total and perfect following of Jesus Christ. . . I am the door, says This Most Lovable Redeemer. If anyone enter by Me, he will be saved, and can go in and out at will, and will find pasture. This is My Beloved Son, says the Eternal Father, in Whom I am well pleased. Hear ye Him.

Heed Him well, my soul. The one Model of holiness sent by the Eternal Father is Jesus. . . By entering through this door, you will find perfection, pure love, and intimate union with God. But remember that there is no more than the one door, and aside from it there is no hope of entry.

Affective Acts

(1) Faith — I well know, my Jesus, how different Thy judgments are from mine. But because Thou art Eternal Truth I believe that true riches consist in suffering poverty, true glory in suffering contempt, true peace in suffering persecution, true liberty in

216

submitting to authority. The true road to sanctity is found in imitating Thee and it consists of a universal mortification and the love for adversities. This I believe, O my Jesus, because Thou hast made it so. And thus by laboring, by loving, and by suffering, as Thou did, I will have Thy Spirit and can hope that even during my life that blessed hour will come in which Thou will admit me into a familiar communion with Thyself, O my Jesus. . . . Any other road one might take is no more than a mirage, an imposture, a pretense, a vanity, which cannot be acceptable in Thy Divine Judgment.

(2) Desire to unite with God — Yes, my Jesus, Thou art my one and Sovereign Good, in which consists all my happiness. I sigh for Thee and desire Thee with all the powers of my heart. . . I wish to love Thee whole-heartedly in this life and love Thee perfectly. I wish to enjoy Thee in an unhindered way hereafter in that glory which Thou hast destined for me from eternity. . . I see that the way is distasteful — the total denial of selfish inclinations, a continual silence when bearing contempt, an affectionate treatment of persons who oppose me.

All these are practices which demand great spiritual strength. But be that as it may, and though nature cry out and complain as much as it pleases, I have decided upon Thy way. Indeed, my Jesus, I want to follow Thee. . . And how could I refuse? Could it be too burdensome for me that I obey a man for love of Jesus after Jesus has obeyed a most unjust judge for love of me? Should it be unbearable for me to bear contempt for love of Jesus, after Jesus let Himself be nailed to a Cross between two criminals for love of me?

Should it be too much that I, for love of Jesus, love persons who dislike me, after Jesus, crucified for love of me, loved those who crucified Him? How can man ever refuse to suffer for God what God has suffered for men?

"God forbid that I should glory, except in the cross of Our Lord Jesus Christ; by Whom the world is crucified to me, and I to the world." (Gal. 6:14).

O my Jesus, I love Thee, I unite myself to Thee. At this moment I wish to follow Thy footsteps, I wish to do what Thou did. I wish to suffer as Thou suffered. . . Ah! Deign to grant me Thy spirit, the spirit of subordination, the spirit of meekness, the spirit of love.

Now pray the Our Father and the Hail Mary and the Concluding Prayers as on page xi.

218

Meditation 22

Three Classes of Men

Preparatory Prayer as on page x

Composition of Place — Picture Jesus Christ, seated and crowned with thorns as a mock king and saying to you, "Learn of Me, for I am meek and humble of Heart; and thus you will find rest for your soul." Indeed, you will find rest in this world and in the next world.

Prayer of Petition — O my Jesus and my Master, instruct me, teach me, enlighten me, and make me teachable so that I will succeed well in Thy school.

First Point

The first class of men consists of those who want to aspire to perfection and follow Jesus Christ, but only in speech and not in their heart. If you would know about this class of men, come with me to a sick man's house. See there a man half consumed with the heat of fever. His ailment is getting worse by the moment and he is near death.

A physician comes to him in this condition. After examining him, the physician says, "The sickness is very dangerous, but if the patient will make use of the medications I will prescribe, he can still recover his health."

Now this is just what the sick man does not like. "With all my heart I want to recover," he says, "but do not oblige me to take medications; for by no means can I nor will I take them." Now tell me, does this sick man have a true desire to get well?

From this man who is sick in his body, let us pass

on to the home of someone sick in his soul. See a person stretched out, as it were, in the abandoned throes of habitual lukewarmness. He is told that his ailment can still be remedied, that it requires no more than that he resolve to make his prayers with fervor, that he conduct himself in a spirit of love and with the pure intention of pleasing God, that he walk in God's presence, uniting himself to Him frequently by means of holy affections, that he zealously mortify himself, that every day he offer God this sacrifice, which is so acceptable to Him; that by doing this, the road that leads to sanctity is still open to him.

But, ah! This is just what the man does not want. "With all my heart I want to gain perfection," he says; "but to put these means of reaching it into practice is something too hard and difficult for me."

Now tell me, does this soul have a serious will to attain perfection? On the other hand, alas! many are the evils that threaten it; for —

(1) A will so lukewarm moves God to let it fall into grave sins — The Lord Himself explains this in two parables. The first is that of the barren plot of ground. The plot that is watered with frequent rains and yields no fruit is close to being cursed. The second parable takes its lesson from lukewarm water which one cannot retain in his stomach without it inducing nausea. "I would that thou wert cold, or hot," He says; "but because thou art lukewarm. . . I will begin to vomit thee. . ." (Apoc. 3:15-16). My soul, who is it that spoke thus? Of whom did He speak?

(2) God allows a soul possessing such a lukewarm will, to finally come to ruin — The Lord also declares this truth with two parables. The first takes

its lesson from a tree planted in a field. Having found on it nothing more than leaves, the Lord cursed it with these meaningful words: "May no fruit grow on thee hence forward for-ever." . . . (Mt. 21:19).

The second parable is taken from a tree in a garden. As it had borne no fruit, it was condemned to the axe, with directions to the gardener to cut it down: "Cut this tree down. Why does it uselessly cumber the ground?" (Cf. Lk. 13:7).

I repeat my question: Who said this, my soul? Of whom did He speak?

Affective Acts

(1) Fear — What fear, what alarm seizes me, my God, when I consider these truths that have come from Thy mouth! I, even I, can be damned — I, who have been called by God to the Faith and to perfection! I, whom God has favored with so many graces! . . . I, who have been chosen by God for an eminent glory in Heaven! Yes, I can be damned, and just for my lukewarmness! . . . Ah, lukewarmness! Accursed lukewarmness! What a great evil you must be when you can cause such nausea to the Heart of the most Merciful God so as to constrain Him to cast me from His mouth!

(2) Repentance — Have still a little patience with me, O my Jesus! With all my heart I detest and hate all my negligence, and the abuse I have made of all the graces and means which in Thy kindness Thou hast given me. Until now I have spent my life without having any care either for the glory of Thy Holy Name, or for the salvation of my soul. Thou, by a feat of Thy Mercy, have this day enlightened me to know my sinfulness. Again, I detest it, I hate it, and

I earnestly resolve to endeavor henceforth to be upright and perfect, as Thou art asking me to be.

Second Point

The second class of men consists of those who have a true will to aspire to perfection, but it is not an all-inclusive, generous will . . . Let us return to the example of sick persons. Behold, my soul, another sick man very different from the first one. He desires to regain his health, and to achieve this he is ready to take medications and other remedies. But he is unwilling to take the iron or the caustic medications, nor other similar disagreeable remedies. (He will take whatever medicine is prescribed, provided it does not taste bad.) Thus he, too, is unwilling to have all treatments that are necessary. What should be said of this sick man? It is true that he has a good will, but it lacks strength, whole-heartedness, and generosity.

A disposition resembling that of this sick man is that in which we find many spiritual people. They want to acquire perfection, and to obtain it they are ready to take some of the means, but not all. To bear up for many years with interior desolation and grave trials, to suffer humiliation and contempt without having given any occasion for it, and other things distasteful to corrupt nature, seems to these souls too great a burden for their shoulders. What should be said of these souls? One will say that they have some good will, but it is like that of the sick man unwilling to take all treatments that are necessary. What will follow for a will that holds back this way? Note this well, my soul, and impress it well in your heart. . . Realize that:

(1) A soul in this disposition will always lack consolation and peace — As it lacks holy indifference of will and complete, unreserved resignation to the Divine Will, the evil inclinations in it will never die. Pride and vainglory, caprice and attachment to one's will and judgment, carelessness of speech, anger, melancholy, and harshness towards one's neighbor, will continue after many years of spiritual reading, mental prayer, frequenting of the Sacraments, and works of mercy. These faults will be as lively as when one began his pursuit of virtue. Rather, they will keep growing with the years and will develop like a sturdy tree which every year always gains more height and firmness. The burden of obedience to superiors will every day weigh more heavily on such a soul, and each experience of contempt will be harder to bear. One's conversation will each time become less restrained, less controlled, and his treatment of his neighbor will become more discourteous and offensive. What peace, what consolation, could ever be found in a heart so ill disposed? One unmortified attachment is to a soul like a snake on a man's body, who has rest when the serpent is asleep and does not bite or poison him; but the instant it wakes up, it bites and torments the unhappy man. This soul will not otherwise enjoy peace and quiet, except when its passions are not provoked. But if they are awakened, either by an offense done to him or some slight that he receives, or by a command that is not pleasing to him — oh, the storm, the torment he must suffer! Yet we are so blind that we do not see the source of our misery; and when we could easily discover it in our own heart, we turn everywhere else to try to find it.

(2) This soul will go through life without making any progress in perfection — It is God Himself Who thus explains the matter, and one may not expect Him to retract... "One ... that doth not renounce all ... cannot be My disciple." (Lk. 14:33). This means: One who does not renounce all creatures that capture the heart and does not completely abandon himself, without any reservations, to My Way of disposing matters, will never be able to attain to My Love nor become one with Me. And why? Listen to the reasons for this, my soul.

(1) God is Infinite Authority. It is a matter for God's choice to grant the particular graces that are necessary for reaching perfection. Now His established way is not to grant them to a soul that holds back and does not submit completely to His Majesty. Can God be criticized, perhaps, for this procedure?

(2) God is Infinite Worthiness. To Him belongs the right that one's whole heart be given Him with all its affections. It will never be possible for Him to surrender this right nor admit to union with Him a soul that fails to give itself to Him unreservedly.

Affective Acts

(1) Confession — This sick man is a vivid image of my soul, O my Jesus. He wants to regain his health, but without labor, without suffering, and without taking unpleasant remedies. This is exactly the disposition of my soul. I would like to have perfect humility, but without bearing contempt; perfect obedience, but without painful commands; a perfect charity and meekness, but without undergoing ill treatment. That is, I want to be holy, but without suffering... Is not this to directly oppose the

224

Will of the Heavenly Father, the doctrine and example of Jesus Christ, the designs and interior inspirations of the Holy Spirit? Oh what a fool I am! There has not been anyone before me nor will there be anyone afterwards, who became holy without suffering and without following the footsteps of Jesus Christ. It is absolutely necessary to suffer, to die to self, to give up all useless, selfish pursuits, if one wants to acquire perfection. Yes, this is Thy doctrine, O my Jesus. This is the road that leads to holiness. And so I wish to suffer with Thee, and to suffer even until all disorders disappear from my heart and all my perverse impulses have been mortified.

(2) Resolution — And why should it not be thus? Will I be so foolish as to want to get rid of a lesser cross to thereby come burdened with another greater one, without gaining anything? Ah, my God, enlighten me! Make me know and see what till now I have not seen nor known. A little pride causes in the heart more unrest, more disturbance than the sting felt in the most humbling experience, the most humble behavior. . . A little wrath rouses up in the heart far greater troubles than any pinch we might feel from practising the most heroic meekness. . . A small resentment voluntarily harbored, torments the heart much more than the stress and strain of the most heroic meekness . . . It is necessarily so, then, that one must suffer, either for virtue or for vice, and there is no escape. I wish to suffer for virtue. I want to suffer for Heaven. I want to suffer for Thee, O my Jesus. . .

Third Point

The third class of men consists of those who have

an earnest, generous will to strive for perfection. I mean that they are ready and willing not only to carry out whatever God wants, but also to suffer all that His designs provide, in order to acquire perfection. The advantages that a soul should promise itself in this state are the following:

(1) This soul infallibly arrives at perfection — The measure with which God gives Himself to a man is exactly the same as that with which the man gives himself to God. Therefore when the soul surrenders itself entirely and without reserve to God in this state of which we speak, so that it is ready to do and suffer all that pleases God, God also, on His part, communicates Himself totally and without reserve to the soul, and in a very short time raises it to this perfection. . .

(2) The soul that has this disposition certainly reaches union with God — Union and intimate familiarity with God is the reward promised for perfect charity. "If any one love Me," says the Divine Redeemer, ". . . My Father will love him: and We will come to him and will make Our abode with him." (Jn. 14:23). Now who is it that has perfect charity, to which is attached the promise of such an outstanding grace? It is beyond doubt one who surrenders himself entirely to God.

(3) This soul infallibly obtains from God many other very sublime graces — If God is infinitely liberal, He will not fail to pour down His Graces superabundantly and will pour them assuredly on my heart which submits completely to Him. These graces consist in a very sweet, quiet peace and joy of heart, in a very tender devotion and affection for God and in other gifts which are properly from the

Holy Spirit. This is that very blessed hundredfold which Jesus Christ promised those who, for love of Him, deny themselves and entirely surrender to Him without holding back.

Affective Acts

(1) Fear — O my God, how liberal and merciful Thou art with me! It is purely an effect of Thy Grace that I now know the road which leads to Holiness, that I certainly know I can attain it, provided I abandon myself entirely into Thy Hands. Oh, what Goodness! Oh, what Mercy! Oh, what Grace! But these very graces make one tremble, O my God. Thy words are, ". . . Unto whomsoever much is given, of him much shall be required." . . . (Lk. 12:48).

And one to whom a great deal has been lent, must likewise restore a great deal. Oh, what a disaster it would be for me, if the very abundance of grace that ought to raise me to a very high level of glory in Heaven, were to plunge me into the depths of hell! This is certain, that for many souls there is no middle state; but they will either be elevated to a very high place in paradise, or they will fall most disastrously into the eternal pit of hell. Could I be one of these? I do not know. Oh frightening thought! I do not know! . . .

(2) Resolution — I will promptly look after my soul's welfare and begin walking the way that Thou, O my Jesus, hast made known to me today. Yes, at this moment I surrender myself entirely to the ways Thou hast designed. One single grace I ask of Thee, and it is that Thou make me worthy of Thy love and let me arrive at an intimate union with Thee. Everything else I leave to Thy Most Holy Will. Whatever

troubles befall me, I will look upon as something designed by Thy Fatherly Providence, and will embrace it with perfect submission as the means of my sanctification. My Jesus, preserve this will in me.

Now pray the Our Father and the Hail Mary and the Concluding Prayers as on page xi.

Meditation 23
Third Degree of Humility

Preparatory Prayer as on page x

Composition of Place — Imagine, my soul, that you see Jesus, after He has been whipped, crowned with thorns, rejected in favor of Barabbas. And now, after He has been taken by Pilate to a balcony, all the people cry, "Away with Him! Away with Him! Crucify Him! Crucify Him!"

Prayer of Petition — O My Jesus, grant me grace to love to be belittled and humbled. When I find myself humbled, grant that I will be quiet and only say, "It is good for me, Lord, that Thou hast humbled me, that I may in this way learn Thy very just precepts." (cf. Ps. 118:71).

First Point

Fairness and justice demand that we love to be treated as of little account — We are so blind and self-esteem is so deep-rooted in our hearts that we think our life is very wretched when we are treated as of little importance and when we are in any way looked down upon. Yet we should be certain that nothing is more suited for us than contempt and that all men together could never manage to belittle us as much as we deserve. Listen with attention, my soul, to some truths which are very plain.

(1) God can and should punish sin — Faith teaches us this. God is Infinite Justice. Now, just as He would not be Infinite Goodness if He did not reward uprightness, neither would He be Infinite Justice if He did not punish evil. Do you believe this, my soul? Let us proceed.

(2) God can punish sin in the way He wishes — Just as God is Infinite Justice, He is likewise Infinite Authority. He can punish sin with bodily pain, or by grief and affliction of soul; but belittlement or contempt seems to be the punishment most proper for sin. For, as sin is a belittlement of God, it rightly deserves to be punished by contempt, and one who has had the boldness to belittle God, may rightly be belittled.

(3) God can use whatever He wishes to punish sin — God punished David for sin by means of a son of David. God punished the disobedient prophet by means of a wild beast which fatally mauled him on his journey. God punished the impious Heliodorus by an angel who gave him a bloody whipping. He punished our sins in Jesus Christ by an Apostle who sold him. God can, then, punish me too, and send me contempt in the way that suits His good pleasure.

(4) No matter how much God punishes sin in this life, He always punishes it less than it deserves — If God prolonged my life to the day of Judgment and I spent it suffering continuous hardships, ill treatment and insults, all this could never satisfy for the contempt that I have shown His Divine Majesty by a single venial sin. Gather your thoughts, my soul, and answer me: Have you committed a sin at any time? Alas! Not only have I committed one sin, but a hundred and a thousand! Can God not punish you and inflict contempt as punishment if He wishes? The fact is undeniable. No matter how many instances of contempt you suffer, they will never equal in number or quality as much as you deserve for a single venial sin.

Consider how true this is! What conclusion follows? It follows that you can have no reasonable cause for complaint for any contempt you receive; for it will never give grounds for complaint. It follows that in the midst of contempt, of whatever sort it is, you ought to praise God and bless Him, inasmuch as it is always less than what you deserve. It follows that it is a proper and right thing that throughout your life you be always shown contempt and disregard.

Affective Acts

(1) Confession and humiliation — It is fair, O my God! I admit it is fair and very just that I live in the midst of contempt and that I regard contempt in no other way than as an effect of Thy Mercy toward me. Alas! What is all the contempt from men in comparison with what I have deserved? O my Jesus, if Thou hadst treated me according to the strictness of Thy Justice, where would I now be? O Infinite Wisdom, Thou knowest the answer. I would be in hell. I would be despised by all the saints for all eternity, by all the angels of Heaven and by all men on earth. Thou hast preserved me from this eternal contempt, O my Jesus, out of Thy pure Mercy, and instead of letting me experience that contempt, Thou hast been satisfied to let me suffer the contempt that comes to me in this life. Is it not right that I look upon these things as effects of Thy Mercy? Should I not regard them with imperturbable peace?

(2) Resolution — This I will do with Thy help, O my Jesus! I will not allow this thought to escape me. I have sinned and I have deserved to be mocked and despised for all eternity by Heaven and earth, by angels, by men, by the saints and by the damned. I

will always keep this imprinted in my memory on every occasion, and in the midst of contempt and insult I wish to praise and bless Thy Infinite Goodness and Mercy.

Second Point

It is to our best interest that we love contempt — Certainly nothing is to be found in contempt except what appears bitter and disagreeable. But consider, my soul, that we appreciate and value many things which are distasteful to nature because we know they are good for us. When a sick man is tormented with bitter pain, one cannot do anything better for him than provide him with a remedy, even if it is distasteful, if it is sure to rid him of his trouble or at least relieve it. And why can we not love an experience of contempt as we reflect on the great and special advantages it brings with it? Now what are these? I will present to you the principal ones.

First Advantage — To be belittled and discredited destroys pride in us. The worst evil and the greatest hindrance that a soul can meet on the road of perfection is pride and vainglory. As long as the smallest selfish regard, the slightest self-satisfaction or petty ambition for human praise lives in the heart, it will never come about that God enters and lives in it with satisfaction. He looks upon such a heart with horror; He shuns it, and leaves it deprived of His heavenly lights, of Holy affections, of devout impulses, of choice graces, and it will lack the very special care of His Providence. Can a greater evil be imagined for a soul that desires perfection? But is there no remedy for such a great evil? Yes, there is, my soul. Believe this as an undeniable truth. The surest remedy, the most effective, most efficient remedy is the experience of contempt. To put out a great fire, nothing is more suitable than a heavy rain from Heaven. To uproot pride, there is nothing more powerful than to receive contempt and belittlement.

Oh, how few are they who, without this means, arrive at true humility! Should you not, then, my soul, wholeheartedly desire contempt? And in the midst of it, should you not be transported with joy, and praise, bless and thank God? We thank a surgeon because, by cutting away an abscess with a momentary pain for us, he delivers us from continuous pain. Should you not thank God Who, by subjecting you to a small ill such as contempt, delivers you from a far worse evil, which is pride?

Second Advantage — Contempt produces humility in us. The best disposition for gaining perfection is humility. As soon as God discovers it in a heart, He quickly enters it and fills it with an abundance of His Grace. The humble heart is like a valley; for just as the waters that run down the mountain all gather in the valley and make it pleasant and fertile, so Divine Grace, which departs from the arrogant and proud heart, symbolized by the mountain, gathers in the humble heart and greatly enriches it. Could a more profitable treasure ever be imagined than this? But what is the means for acquiring a virtue so pleasing to God? Turn your gaze to Jesus, my soul, and from Him learn to acquire it. This dear Redeemer has been our example for all virtues and has taught us also the most effective means of acquiring them. But what means has Jesus given us for gaining humility? No other than the observance of continual silence when we receive contempt and are disregarded. If you, O my soul, learn to be silent during contempt and love contempt, then without doubt He will give you the spirit of humility, which is His spirit, and you will enter into the possession of it when you begin to practice it.

Affective Acts

Ah, my Jesus, my Redeemer and my All! Now I know perfectly what displeases Thee in my heart and what keeps Thee from making it Thy dwelling place. It is that desire to be honored and esteemed by men, that pursuit of praise and honor, that ambition to be preferred to everyone in everything. That is what it is, O my God, that makes Thee hate to live in my heart. O accursed ambition! Of how many graces you have deprived me! How many heavenly lights you have prevented me from gaining! Of how many Divine consolations you have cheated me! Oh, how much you have withdrawn me from God! And how many other evils you can still bring on me! I will weary myself in vain and will gain no access to Thee, O my Jesus, if I do not uproot from my heart this very bad inclination which has planted such deep roots in it. A God so humble and a creature so proud cannot have familiar and mutual friendship. O my Jesus, Thou must change Thy Heart, in the future loving haughtiness and pride; or else I must change mine, from now on, loving humiliation and contempt. Forgive my simplicity, O my Jesus. I know well that it is I who must change. I will do it, indeed, my beloved Jesus! But if Thou do not strengthen me with Thy grace, all my resolutions will be in vain. I do not dare go forth trusting in my promises. This accursed ambition is so rooted in my heart that I do not find the strength to uproot it. I have detested it a thousand times, and even so it would sprout forth more vigorous than before. I should not put the blame on anyone but myself; for my resolves have been no more than empty words with which I have deceived myself and have made myself the more guilty before Thee. If I were to sincerely resolve upon this, I would have to give thanks, with hands joined, to the one who despises me, and gladly embrace all occasions that are allotted me to be humbled. But the truth is, O my Jesus, that here there are roots that no one can pull up except Thy Almighty Hand. Turn, then, Thine Eyes toward me, O loving Jesus! Uproot in me every desire for vainglory. Let only Thy Spirit and the love for contempt reign in my heart.

Third Point

Contempt is deserving of our love on account of its excellence and preferability — If you but knew, my soul, how valuable in God's eyes belittlement is, oh with what eagerness and what pleasure you would go hunting for it, no matter how distasteful it might be to frail nature! Therefore consider with attention the excellent qualities that are contained in itself, in an instance of contempt borne with patience.

First excellent quality — To bear contempt in silence is the most worthy sacrifice that we can make of ourselves to God in this life.

The desire to be prominent and gain respect and honor from men is a passion so common and universal that perhaps no man is always completely free from it. There are some people who have no difficulty in depriving themselves of convenience and weakening their bodies with fasts and other austerities; there are others who love solitude and spend many hours in prayer; there are those who, no matter how afflicted they appear to be with aches and sickness, show an immovable patience and who seem to have an unquenchable thirst for suffering. But even though all these people appear so advanced in virtue, few know how to bear in silence a contemptuous affront, a calumny, or even a disrespectful word. Here is where their virtue falls short and where ordinary holiness fails, because this evil appetite is so deeply rooted in the human heart and so hard to uproot. And so, since an extraordinary effort and violence is necessary in order to conquer it, who does not see what an excellent sacrifice one offers to God if he makes this effort and proves victorious?

Second excellent quality — To bear contempt in silence is the marrow, the essential part, of the following of Jesus Christ. If you give attention to the actions of Jesus Christ, my soul, you will find that throughout His Life and at every age of His lifetime He underwent contempt. He was made light of at His birth in the stable at Bethlehem; despised in His Infancy as He fled to Egypt; despised in His youth at the workshop in Nazareth; despised during His manhood as He preached and suffered death on a Cross.

He was despised in Himself and in all His works. He was despised in His divinity and humanity; despised in His virtues; despised in His doctrine; despised in His miracles. Whatever He said or did was given a bad interpretation and was despised.

He was despised by all sorts of people. He was despised by His fellow citizens and by foreigners; despised by priests and lay persons, by royalty, by nobles, by common people; despised by soldiers and by civilians.

Educated people despised Him. Seeing that He had not been taught by them, they would say, "Where did He get such wisdom, since this Man has not even learned His letters?" But Jesus kept silent and made no comeback to save His Honor; for He could have told them that He was the uncreated Wisdom, that He knew all things and had no need to learn anything, that He was sent to be Teacher of all and was to be no one's pupil.

The rich despised Him. The Lord Jesus is owner of the world and all that there is in it. Yet, for love of contempt He chose poor parents, poor companions, poor food, poor clothing, a poor occupation, a poor home, and in everything He loved poverty and abjection. That is why He earned the contempt of the rich, who love wealth, high living and vanity.

His young countrymen despised Him. Hebrews were accustomed to marry at nineteen years of age. On seeing Jesus young, elegant, handsome and genteel, but not caring about women nor about things of the world, on seeing Him live a life withdrawn from bad companions and youthful amusements, what sport they made of Him, what mockery!

With the exception of the Blessed Virgin Mary and Saint Joseph, His relatives despised Him on noticing that He did not marry nor try to make any fortune. They criticized Him and considered Him as a man deserving contempt. As soon as He began to gather disciples and preach, some of His relatives came to seize Him, for they said He had gone mad (Mk. 3:21). Jesus did not trust them, nor would He go to Jerusalem to the feast with them. Considering how He appeared despised by relatives and country-men, He went so far as to say, "There is no prophet without honor except in his own country and among his own people," and, "The chief enemies of a man are those of his own household."

After all that has been said, should you not admit this, my soul: To suffer contempt with patience and silence, to love to be disregarded — this is the essence of the spirit of Jesus Christ, and one cannot acquire His Spirit without loving contempt.

Third excellent quality — To suffer contempt in silence is the key to Jesus' Heart and the means of uniting with Him. You will waste your efforts, my soul, if you search for Jesus without searching for contempt. Prayers, sighs, fasts, night vigils and other devout exercises are not enough. It is necessary for you to die, and that you die under blows of contempt. I mean it is necessary for you to put on Jesus Christ by loving contempt as He did, if you want to gain entrance into His Divine Heart. It is the souls that do this, whom Jesus loves. He enlightens them to know the secrets of His Greatness and Majesty. He con-soles them and lets them taste the sweetness of His Love. He deals familiarly with them and admits them to union with Him. They are the ones in whom He fulfills even in this life the promise He made with these words: "Lo, I stand at the gate knocking; if anyone hear My Voice and open to Me, I will enter and will dine with him and he with Me." Tell me now, O my soul, are we not completely blind and should we not deplore our folly with bitter tears, when we grieve over contempt? Should we not sigh with ardent longing for a good which Jesus has loved so much? Should we not even rate it above everything we have? Should we not embrace it with great joy? Oh, that we should so hate ourselves as to deprive ourselves of a good so valuable which has no equal on earth! Ah! We are that sick man who wanted to be cured, but would not use the remedy.

Affective Acts

Oblation —O my dear Jesus, I am well enough aware that as long as love for worldly glory takes up room in my heart, that Thou wilt never come to me nor can I ever familiarly approach Thee. It is necessary to remove the desire for honor and make every effort to put in its place the love for contempt. This I resolve upon, my most loving Jesus, and from this moment I offer myself in sacrifice. Vouchsafe to hear my prayer and grant me strength to fulfill the following resolves:

(1) I detest, I abhor, with all my heart, all desire for honor; — and I surrender it at Thy feet. I do not want there to be a man in the world who gives me a thought, who esteems me, who loves me and honors me, not even for a moment. And if, against my will, this should happen, it is my intention to detest all satisfaction arising therefrom as something loathsome in Thy sight.

(2) I love and embrace contempt with all my heart — Whatever happens to me by Thy Mercy, I will bear in silence for love of Thee. I will even praise and bless Thee for it as a great favor and benefit coming from Thy Hand.

(3) From this moment on, I surrender all claim I might have before the world for reputation and honor — I submit it all to Thy will. From now on I will care no more about all this and will look upon

it as another's property and not mine. Be good enough to accept this, O my Jesus! Just as Thy Eternal Father for His glory availed Himself of the claim Thou had to good repute, allowing Thee to be despised and belittled, so do Thou avail Thyself of the claim I might have to a good reputation. This, O my Jesus, is the sacrifice I choose to make. I will renew it each day and hope to live and die living up to it outwardly and inwardly.

Petition for the spirit of humility — But who will grant that my heart stay in these happy dispositions? Thou, alone, O my Jesus, Thou alone can do it. Without Thee, my good desires will vanish like smoke. Without Thee, my good resolves will never be worthily carried out. Without Thee, my good intention cannot last even an hour. Turn Thy merciful eyes to me, O Dearest Jesus! Grant me a heart that will completely agree with Thine. Grant that I may love what Thou hast loved, may hate what Thou hast hated. Grant that I may hate all vanity and esteem from men, just as Thou hast hated it. This grace I beg of Thee. This favor I long for.

Now pray the Our Father and the Hail Mary and the Concluding Prayers as on page xi.

Meditation 24

Interior Suffering
of Jesus Christ

Preparatory Prayer as on page x

Composition of Place — Imagine, my soul, that you see Jesus in the garden of Gethsemane, sorrowful, afflicted, in agony, sweating blood.

Prayer of Petition — O my Jesus, grant me constancy, silence, and patience so that I will suffer according to God's Will all the pains that it serves Thy interest to send me.

First Point

Jesus Christ has suffered before we have, all the interior pains that we are met with on the road to perfection.

O my soul, with lively attention let us suppose you see your Divine Redeemer in the garden of Gethsemane. In your imagination try to penetrate deep into His Heart and understand those terrific pains with which He was oppressed . . . But bear in mind that the Divinity offered no relief to His Holy Humanity in this suffering, just as a holy soul that has gone to Heaven gives no aid to its body which it has abandoned to rot in the grave. Jesus suffered just as He would have suffered if He had been purely human and created as we are. With these thoughts, begin our meditation.

The first suffering of Jesus Christ was an immense sorrow — There were two causes of this. The first was His burning Love. There was never a mother so devoted, who loved an only son with such tenderness as Jesus Christ loved each and every human being in particular. The second cause was His Infinite Knowledge. The Lord knew that, in spite of His Passion, the majority of men would come to perish eternally.*

From this came a sorrow which was enough to cause Him death, even if there had been no other pains. To conceive an idea of this, suppose, my soul, there is a mother who has left her little children, whom she loves devotedly, playing in a field. Suppose she turns to see them all mangled by a beast which has come out of a nearby forest, and after the horrible slaughter, tender members of their bodies are left scattered here and there, clawed and torn to pieces. Could one ever sufficiently understand the pain of that devoted mother at the sight of her dear little ones so tragically slain?

Enter now, O my soul, into Jesus' Heart and see if you cannot find a similar pain there at the sight of so many souls purchased by the shedding of all His Precious Blood and lost forever in hell.

The second interior suffering of Jesus Christ was fear — There is nothing that more cruelly crushes a man's heart than fear of death close at hand. Not seldom has it happened that persons told of approaching death — even young, robust persons

---

*NOTE — This does not say a majority of free creatures; and we know, according to the holy Fathers, that angels vastly outnumber men and that just a third of them were lost. (Apoc. 12:4). Nor does this say a majority of all human beings, including infants; and we know that the majority of human deaths are of infants and fetuses, and an especially large majority when times are very wicked. "God bears up with men," writes Saint Alphonsus Liguori, "but He does not bear forever. Were God to bear forever with sinners, no one would be damned: but the most common opinion is that the greater part of adults, even among Christians, are lost." "Wide is the gate, and broad is the way that leadeth to destruction, and many there are who go in thereat." (Mt. 7:13).

— have broken down overnight so as to appear aged and very feeble. What impression would fear of approaching death not make on Jesus' Heart — a death He plainly foresaw with all the terrible circumstances that made it so bitter to Him?

The third interior suffering of Jesus was the battle waged within Him — Nature and grace joined in Jesus' Heart to bring on this battle. Nature made His Passion unbearable in view of the horror of the death and the bitter pangs experienced from man's ingratitude; therefore He turned to His Father with these words: "Father, if it be possible, let this chalice pass from Me." Grace called for the great sacrifice and induced Him to add: "Father, not My Will, but Thine be done . . ."

Who will explain the violence of this battle waged within Him? It is enough to know that His Sacred Humanity could not stand it and was forced to sweat an abundance of His Blood through all His pores.

The fourth interior suffering of Christ was His mortal agony — A man's greatest trial and torment is surely his death agony. Imagine, my soul, that you see a dying man. His forehead yields a cold sweat caused by the struggle within him, which is most bitter. His hands and feet are limp and cool. Only with the greatest effort can he breathe. His heart pounds and putters. One pulsation does not yield place to another, for all is continually irregular and abnormal. The mere sight of him is pitiful. Consider now, my soul, your Jesus in the garden of Gethsemane, reduced by inner pain to this agonizing state, and have no doubt that He would have died if an angel who had been sent from Heaven, had not comforted Him in that crisis so that He could complete His Sacrifice.

Affective Acts

(1) Shame — O my Jesus, how great are Thy Sufferings, and how great is Thy fortitude in the midst of them! Thou art abandoned in a sea of bitterness, of anguish and sorrow. Weariness, horror, affliction, desolation without relief, and mortal agony, are like great ocean waves stirring up Thy Heart. But in the midst of this terrible storm Thy unconquerable constancy lets itself be seen.

Yes, Thou dost continue at prayer and even make Thy prayer all the longer. Thou conform Thy Will with that of the Eternal Father. Thou dost not turn back at the sight of torment, nor dost Thou even refuse the death of the Cross. Oh, this indeed is true charity! This is true faithfulness to God! This is perfect fulfillment of the Divine good pleasure.

Compared to Thy Suffering, what is mine, O afflicted Jesus? Ah! My suffering, compared to Thine, is very slight. Yet any suffering, however small, is enough to make me quit what I had started well. Distaste and sadness at time of prayer, lack of mortification, fickleness about good resolutions, dissipation of mind, faint-heartedness, mistrust - these are the unhappy results from the pains which you offer me so that I may be approved and gain merit. Oh, how I should blame myself and be filled with shame in Thy presence! Thou, Who are Innocence Itself, submitted to pain; and I, who am a sinner, want only consolation.

(2) Resolution — What a shame to the eyes of all the Heavenly Court! Jesus is afflicted unto death,

without having any sin; and I want to have consolation until death, after so many sins! I know my foolishness, O my Jesus, and I detest it. Never any more will I grumble at my inner pain. The desolation which Jesus suffered for love of me, I want to suffer also for love of Him. It is enough for me that I please Him. Him alone do I choose to seek. Him alone do I choose to love, in darkness as well as in light, in affliction as well as in consolation. This I resolve upon, O my Jesus. This I will do, by Thy Grace.

Second Point

The state of desolation is far more to our advantage than that of consolation. O my soul, in what peace you could live in the midst of darkness and desolation, if you knew the advantages which desolation brings with it! From the following truths you can form a fair concept:

First Truth — The state of desolation is more suitable for our offering God an acceptable sacrifice, than is the state of consolation. Oh, my soul, how we deceive ourselves, even in spiritual things! If by luck one enjoys a bit of inner peace, if he experiences a little more tender devotion in his heart, if his eyes moisten with sweet tears, he counts the day on which this occurs a happy one. But, oh how much more valuable beyond comparison is a day of desolation!

For on the day which you call fortunate, God gives you something; but you give nothing to God. When He has feasted you at His table and given you a taste of His Sweetness, it is a generosity that is all His. Nothing comes from you for Him. Ah! How many there are who show themselves faithful to God in

245

time of consolation; but how few there are who show themselves equally faithful in time of desolation!

When one finds oneself without any light and zest, and with his emotions stirred up in rebellion, and assaults of temptation of every kind at every turn, and yet he continues faithfully in silence, in prayer, in recollection, in mortification, and in all other virtuous practices, then we have the sacrifice which is the most acceptable to God, the gift of ourselves which His Majesty regards with eyes of most devoted satisfaction.

Second Truth — The state of desolation leads the soul to perfect love for God more securely than does the state of consolation.

To love God perfectly is nothing but to seek solely and purely His good pleasure, and outside of this to care about nothing else, neither on earth nor in Heaven. He that reaches this state enters in an instant into the possession of the most perfect love for God and becomes perfected in His Divine Presence. How to arrive at this, the surest way one can take is the road of desolation; for when a faithful soul in this state is without all consolation from the outside world and God withdraws all inner sweetness, he becomes practically crucified and little by little he dies to self and to all creatures. As he finds no satisfaction in anything else but the Divine good-pleasure, in this he finds rest and in God he finds perfect Divine Love.

Third Truth — In preference to the state of consolation, it is the state of desolation which leads a soul more surely and more promptly to close union with God. You should know, my soul, that just as fire purifies gold, and as it rids it of all impurity and leaves it beautiful and shining, so the state of desolation purifies the soul, and as it burns up within it all affections that do not refer to God, it very promptly makes it pleasing to God and puts it in immediate readiness for close union with the Supreme Good, enlightening it with His Heavenly Light and inflaming it with a holy love for Him.

The same thing happens to it as happens to a room which the sun brightens and warms only when the shade which is blocking the passage of its rays is lifted. One cannot say this of the state of consolation; for as it agrees so much with selfishness, out of a thousand souls in that state there will scarcely be one which reaches union with God. Therefore how much more desirable is the state of desolation!

Affective Acts

(1) Oblation — What, then, will I do? I see Jesus in the state of desolation. He is sorrowful even unto death. (Mt. 26:38). I realize that this state is supremely profitable to me, as it is the one which brings me to union with God. Why, then, am I unwilling to experience it? Ah! No! I am not unwilling.

At this moment I bow, kneeling at Thy Most Holy Feet, O my Jesus, and I consecrate and dedicate myself entirely to Thy Divine Will. My heart is ready to be left without any light, without any consolation, without any satisfaction, to suffer darkness, to be forsaken, as Thou were in the garden. I am ready to experience grief, temptation, and whatever else Thou wish me to suffer, my God.

Henceforth my only contentment and consolation will be the fulfillment of Thy Divine good-pleasure. My only joy, my only relief is in being deprived for

Thy sake and in Thy company, of all consolation and rest, and in knowing that in this way Thy Holy Will is fulfilled in me.

(2) Prayer to obtain fortitude — But here is where I see that I must raise my hands, my eyes, and my heart to Thee, O my Jesus, to beg Thy Sweet Mercy on my behalf. To see no relief in creatures and to be faithful to Thee; to have our mind clouded with heavy darkness, our will distressed with painful dryness, our heart afflicted with continual desolation and yet not falter; to bear the attack of horrible temptation, to have our mind harassed with frightening thoughts, but not yield to discouragement; to experience feelings of bitterness, anxiety, rebellion, when it seems that all our wild impulses are let loose on us, and yet to remain constant in God's service — this is virtue without equal. (For we know it is one thing to experience wayward tendencies, another thing to consent to them.)

Herein lies true self-denial, complete detachment from all creatures, true faithfulness, pure love, and the surest pledge of union with God. But for an achievement so generous, no less is required than a powerful and effective grace from Heaven. Therefore I appeal to Thee with all my strength, O my Jesus. Do Thou help me, Lord.

Now pray the Our Father and the Hail Mary and the Concluding Prayers as on page xi.

Meditation 25

The External Sufferings of Christ

Preparatory Prayer as on page x

Composition of Place — Imagine, my soul, that you see Jesus after being nailed to the Cross and shortly before He died, that you hear Him say, "O all ye that pass by the way, attend, and see if there be any sorrow like to My Sorrow..." (Lam. 1:12).

Prayer of Petition — O my Jesus, grant that I may ever meditate on Thy Sorrows, keeping them ever in mind.

First Point

During this life in these bodies of ours we will never suffer as much as Jesus Christ did in His. In order to conceive an idea of the cruelty of the pain Christ suffered in His Passion, consider with attention, my soul, the following circumstances:

First Circumstance — Christ's pains were all-extensive, so that no part of His Body was exempt. Direct your gaze to Christ, my soul, and observe His Members one by one and tell me if you can find even one that is exempt from great pain.

See His Cheeks, swollen and blue from beating. His Mouth is tormented with thirst and soured with gall. His Hair and Beard have been cruelly yanked from the roots. His Eyes are covered with blood. His Head is pierced with rough thorns. His Flesh, Nerves, Back, Chest, Abdomen, Sides, right and left, are pitilessly mangled. His Skin has been ripped and torn; His Veins cut, and they discharge blood; the arteries are wounded; muscle fibers are exposed; and

His Body is so cut up that one sees even bones. His feet and hands have been pierced through with rough nails, and His whole Sacred Body has become one wound.

Isaias, who saw Him long before, described Him as follows: "There is no beauty in Him, nor comeliness . . . a Man of Sorrows . . . Surely He hath borne our infirmities and carried our sorrows: and we have thought Him as it were a leper, and as one struck by God and afflicted." (Is. 53:2-4).

Second Circumstance — Jesus' pains were supremely cruel, and incomparably greater than all any man could ever endure. This was due, first, to the tenderness and delicacy of His Most Holy Body; for, as Saint Bonaventure teaches, He had a Body so tender and delicate, so fine and sensitive — which was a work of the Holy Spirit — that a pain in the sole of His Divine feet became more perceptible to Him than an injury to the pupils of the eyes would be for other men.

It was due, secondly, to His being tormented in His most sensitive parts. What torture did He not feel as men pressed on His Head a crown of rough, sharp thorns which went through not just the skin, but the skull-bone and temples as well, and drew blood that streamed down His cheeks and eyes! . . . What pain He surely suffered when, swinging their hammers, men drove rough nails into His feet and hands, tearing flesh, bursting veins, passing through nerves . . . What a martyrdom did He not surely suffer, with His Body suspended between Heaven and earth, when He hung by the nails driven into a wretched cross, and found no relief in any position to which He might turn Himself.

Third Circumstance — Jesus' pains were without relief. He had been hanging on the Cross several hours, He had shed His Blood, and none of it remained but a few drops in His Veins, when, tormented by an unbearable thirst, He asked for a drink. Might not one give a God-Man the bit of relief of a cup of water when His Strength is wasting away and He is dying in a sea of affliction?

However, not even that was granted Him. Instead, they gave Him vinegar mingled with gall to torment Him more, and so that His final pains might be without relief, as were all the other pains which He suffered.

Affective Acts

(1) Thanksgiving — I know not what to say nor what to think at the sight of such a tragedy, O my Jesus. If You had committed as many sins as I have, and if Thy Heavenly Father had been as offended as He has been by me, or Thou had deserved hell as I have, could Thou have suffered more or done a penance more rigorous than the one Thou did? Ah! Thou submitted to such terrible pains not because of any sins Thou had committed (for being Holiness by nature, Thou could not sin), but it was because of my sins.

Yes, faith tells me that His whole Body was cut up with lashes; for my sins He was mocked as a fool; for my sins He was to die, and die as a criminal on a cross. O Jesus! O most lovable Jesus! What kindness, what mercy Thou dost show!

Would that I had a thousand tongues so that I could praise and bless Thee as I would like! My boundless thanks be to Thee for all the drops of Blood Thou shed for love of me, for all the blows and lashes Thou suffered for me, for all the insults, mockeries and abuses Thou endured for love of me, for all the aches and pains Thou bore on the Cross for my sake. . .

(2) Resolution — But this is not enough. Jesus was not satisfied to just appeal on my behalf. He also wanted to suffer for me. From this I should detect the need to suffer. In this way I want to respond to Jesus' love for me . . . I know how right it is in absolute justice, and I want to carry it out. And so I offer myself, from this time on, in a sacrifice from which I desire never to withdraw myself. . .

First, Thou knowest all the pains, ailments, and other misfortunes which Thy Eternal Father has determined to send me. From this moment on, I adore and humbly accept all these decisions and I desire that they be perfectly fulfilled in me. Second, Thou likewise knowest, my Jesus, the manner and the time that the Eternal Father has determined to call me to Himself out of this world by means of death. I also profoundly adore this decree, and agree to it with all my soul. I wish to suffer and die, and to suffer and die for the sake of pure love, just as Thou didst suffer and die for me. . .

Second Point

Just as Jesus Christ's pains were extreme and cruel, all the more so was His patience very marvellous and astonishing. These are the circumstances whereby you can conceive some idea of this, my soul:

First Circumstance — Jesus endured His sufferings in silence and without complaining. The Holy Spirit, speaking of Jesus Christ, compares Him to a lamb. This is because, being a guileless, harmless animal, it allows itself to be shorn and led away to the slaughterhouse without bleating nor offering the least resistance. Likewise Jesus allowed Himself to be extremely mistreated without resisting or even uttering a complaint.

Yes, He was whipped and His whole body torn, and He held His peace. He was crowned with rough, sharp thorns, and kept silent. He went through the greatest agony and, though He was extremely weakened, men burdened His shoulders with a heavy cross, and He kept quiet. . . They pierced His Hands and Feet with nails and crucified Him on a cross with unheard of cruelty, and He remained silent. "I . . . (was) as a dumb man not opening his mouth." (Ps. 37:14). He Himself says by the Royal Prophet. Thus did Jesus conduct Himself during His extreme sufferings. . . How do I conduct myself?

Second Circumstance — Jesus bore His Sufferings with unswerving meekness. There has not been a man in the world who has had such good grounds for being angry as Jesus had on the cross. The grounds were:

(1) The hatred that was all around Him. Before His eyes there was a countless multitude of people of all classes, and He saw into the depths of their hearts. Now what did He discover therein? Nothing but hate, ill-will, animosity, with satisfaction and glee at His sufferings and death, and a wish and hope that His Name disappear from the world and be wiped from everyone's memory.

(2) The mockery, the blasphemy, the insults with which the scribes and Pharisees abused Him, wagging their heads in harsh sarcasm, saying, "Bah,

Thou that destroyest the temple . . . and in three days dost rebuild it: . . . He saved others: Himself He cannot save." (Mt. 27:40, 42). "If Thou be the Son of God, come down from the Cross." (Mt. 27:40).

In the face of these cutting taunts that men made at the height of His suffering, did Jesus Christ not have good grounds for showing anger? Yet He shows none, but suffers everything with complete resignation, with a marvellous love that forgets the wrongs and the pains, and only shows a care for the salvation of His enemies. That is why, instead, He had spoken to the women these words that showed His compassion: "Daughters of Jerusalem, weep not over Me; but weep for yourselves and for your children." (Lk. 23:28)

Third Circumstance — Jesus endured His pains with fortitude and a desire to suffer more. Jesus is hanging on the Cross. His strength is now exhausted. His pain has reached its height. His Body, drained of its Blood, can no longer resist the power of death. . . What, then, does He do? O my soul, take an inward gaze, and marvel at His astonishing fortitude! Two loves with which He burned, ignited in Him two desires . . . He loves His Heavenly Father, and out of this arises the desire to live longer so as to be able to suffer more for the sake of love . . . He also loves us men, and from this there springs the desire to live longer so that He can, out of His love, suffer yet a longer time. . . This is just what He meant when He showed His thirst, and when addressing His Father, He said, "Father, why hast Thou forsaken Me?" As though He would say, "O Father, why dost Thou not give Me strength to live longer and to suffer more for love of Thee and for love of men?"

Affective Acts

(1) Shame — Oh, the fear, the shame I should feel, O my Jesus, at the sight of Thy body hanging on the cross! Ah! how hast Thou sinned, venerable head of my Redeemer, that Thou should be wounded with such rough thorns? What hast Thou done wrong, O beautiful eyes, to be so sunken, so clotted with blood? O all-powerful hands and feet, how hast Thou offended, that Thou shouldst be bored through with rough nails? What hast Thou done, O most loving Heart, that Thou should be pierced with an unmerciful lance? But indeed Jesus is innocent! How the flower of innocence fully shines out in Him! ... And why, then, do so many and such cruel torments afflict this Innocent One? Alas for me! Jesus suffers not for His sins, but for mine. My sins brought Him to this unhappy plight. My sins nailed Him to the Cross. My sins brought on His death.

(2) Confession and Resolution — And I, guilty of much sin, feel unwilling to suffer. And — all the worse for me! — I do not want to believe that many times I have deserved to suffer. But eternal praise to Thee, O my Jesus! For at present I am convinced of this: That there is no pain nor torment in hell that I have not deserved by my sins. No matter how much I have suffered up to now or will suffer in the future, it is not enough to wipe away even one of my many sins nor make up to Thee in the least for them. Oh, how unjust it is for me to complain in my troubles! No matter how much I suffer, I will always suffer less than I deserve. Is it not quite right, then, that I surrender to Thy Most Holy Will in everything, and that in the midst of my troubles I praise and bless

Thee for all Thy loving designs concerning me? Yes, it is quite right; and I resolve to do so in the future.

Now pray the Our Father and the Hail Mary and the Concluding Prayers as on page xi.

Meditation 26

The Insults and Pains
which Jesus Suffered

Preparatory Prayer as on page x

Composition of Place — Imagine you see Jesus
at the tribunals and palaces of Annas, Caiphas,
Herod and Pilate. Note the patience with which He
bore horrible insults and atrocious pains.

Prayer of Petition — O my Jesus, grant me the
grace I need in order to bear with silence and humility the degradations and pains that I must undergo in
this world.

First Point

There has not been and will never be a man who
has suffered or had to suffer such great wrongs and
degradations as Jesus Christ suffered. It is not possible to combine in a single meditation all the degradations to which Jesus Christ submitted. Therefore
we will only consider some of them. These alone,
my soul, will be enough to make you ashamed of
your pride.

*The first kind of degradation was the false
charges and the calumnies* — There is nothing that
more keenly wounds a man of noble and sincere
heart than piling up false charges against him of
things he would not even dream of doing. Enter, O
my soul, into the tribunal of Annas and Caiphas and
hear the outrageous crimes that are charged against
Jesus.

The witnesses are lined up and here are the
charges they make: They say He is a lover of wine;

that He likes to eat with publicans and sinners; that He is ruled by an intolerable pride, going so far as to claim to be Divine; that He would destroy the temple in Jerusalem; that He spreads impious doctrine and is introducing the people to idolatry; that He is a sorcerer and works prodigies with the help of the devil, with whom He has a secret compact; that He is a seducer and astutely plots the ruin of the chosen people... They charge Jesus with all these crimes in the tribunals of the High Priest and of Pilate. These charges are circulated among the people and are spread in the neighborhoods and public squares of Jerusalem.

The second kind of degradation was the scoffing and mockery — The wickedness of calling Jesus a blasphemer and criminal was not enough. It was also necessary to call Him a senseless fool. See Him in Herod's presence. Because He makes no answer to repeated questions but in His Infinite Wisdom keeps silent, men call Him a fool, at the prompting of the king and courtiers, and, like a fool He is covered with a white robe, and amid the mockery and laughter of insolent people they lead Him through the public streets to Pilate.

After this insult another follows of which I would not know whether to call it more savage or more contemptuously insulting, this time in the palace of the Roman Prefect. Incited to do so by the Jews, the soldiers decide to make sport of Jesus in a way no one but the devil could suggest. They throw a purple robe over His shoulders. Then they place a reed in His hand. Weaving together a crown out of rough, sharp thorns, they press it down on His head in order to make fun of Him as a make-believe king.

Their mockery does not stop here. To ridicule Him more, they bend their knees to Him in mock reverence; then they spew their filthy spittle into His Face and give Him a cruel beating. While the Heavens darken at the sight of this and the angels are bitterly weeping, a countless throng pauses to look at the unusual spectacle, and add to the injury and mockery in their festive way by their applause.

The third kind of injury that was done to Jesus was the passage of the death sentence with all its bad implications — Pilate, who was perfectly aware of Jesus' uprightness and innocence, in order to deliver Him, placed Him before the people, who had gathered beneath the balcony of his palace. They were there to choose a man sentenced to die whom Pilate would do the favor of sparing in honor of the Pasch.

They were to choose between Jesus and Barabbas. And who would believe it? Against Pilate's expectations the choice fell on Barabbas, as all the people cried out that Barabbas should go free and Jesus should be condemned. Now how is it that people want Jesus condemned and Barabbas released? Who is Barabbas? He is a criminal found guilty of sedition and murder.

And ought he be released and Jesus condemned? "Indeed, that is what we wish. Let Barabbas live and let Jesus die!" What evil has Jesus done? . . . Now if Jesus must die, what kind of death should He be sentenced to? It would be very harsh to put Him to the sword.

Even so, He must die the most bitter kind of death and at the same time the one most disgraceful. He must die nailed to a cross — the way the most

259

infamous, the most wicked criminals are accustomed to suffer death. And He must die in between two criminals, so that all may know that He surpassed everyone in wickedness. This was what the people wished and was the sentence Pilate gave Him.

Thus Jesus was led to His death on the Cross amid the festive joy of the high priests, amid the blasphemous insults of the scribes and pharisees, and amid the harsh mockeries of an immense throng. It was exactly then that was fulfilled the prediction of the Prophet who, in the person of Jesus Christ, testified, "I am a worm and no man: the reproach of men, and the outcast of the people." (Ps. 21:7).

Pause here a little, my soul, and answer the questions that I am going to ask. First, I ask: Did the Eternal Father give an unjust sentence when He decreed such great, such shocking degradations for His Only-Begotten Son? No, my soul, certainly not. Jesus had taken on Himself the liability for our sins by His own choice, and our sins called for this payment . . .

Secondly, I ask: Would the Eternal Father do you any wrong to allow against you insults and disgraces as great as the ones that He willed for His Only-Begotten Son to undergo? No, for sin deserves as much; and rightly do you come to realize this from the outrages and insults done to Jesus, and rightly does your conscience accuse you of being guilty of many sins.

Thirdly, I ask: If you believe that sin is something that deserves such ill treatment, knowing as you do that you have sinned, would your pride not be intolerable if you refused to bear even a slight contempt? What could be the ingratitude if you were unwilling to suffer a bit of offensive treatment for love of Jesus, after He has suffered such great wrongs and such extraordinary offenses for love of you?

Affective Acts

(1) Admiration of the humility of Jesus — O my beloved Jesus, my Redeemer, what astonishing wonders are put before my eyes by Thy humility! Thou, Who art Infinite Wisdom and govern Heaven and earth, are declared a dull-witted fool! Thou art mocked as a make-believe king and people spit in Thy Face as though Thou were the vilest man in the world! Thou, Who are Holiness Itself, from whom come all gifts and Heavenly Graces, are counted a hypocrite and a lover of wine!

Thou art charged with being a seducer and blasphemer; Thou art called a Samaritan and a sorcerer, and are counted worse than a murderer and an assassin! All this Thou suffer, and suffer it with awesome silence without the least complaint, with a meekness beyond comparison, without bitterness and with full resignation, without any regret that Heaven decreed this. . . Oh, what humility! Oh, the reticence of my Jesus! This is truly a sacrifice which, of itself, is enough to give infinite pleasure to the Eternal Father and to give the hearts of all men a lesson of humility . . .

(2) Shame — But this humility of Thine, oh, how hateful it makes my pride appear in Thy sight. O my Jesus! I, a lowly little mortal with a mind so very ignorant, so darkened — I want to be counted wise and prudent; while Jesus, Who is Wisdom Itself, is led in the garment of a fool through the public streets to be the laughing-stock of all the people! I, a sinner,

want to be counted blameless, while the blameless Jesus is being counted as a seducer, a blasphemer and a sorcerer!

I, poor in every virtue and full of evil ways, endeavor to win preference above all others; while Jesus, Who is Holiness Itself, is ranked below Barabbas and sentenced to die on the disreputable Cross! Oh, how hateful, how abominable my intolerable pride must seem in my Redeemer's eyes! O my Jesus, have mercy on me and grant that in my mind I may have an entirely different outlook, and in my will my sentiments shall be quite contrary to what they have been up to now.

Second Point

There has not been a man in the world who has borne degradations and outrages as Jesus bore them. The royal Prophet describes the truly awesome humility with which Jesus bore insult and outrage, and he uses these words: "I, as a deaf man, heard not: and as a dumb man not opening his mouth." (Ps. 37:14). Ponder these brief words, my soul, and wonder at the immense humility that is hidden beneath the awesome silence.

(1) Jesus was blameless — and could never be charged with anything that was not upright, and He could never be rightly rebuked. The crimes with which men charged Him were evil inventions of His enemies. If Jesus had chosen to speak, in a moment He could have made His innocence very obvious to everyone. He could have silenced His enemies before all the people and could have covered them with shame and embarrassment.

(2) Jesus was All-Powerful — One word of His

was enough to cause bolts of fire to shoot down from the clouds upon all His enemies and hurl them all into the abyss of hell. With just a word He could have caused all men to know His Divinity and He could have caused all Jerusalem to adore Him as the long-awaited Messias.

(3) Jesus was Infinite Wisdom — He knew that His enemies would become abusive on the occasion of His silence, and that they would not rest until they had seen Him die a disreputable death on a Cross. He knew that from His silence His beloved Mother and the Apostles would suffer extremely. . . .

He knew that when He would hold His peace as He did, men would make it an occasion to discredit the miracles He had worked, to condemn His teaching as erroneous and to vent their rage against His newly founded Church. He knew all this. Nevertheless these considerations were not powerful enough arguments to draw one word from His mouth to prove His innocence. He wanted to keep silent, and to keep silent up to His last breath.

O Jesus, my wonderful Jesus, how astonishing and how eloquent is this silence of Thine! How sublime is this lesson of Thine! But alas! How few there are who imitate it! Where are those souls who, when they suffer insult and reproach and outrage, know how to join Jesus in keeping silent? There may indeed be men who know how to adapt themselves to other difficulties and mortifications, above all if they are undertaken through their own decision. But to be quiet when people disparage us, to love our cross of insult and calumny, to avoid explaining away unjust accusations against us — Ah! This is a burden few backs would carry! . . . But meantime it will always be an undeniable truth that Jesus Christ's example is the only road to holiness, and one who does not imitate Him will never be very worthy in His sight and will have no hope of reaching perfection at any time*.

Affective Acts

(1) Esteem and appreciation for contempt — Oh how wonderful is Thy teaching, my Jesus! How far it outmatches all the wisdom of the world! In suffering unkind criticism, contempt, and ill treatment, Thou found only the beauty and desirability of these things. When with a single word Thou could draw on Thyself as much honor as there was contempt that Thou received, Thou preferred contempt rather than honor. So far removed were Thy affections from being set on honor, that Thou showed a desire for the humiliations.

Now why should I not have the same sentiments that Thou had and why should I not love what Thou loved? Indeed, my Jesus, in the future I will regard

---

*Note — This point deserves a clarification. Even though Christ did not answer all of Pilate's questions, He did respond truthfully when Pilate asked Our Lord if He was King. (*Matt.* 17, 11). Further, Our Lord proclaimed His innocence and defended Himself during His trial before the high priest. When He was struck by the officer at the Temple, He said: "If I have spoken evil, give testimony to the evil; but if well, why strikest thou Me." (*John* 18:23). At this trial, Our Lord proclaimed His Divinity to the high priest (*Matt.* 26, 63-64). Also, during Our Lord's public life, He gave testimony to His sinlessness: "Which of you shall convict Me of sin?" (*John* 8, 46). Hence, St. Anthony Mary Claret is actually speaking here about the holy and meritorious virtue of remaining silent in the face of detractions and calumnies, that is, when we are attacked *personally*. But if we see the rights of God under attack, then we may not be silent. We must publicly and steadfastly defend the rights of God at all times. Pope Leo XIII reiterated this truth when he said "About the rights of man, people have heard enough. It is time they should hear of the rights of God." (Encyclical Letter *Tamisti*, Nov. 1, 1900) contempt as something that overthrows my fiercest enemy, which is pride, as something that opens for me the entrance into the Heart of Jesus, as something that ought to form the loveliest part of my glory in paradise.

(2) Contrition and Resolution — Ah how blind I have been in the past, my Jesus! I have desired to be able to love Thee as Thou art loved by the Seraphim in Heaven and especially I have wanted to be able to show Thee my love by offering Thee a sacrifice that Thou would like and accept. And what other sacrifice could be more agreeable to Thee but that of forsaking my high rating of self, by bearing humiliation and insult in silence? And why have I not conducted myself in that way?

Ah, the most beautiful moment of my life was not when my heart was penetrated with a tender, sentimental affection for God and felt carried away with love for His Infinite Goodness. No; rather the loveliest instant was when my actions were being unfairly interpreted and discredited, and the most beautiful occasion of offering God a perfect sacrifice was when people downright despised me and ceremoniously mocked me.

I was wrong, then, O my Jesus; I was wrong in grieving when I should have rejoiced, and in running from what I should have sought, and in grumbling when I should have kept quiet. Now that I know my mistake, what should I do, O my Jesus? I should do just what Thou did when the hour approached for Thee to suffer disgrace. "That the world may know, that I love the Father: . . . Arise, let us go hence." (John 14:31). This is how Thou spoke when, full of fervor, Thou submitted Thyself to Thy enemies, from whom Thou could hope for nothing but ill treatment and slanderous insult. When an occasion comes to me to suffer contempt and humiliation, I, likewise, will lift up my heart, saying: That Heaven may know that I love Jesus, come, my soul, let us proceed to embrace these things gladly for love of Him. . .

Now pray the Our Father and the Hail Mary and the Concluding Prayers as on page xi.

Meditation 27

Jesus Proves on the Cross His Love for His Enemies

Preparatory Prayer as on page x

Composition of Place — Envision Jesus nailed to the Cross and enduring His greatest pains. You hear Him pray to His Father on behalf of those who crucify Him.

Prayer of Petition — O my Jesus and my Master! I beg of Thee the grace not only to forgive my enemies, but to love them and do good to them.

First Point

Jesus showed an astonishingly great love for His enemies. Go back in your thoughts, my soul, to Calvary, and ponder with attention Jesus' Love for His enemies. See Him suspended from three nails on an infamous gibbet. He is wounded all over, dripping with blood, plunged in a sea of pain, and is close to breathing His last. See, also, the throng of people of every age, condition, and state — young and old, lords and ladies and common people, Hebrews and Gentiles, scribes and pharisees, elders of the people and high priests — and these people, instead of having pity (which only a few show at the sight of pain), are all burning with an implacable mortal hatred for Him. As we ponder the more noteworthy circumstances of this hatred, consider whether it should have been hard and difficult for Him to love a people so savage and inhuman.

The first circumstance was the triumphant glee of His enemies — Here, my soul, you should not consider Jesus as a mere man, but as both God and Man (as indeed He was), to Whose gaze everyone's heart lay bare, as He saw even their most secret thoughts. As He hung suffering on the Cross, what evil did He not find in the hearts of those cruel people? He perceived some who rejoiced at the sight of Him nailed to the Cross, who were congratulating themselves on the arrival, at last, of the hour they had hoped for — the hour of seeing the One they accused of being a seducer, an impostor, a deceiver, hanging from a Cross. He perceived that others were approving the sentence passed against Him, and were judging that it was quite just (because they thought He was a scoundrel and blasphemer) to be assigned no other execution than one on a cross. He saw that these men took great delight and danced, as it were, with glee at seeing Him suffer, at seeing Him refused the smallest relief for His thirst, at seeing men rather increase His thirst and add to His torments by giving Him gall and vinegar to drink. He perceived others impatiently awaiting His death and wanting His Name blotted out from everyone's memory. All of this Jesus saw, and saw it in the hearts of the very ones for whom He came down from Heaven to earth, leaving an immensely happy condition and submitting to human miseries. Yes, He saw these things in the hearts of those on whose behalf He had worked so many miracles and for whom He was dying. At the sight of all this, what must have been the quality of His love for such people?

The second circumstance was the jeers and insults of His enemies — When someone is in his death agony, having been turned over to an executioner to be put to death, it is an act of compassion to show him sympathy . . . something that is not refused even the most wayward criminal. When a criminal is presented on the gallows, no matter how deserving of death he may be, a great silence is observed by everyone, and even the hardest hearts show him some indications of pity and compassion; and the more painful the execution to which the man is condemned, the more apparent is this sympathy. But Jesus was not counted worthy of this much. The more cruel His pains were and the more savage the execution procedures, so much the more bitter were the jeers, so much the more cutting was the mockery with which He was insulted by His enemies.

"Bah!" some were saying, "If You boasted that You would destroy the temple and rebuild it in three days, show Your Power now and rescue Yourself from the Cross!" Others argued, "If You made such a boast of being the Son of God and of always trusting in Him, why does He not come now to deliver You?"

The third circumstance was His enemies' stubbornness — It would not have been difficult for Jesus to love His enemies if in the end they had recognized and detested their sin; but the obstinacy of these wicked people was too great. The elements, even though they were lifeless, bore witness to Jesus' innocence. The sky shrouded itself with mourning. The sun grew dark. Boulders cracked in pieces. The veil of the temple ripped into two parts. The earth trembled and quaked. The people were eyewitnesses of these astounding events; but in spite of them, they did not stop abusing Him. Rather, becoming even more furious against the Lord, they kept mocking Him, cursing Him and blaspheming Him. They did not cease tormenting Him until they saw that He was dead. And yet Jesus bore it all with an heroic patience. And even forgetting His Pains and the many abuses they were vomiting forth against Him into His very Face in His agonizing condition, turning to His Eternal Father He pleaded with Him and took up their defense, so that He might obtain pardon for their wicked behavior . . .

Could a love be found that resembles this? It would not have been hard for Jesus to love His enemies if He had foreseen that they would stop hating Him, at least after His death. But He could not even have this consolation. He foresaw that most of them would make a joke of all those miracles which would be worked on His behalf after His Resurrection. He foresaw that they would persecute even to death His Apostles, who were to proclaim His Name. He foresaw that they would continue in their obstinacy until death and that they would blaspheme forever in hell even more than the demons do. It surely must have been a very hard thing for Jesus to love a people so unjust and evil. But in spite of all this, instead of giving Himself over to anger and seeking vengeance for His extremely painful, degrading death, He ceased not from loving even the most sinful ones, nor from wishing that His Divine Blood might give life to those who had shed it so brutally . . .

My soul, enter within yourself here, and see who those persons are whom you find it difficult to love. Are they, by any chance, false witnesses who have falsely accused you in court? Are they cruel characters who have sometimes made you drink the gall and vinegar of pain, hardship, privation and injustice? Are they assassins who are thirsty for your blood and want to nail you, like Jesus, to a cross?

Ah! There may be someone perhaps who gives you an unpleasant look. There may be someone who lets a thoughtless word escape from his mouth. And will you have difficulty loving these persons, after seeing Jesus love even His unmerciful persecutors? Compare well your enemies with those of Jesus.

Affective Acts

(1) Shame — O Jesus! O most lovable Jesus! I marvel at Thy generous charity, and at the sight of it I know how weak mine is. In Thy Heart Thou preserved a love that remained steadfast in the midst of every outrage. With Thy vision Thou dost perceive those who harbor for many years in their hearts a hatred for Thee that is more than diabolical. Thou dost recognize those who curse and blaspheme Thee as if Thou were the greatest criminal in the world. Thou knowest those who make a boast of reducing Thee to this condition in which Thou become unrecognizable, and those who jeer at Thee and mock Thee when Thou art in the throes of the most horrible torment.

With Thy Own eyes Thou seest them; with Thy Own Ears Thou hearest them; and all the hate and raving of their hearts is quite known to Thee. But all this is not enough to cool off Thy Love, nor does Thy Heart yield to a shadow of irritation, nor do Thy lips utter one word of grumbling, nor do Thy hands make any move to take revenge. Instead, Thou lovest them all. Thou dost press them all to Thy bosom. Thou didst shed Thy Precious Blood for them all. Not one dost Thou shut out from Thy Heart. This is how strong and generous Thy love is, O my Jesus. And mine? Ah, it is a love that does not deserve to be called love, because any petty injury is enough to cripple it, and sometimes it manages to extinguish it and perhaps to change it into hatred.

(2) Repentance — In this light, I am a man truly lacking love! Oh, what a sad, distressing thought! — That I am a man who is poor and needy as regards love! And yet, who am I? I am a soul chosen from among thousands and thousands to follow Jesus. I am a Christian soul who spends so much time daily meditating on the example of Jesus Christ, Who even loved those who crucified Him. In spite of all this, I am a creature poor and needy with regard to love! This is so, after so many years of my life as a Christian have passed, after so many insights, graces, and interior inspirations, after so many aids and opportunities! Ah! What reason I have to detest my sluggishness!

Second Point

In view of the circumstances in which He loved His enemies, Jesus' love was something astonishing. Up to now the circumstances we have considered have been the hate, the rabidness and the unheard of savagery that His enemies displayed against Jesus. Now, my soul, ponder the circumstances of that love Jesus showed them at the very time of their rage. I do not doubt that a consideration of these two points will supply the weightiest motives for admiring a love so immense.

The first circumstance was the time in which He prayed for those who were crucifying Him — Jesus needed to say a number of things from the Cross: to His Eternal Father, to commend His Spirit to Him; to His beloved Mother, to entrust Her to His Disciple John; to John, to charge him with the care of His afflicted Mother; to bystanders, to ask relief in His extreme thirst. But for whom did He give first attention when He spoke? Ah! His sorrowful Mother would wait, the faithful disciple would hold off; Jesus' personal affairs would be forgotten; and the first words would be directed to His Eternal Father in favor of His enemies, begging pardon for them: "Father, forgive them." (Lk. 23:34). What love! What wonderful love!

The second circumstance was His enemies' malice — This was growing more and more on each occasion, the more ardent Jesus' love appeared to be - One might think that, before setting about to obtain the pardon of His enemies, Jesus would wait until they first recognized the enormous misdeed they had committed and with humility and regret begged for pity and mercy. But His Charity was of another quality, which did not allow Him to wait until they recognized their great fault; but He at once became their Mediator with the Eternal Father to obtain their forgiveness. I love them, Jesus said; and because I love, I intercede. I love and I intercede at the very moment in which I hear their ridicule and blasphemy, and I see their hate and experience all the effects of their rage and fury. I love them and I intercede for them and I offer all My Blood for them. . .

What do you say, my soul, at the sight of a love of this fine quality?

The third circumstance as the reason which

Jesus presented in His prayer — It is undeniable that the Jews had committed against Jesus an injustice of the most horrible, abominable kind, choosing for Him the most cruel kind of death. The miracles that He had worked and which they had seen with their own eyes, the blamelessness of His life, known even to the Gentile prefect (Pontius Pilate), the very accusations which they had invented and had produced at the trial — all in an evident way proved their bad will. In spite of this, Jesus prayed for them, and to excuse them He pointed to their ignorance, saying, "Father, forgive them, for they know not what they do." (Lk. 23:34). It was as if He wanted to say, "Father, I do not say that they have not sinned. I only say that their impiety can be pardoned, that ignorance plays a great part in it. Otherwise they would never have treated Me this way. Therefore I beg Thee, My Father, to forgive them as I forgive them, and that Thou love them as I love them. . ."

Oh, the wonderful love of Jesus for His enemies, which moved Him to love them with such love! My soul, you, too, learn to love the person that has offended you, and, if you please, look at your enemies with those eyes with which Jesus looked at His enemies from the Cross and it will become very easy for you. What did Jesus find in His enemies that could incline His Heart to love them? Ah! He saw in them the weakness of fallen nature that is prone to evil from birth. He saw in them precious souls fashioned to His Own Image and Likeness and called to share His Glory. He saw in them the most profound designs of His Heavenly Father, Who, by the very hands of His enemies, offered Jesus the chalice which He, the Father, had prepared. Finally, He saw that very great number of sins for which He had freely obliged Himself to make due payment to Divine Justice and which that Justice was punishing in Him by means of His enemies. These reasons were the strongest ones that persuaded Him to earnestly plead and intercede with His Eternal Father, to win for them the forgiveness of the great crimes that they had committed.

Affective Acts

(1) Repentance — Ah, my Jesus! Now I understand the true cause of the difficulty I have always experienced in loving people by whom I have been offended. The cause is that I have never looked at them with those eyes with which Thou looked at Thy enemies; and this is also the true cause of my bad state. If only I had always regarded people who offended me as persons by whose hands my Heavenly Father was offering me the chalice He had prepared for me; if only I had always regarded them as persons whom Divine Justice was using to punish my sins — ah! — how many perfect acts of love might I not have made up to now, and how closely my heart would come to resemble Thy loving Heart! But now — what is the state of my heart? What kind of charity do I have? Ah, my beloved Redeemer, let me be silent and hide myself from Thy eyes, because the great shame I feel restrains me from talking to Thee and looking at Thee. But what would be the benefit of being silent and hiding from Thee? It is better that I sincerely confess my folly and humbly beg the forgiveness of Thy Mercy. Ah, my Jesus! I have certainly reflected on the outstanding ways in which Thou hast been an example of love. I have

admired this and have praised it. But when have I taken up the task of imitating it?

(2) Resolution and Prayer of Petition — Then, will I always behave as I have, O my Jesus? No, please! For the attitude I now feel is, by Thy Grace, different, and my heart feels changed. What I propose is to love those who have offended me with all my heart, to bear meekly and silently the injuries that are done to me, and I will make it a special endeavor to return good for evil. This is the way Jesus loved. It is the way I, too, should love, and indeed, choose to love. But how will I do it without a light to clear up my mind and a powerful impulse, a help, to give strength to my courage? I turn to Thee, my Beloved, my Crucified, my only Teacher of Love. I call upon Thee by that wonderful meekness with which Thou forgave Thy enemies, by that affectionate prayer Thou made on their behalf, by that Precious Blood which Thou shed for them. Grant me a charity that extends to all men, a charity that gives me strength to patiently suffer and bear everything, a charity that is always moving me to react to the evil done to me, by rendering some good turn that matches it. *Amen.*

Now pray the Our Father and the Hail Mary and the Concluding Prayers as on page xi.

Meditation 28

Conclusion of the Fourth Section on the Illuminative Way, and the Step Preparing for the Unitive Way

Preparatory Prayer as on page x

Composition of Place — Imagine you see Jesus on Calvary, nailed to the Cross, and on Mount Tabor transfigured, and you hear the Eternal Father's Voice saying, ". . . This is My beloved Son in Whom I am well pleased: hear ye Him." (Mt. 17:5).

Prayer of Petition — O my Jesus, I beg to fulfill all that Thou art teaching me by word and example.

First Point

Truths one must keep before oneself — Now, my soul, we have already reached the most important point on which depends your whole welfare in the spiritual life. This point is that one must tread in the footsteps which Jesus Christ left before us, and keeping Him faithful company, patiently bear the desolation and affliction in one's spirit, pain and hardships in one's body, outrages, injuries, ill-will and persecution from whatever source they come. One who has no willingness to walk this road will never find God, and much less will he come to a pure and perfect love for Him — which is the object of these spiritual exercises and for which we must adjust our whole life. Consider the following truths; then, with attentive reflection and determination, resolve once and for all to enter with generous heart on this road with your Crucified Redeemer and to continue on it as long as it pleases Him.

First Truth — The road of suffering is the noblest road that a soul can take. There were two purposes for which the only-begotten Son of God came down from Heaven. The first was to offer His Heavenly Father a sacrifice whereby He would be paid a supreme honor, and which would both be worthy of His Father's Infinite Greatness and serve as a just satisfaction for the sins of the world. In this way Christ fulfilled the role of Redeemer.

The second purpose was to give man an example of that perfect holiness for which one should strive. What was the road Jesus picked to carry out these two purposes? No other than the road of suffering — a suffering that started from the first instant of His Incarnation within His Mother, and did not end until His death. One rightly says, then, that either this is the noblest road, or that Jesus Christ has not given men an example of the most perfect holiness.

Second Truth — The road of suffering is the most profitable one a soul can walk. One cannot explain in a few words the very precious fruits one gains on the road of suffering. I will mention only two. Whenever God wants to admit a soul to union with Him and make it share the sweetness of His holy love, He requires chiefly two things of it. These are perfect purity of heart and perfect possession of the virtues. Now, for gaining these two things, no other way better suited can be found than that of suffering. As for the purity of heart, it appears impossible to doubt that by this road one may obtain it; for as the soul finds on it nothing to satisfy itself but God alone and His Divine good pleasure, little by little it learns detachment from creatures, it learns to disesteem all creatural satisfaction and consolation, and to turn all the affections of the heart to the Supreme Good in Whom alone it can find all that can content one's desires . . .

By this same road one also arrives at perfect possession of the virtues; for as the soul cannot fulfill all its duty in time of suffering without exerting extraordinary and heroic effort, thereby overcoming all the perverse inclinations opposing the virtues, these virtues become more deeply rooted in the heart and gain new luster and perfection. Thus souls which are led along the road of suffering, more quickly reach an intimate union and familiarity with God.

Third Truth — The road of suffering is the most secure one that a soul can walk. There have been persons favored by God with very sublime lights imparted to their minds and lofty consolations given their spirit, who seemed to touch the summit of holiness, and who led a life more angelic than human; but as they were not well enough proved and established in virtue, especially in humility, they became puffed up over their favors, and fell headlong from the heights where they stood, into the depths of total ruin.

One should fear none of this for a soul that travels the road of suffering. It is always profitable, always safe. For on it the most perfect virtue is practised — humility, submission, meekness, charity, resignation to the Divine good pleasure; and with these a solid foundation is laid upon which can then be built the greatest graces and most sublime holiness.

This is the true imitation of Jesus Christ, and the

way He has taught us by His doctrine and example; and it never fails.

Second Point
Practices

After you have reflected well on these truths, my soul, learn the practices you must observe along the road of suffering.

First Practice — Using the power of prayer, impress deeply upon your mind certain maxims and truths which can lift up our hearts in time of suffering ... These, for example, can be:

(1) I can never suffer enough to pay a fair price for gaining God; for though I suffered all imaginable pains for a thousand years, this would be nothing in comparison with that Good.

(2) I can never suffer as much as I deserve for my sins; and no matter how much I suffer, it will never be a hell of suffering, though that is what my guilt deserves.

It is good to meditate on these truths very often and with enough attention for them to be thoroughly familiar to us and so that we may keep them before us on all occasions that come up.

Second Practice — Suffer in silence little day by day troubles, and in this way gather courage and be prepared to endure other greater things. On these occasions it is well to do the following:

(1) Call to mind one or other of the maxims given here.

(2) Keep perfect silence. Do no grumbling, no matter what the trouble is.

Third Practice — During your greater and lengthier misfortunes, offer yourself to God as a victim. To carry this out, you need to do these things:

(1) Start off in the morning submitting perfectly to God's Will and to all that God provides, and confirm this submission during the day.

(2) Every hour offer to God with the pure intention of pleasing Him and with earnest love, the sufferings you are undergoing.

(3) Never grumble about God's arrangements nor about anyone.

(4) As you practise these acts with humble patience and childlike confidence in God, patiently await the time He has appointed to deliver you.

These practices, O my soul, amount to the eminent virtues in which lie the true imitation of Jesus Christ and which open the way to intimate union with God. If you choose to practise them without delay, offer yourself humbly to your Lord and tell Him earnestly:

Resolution — O Jesus! O my dear Jesus! What a scene is presented to me when I see Thee hanging on the Cross! One Who is by nature Joy and Blessedness, is afflicted unto death! One Who is Innocence and Infinite Holiness is condemned to die! One Who is Infinite Majesty, is placed on a cross in company with two notorious criminals! . . . He Who is Immense Love, is hated! . . . And Thou didst suffer all this for me!

For my sake there is that Blood that flows in torrents from Thy Innocent Body! For my sake are all those aches, torments, and insults which Thou suffered . . . I believe all this, O my Jesus.

And yet — alas! oh, the detestable mischief in my heart! — and yet I still fail to love Thee. Ah, I know quite well the tragic cause of this. It all comes from my great self-love, my unwillingness to do any violence to myself, my unwillingness to suffer. When I love myself this way, no room remains in my heart to love Thee.

O my soul, will you forever persist in this condition? Will you not ever die to your selfishness? Will you not, O my soul, resolve to bear your sufferings for your Crucified Lover? O my God, how tragic and shameful my life would be for me if I did not so resolve!

I have deserved to burn in eternal fire; and am unwilling to suffer a small hardship; I have deserved to live in eternal despair down in hell, and I am unwilling to bear a little desolation of spirit. I have deserved to be forever hated by creatures, and I am unwilling to suffer a little contempt.

I have deserved to dwell forever in company with demons and damned souls, and I am unwilling to put up with frailty in my neighbor, even when perhaps he is blameless. How shameful this is of me! At the same time, what ingratitude this is toward Thee, O my Jesus! But may Thou be blessed!

For now, enlightened by Thy Grace, I know the evil of my ways up to now. I call on Heaven to witness my sorrow for my lukewarm past and the resolution I now take to faithfully follow in Thy Footsteps, O my Jesus! Do Thou strengthen me.

Now pray the Our Father and the Hail Mary and the Concluding Prayers as on page xi.

SECTION V

Meditation 29

The Resurrection of Jesus Christ

Commentary — In order to understand the purpose of this, the fifth section (Meditations 29 through 35), it is well to consider the sequence of these exercises. In the beginning we made our meditation on our Last End, which is to love God perfectly in this life and to enjoy Him hereafter in the next; and we resolved to seek this End at any cost.

To achieve this, we must first weep for our sins, uproot our evil inclinations, and keep our hearts free from stain. This is something one is to accomplish in the meditations of the first and second sections (Meditations 1 through 15).

Then we must imitate Our Lord Jesus Christ and adorn our souls with the virtues which He taught us by His Doctrine and example. This we do with the meditations of the third section (Meditations 16 through 20).

However, as we cannot put this into practice without great difficulty and without dying to self, we set forth in the fourth section (Meditations 21 through 28) the consideration of Our Divine Savior's Passion and Death in order to make the task easier.

After the soul has done all this and reached the stage of completely dying to self, it will then enter into perfect love for God, in which our last end here on earth consists. This perfect love for God will be the matter for the meditations that will be made in this fifth section.

The meditation on Our Lord Jesus Christ's Resurrection will make up the introduction to this, so that, with a reflection on this tremendous benefit, we will make light of earthly things, will have a love for suffering, will strengthen the resolves we have made, and enable ourselves to enter into perfect friendship and communion with God.

Preparatory Prayer as on page x

Composition of Place — Picture to yourself the risen Christ — beautiful, glorious, triumphant — and consider that you hear Saint Paul's voice saying, "We suffer with Him, that we may be also glorified with Him." (Rom. 8:17).

Prayer of Petition — Grant me, O Lord, the joy and gladness of keeping Thee company, and the strength to imitate Thee in the patience with which Thou suffered Thy pains and hardships, so that I will share in Thy Glory.

First Point

As great and horrifying was the bitterness of Christ's Passion, likewise great was the gladness and glory of the victory of His Resurrection. Four principal things that Jesus experienced in His Passion were bitter. They are: terrible bodily pain; extreme affliction in His Soul; unheard of abuse to His Honor; the unbelievable ill will of His enemies. Now we will consider, my soul, the blessings into which these bitter elements turned.

(1) Jesus arose with wonderful bodily beauty. In order to form an idea of this beauty, my soul, consider first that if the glorified body of any one of the saints were to replace the sun in the sky, it would give such light that all the world would be illumi-

nated with a brightness greater beyond comparison than that of the present sun, bright as it is.

Second, consider that if God gathered into one body the combined beauty of all the saints, this beauty would fade away to a pin point beside the beauty of the single Body of Jesus Christ. Yet this is that Body which, three days previously, was the target of cruelty and barbarity, and appeared as the body of a leper, made into one wound.

(2) The Risen Jesus had immense joy in His Soul. To understand this joy, reflect, my soul, that just as the bitter pain which Jesus' Soul experienced in the garden of Gethsemane was such that, were it distributed among all human hearts, it would be enough to cause their death, likewise the joy which He experienced in His Resurrection was such that, if it were parcelled out to everyone in the world, it would be enough to take their lives away, so powerfully delightful would be the sweetness with which these hearts would be flooded. Such was the joy that penetrated the Soul of Christ.

(3) Jesus Christ arose infinitely exalted in dignity. Ah! What a difference now, my soul! Jesus is the Glory of the angels who came down from Heaven to take delight in the Glory of His Resurrection. He is the joy of the ancient Fathers, who all kneel to honor and praise Him as their Redeemer. He is Judge of the living and the dead; and so the saints and the damned alike will reverently adore Him on that day of General Judgment.

He is the crown of those who will reach Heaven. Everyone among them will ceaselessly bless Him for all eternity. Yes, this is the glorious sight that Jesus presents for those who see Him on that day — that

Jesus who three days previously was treated like a fool by Herod, ridiculed as a mock king by soldiers, nailed to a cross like a criminal by the Hebrews.

(4) As He rose again, Jesus achieved the happy status of Someone universally loved. I am not speaking of that love with which all the blessed angels burned for Jesus on that day; nor do I speak of the love of the Fathers in limbo, who had access to His most Sacred Heart and took their delight in it. I speak only of the love with which everyone in Heaven was penetrated.

There, for all eternity, there will not be a single moment in which they fail to consider Jesus, nor an instant in which they fail to praise and bless Him; nor will they ever cease to tenderly love Him.

Affective Acts

(1) The joy of the glory of Jesus — Now Thy Suffering has ended, O my Jesus! At last, the day of Thy Glory has dawned and Thy Most Holy Body, now the jewel of all paradise, shines forth more than all heavenly bodies. Thy Soul has been plunged into joy, Thy Most Sacred Heart is a sea of delight. We see Thy Name adored by Heaven and earth. Thou art the joy of all the saints, are fondly desired by all of us pilgrims on earth and by those beholding the glory of Heaven.

I rejoice at Thy Glory and Blessedness and take my delight in it more than if it were my own. I am glad for Thee with all my heart. Let gladness and joy crown Thee forever. It is Thy due to be rewarded with such great glory, Thou Who, with great long-suffering, chose to die for the glory of Thy Eternal Father.

(2) Desire for a similar blessedness — Oh, what happiness would be mine if I should have the fortune some day to also rise again gloriously! Who could ever express my joy at seeing the beauty of Jesus' Face with my own eyes, of hearing His kind voice, of loving Him and being loved by Him, of embracing Him and being embraced, of being forever in His company, and of never being separated from it for all eternity! Oh, what good fortune! It is Thou that shall be the object of all my desires and the goal of all the affections of my heart!

Second Point

Holy considerations and resolutions that should be drawn from this meditation — After having reflected well on Jesus Christ's Resurrection, turn your gaze, O my soul, on yourself and apply yourself to making these considerations:

First Consideration — Just as it is certain that Jesus Christ rose glorious from the grave, it is also certain that one day you will rise glorious if you imitate His example. After Jesus suffered so much in the flesh, it is your place, says the Apostle, to arm yourself with like sentiments, realizing that He Who raised up Jesus Christ will also raise you up with Jesus Christ.

Oh how full of consolation is this doctrine! How well able it is to banish all sadness from the heart! The eyes with which you see on earth, you will open one day to paradise! With those hands of yours you will one day embrace Jesus! With those ears of yours you will one day hear the melodies of the angels! With that mouth you now have you will one day taste the heavenly sweetness! With those feet of yours you will one day walk above the stars!

Second Consideration — As it is certain that by His Cross and Passion Jesus obtained the glory of His Resurrection, it is likewise certain that there is no better way to reach the same glory than by the Cross and by tribulation. This is what the Apostle teaches us also. These are his words: "If we be dead with Him . . . if we suffer, we shall also reign with Him . . ." (2 Tim. 2:11-12).

O my God, what then will I think of my past afflictions and reverses? "O blessed sorrows!" I will say; "O blessed afflictions! which have earned for me such great glory!"

Third Consideration — The more we resemble Jesus in His Sufferings, the more we will be like Him in the glory of His Resurrection. Listen again to the Apostle to the Gentiles when he says, "*If* we be dead with Him . . . *if* we suffer, we shall *also* reign with Him."

Note carefully, my soul, these two words, *if . . . also*; for they mean that the more one suffers with Jesus on earth, the more he will rejoice with Him in Heaven in the Resurrection; the heavier are the hardships borne in company with Jesus on earth, the more splendid will be the glory one reaches in the Resurrection. (cf. Rom. 8:17).

In view of this truth, in what way, my soul, do our troubles, our humiliations under contempt, our desolations and pains, appear to us? Are they not some of the most loving designs of God, the most effective means for reaching holiness, the most beautiful inheritance of Jesus Christ, the surest pledge of our resurrection and of our eternal and immortal glory?

Yes, it is truly so; for Jesus Christ has taught this to us. And you will afflict yourself and call yourself unfortunate if these things come upon you? Oh, how blind you would be! You should rather raise your hands to Heaven and bless the Divine Mercy if God is so generous with you. If men rose up against you and heaped insult and injury upon you and mistreated you in other more outrageous ways, then know, O my soul, that these are just the means whereby God would fulfill in you His loving designs.

They would be putting in your hands the most beautiful means for your sanctification. They would be the means that would make you like your crucified Lord, would increase your glory in Heaven, and would fashion for you the crown that you would wear forever on your head.

Yes, without the slightest doubt that is what they would be. Jesus Christ teaches us so. And — I have regarded them as loathsome? Alas! O evil self-love! How many beautiful and excellent truths you have hidden from me until now! How far you have pushed me aside and have taken me off the road of holiness, the road that follows Jesus Christ!

Affective Acts

(1) Faith — It is true, Jesus is alive. He has risen from the dead. He has entered into His Glory, and now, in His Body and His Soul He is enjoying a sea of delight. Indeed there can be no doubt, and I believe it, O my Jesus. I believe it because Thou hast told it, Who are the Truth by Thy very nature. Furthermore, I will also live forever if I follow Jesus. I will be victorious over death and will enter into the heavenly Jerusalem, and these eyes of mine will see Jesus my Redeemer.

Yes, I am sure of it and I believe it, O my Jesus; for Thou, Who art the eternal Truth, hast revealed it. Furthermore, I will then receive the reward for all the pains I will have suffered. For a momentary grief I will have eternal blessings. For having borne insult, I will receive an eternal glory. For a brief bit of sorrow, I will gain eternal joy. Indeed there is no doubt, and I believe this because Thou, the Infallible Truth, have declared it. O Holy Faith, what stupendous truths you show me and what consolation you give to my heart!

(2) Repentance — O brilliant light of Faith, how I must reproach myself in what I see! If it is true that God grants a special reward for every mortification, hardship, and pain that we suffer, how many of these rewards have I not forfeited by my impatience and self-love? If it is true that all the humiliations, injuries and insults which we have patiently borne for love of Him, God will reward in the Resurrection with a crown of special glory, how many crowns have I not forfeited by my pride and vanity?

If it is true that for every act of resignation during trials and interior desolations, God will grant a special blessedness, of how many such blessings have I not deprived myself by my faintheartedness and laziness? Yes, I have forfeited all these benefits! And why? Oh! How this loss should fill me with bitterness! What abundant, bitter tears I ought to shed! But console yourself, O my soul, because, knowing how Jesus entered into His Glory, you too can enter with Him by following, and you can repair this loss. Kneeling at Thy feet, O my Jesus, I resolve to do this.

Now pray the Our Father and the Hail Mary and the Concluding Prayers as on page xi.

Meditation 30
On the Love of God

Preparatory Prayer as on page x

Composition of Place — Imagine that you are in God's Presence and that all angels and saints are interceding for you.

Prayer of Petition — My God and Lord, grant me a clear knowledge of the Divine benefits, so that, knowing them and being grateful for them, I may love and serve Thy Divine Majesty in all things.

First Point

God deserves to be loved for the infinite goodness and affection with which He has loved and favored us until now. In order to understand the depths of this goodness and affection, consider their circumstances. Collect your thoughts, my soul, and pay attention as much as you can in order to consider well three things:

(1) God's kindness and affection toward you is eternal — Just as God never had a beginning, but always existed, likewise His kindness and love for you, my soul, had no beginning and is as ancient as God Himself; that is, it is eternal. In Holy Scripture God tells us: "I have loved thee with an everlasting love; therefore have I drawn thee." Jer. 31:3.

Bring to your mind another age of two thousand years ago and tell me, What were you then? You were simply nothing. And what was God doing then? Ah, He was loving you, and with the very love that moved Him then to shed all His Blood for you.

Go back with your mind to a time just before the

291

creation of the world and again tell me, my soul: What was there then? There was absolutely nothing, neither Heaven nor earth nor angels nor men — nothing. And God at that time, what was He doing? He was engaged in loving you. He loved you so much that for love of you He created Heaven and earth— earth, to serve as your dwelling place in this short life; Heaven, so that you might rule in a kingdom there for all eternity in the next life.

Go back further with your thoughts, my soul, and plunge into that beginningless period as far back as you can, and tell me: What was there then? There was nothing but God alone, infinitely glorious and infinitely happy in Himself and all by Himself (Father, Son, and Holy Ghost). And what was He doing during all that immense eternity?

He was — if you do not know — He was occupied in loving you, and there was never a moment in which He was not thinking about you, and in which He was not settled in His choice to die for your sake and in His wish to have you share all His goods, all His riches, all His happiness for ever and ever. Is this not a wonderful, amazing instance of kindness and love?

(2) God's kindness and affection for you is generous — In order to convince you of this truth it is not necessary to list one by one the favors God has granted you. Just the mystery of the Incarnation, which you might bring to mind, would be enough to make this well understood.

Suppose that an official in the service of a prince has by trickery robbed him and taken a large sum of gold which had been entrusted to him. Suppose that the man has been convicted for this and has been condemned to prison, to continue his life in tears and grief until he has paid back all of the theft.

Imagine that a rich, highly respected man, in order to put this unfortunate one at liberty, sells all of his own property and makes full payment to the prince, and then, finding himself extremely poor, he is forced into the unpleasant lot of going to work in a shop in order to earn by the sweat of his brow what is necessary so that he will not die of hunger.

Would this not be a wonderful, amazing example of love? Now do you know, my soul, to whom this illustration refers? Who was the unfortunate prisoner? Who was his merciful rescuer? Think about it, my soul, and consider it attentively . . . Mankind is the prisoner, and the Word, the Son of God, is the rescuer.

(3) God's kindness toward you is patient and constant — Turn your gaze, my soul, into the prison of hell and see a sight that you have never seen! What do you see? You see a numberless throng of condemned souls who burn in the flames of a devouring fire. Then, behold, Jesus comes down from Heaven, and out of the many souls that are suffering He picks just one, and drawing it out of hell He joins it again to its body and gives it a period of time for repentance.

What do you say, my soul, at seeing this? Do you not admit that Jesus' love for that soul is incomprehensible? Perhaps you will remark, "That soul deserved hell just as much as the others. It deserved it even more than a thousand others who were less sinful." Yet all the others remained imprisoned down in hell for all eternity.

Only this one was drawn out; or, what is even greater, just this one has been kept from falling into hell. To this soul alone is the favor done; to this one alone is a period given for repentance. Oh, how great, how special, must be the affection with which Jesus loves this soul!

Now will you, perhaps, have a fear of deceiving yourself, my soul, if you recognize yourself in that chosen soul? And what fear should there be? Is it not certain that thousands of souls who have sinned less than you, are in hell, who have not made bad use of as many aids as you have, who have not treated lightly as many graces as you have treated lightly and have disregarded, who have not grown as hard in lukewarm dispositions as you have, and who have yet been condemned for all eternity, whereas you are still alive, plentifully supplied with all kinds of grace and with Divine favors?

You have been indeed favored, but not with the favoritism some might presume; for Christ admonishes us: "And unto whomsoever much is given, of him much shall be required: and to whom they have committed much, of him they will demand the more." (Lk. 12:48)* Should not one say of you what the Jews said when they watched Jesus weep over Lazarus — "See, see how much He loved him?"

Affective Acts

(1) Confession and admiration for the love of God — Everything belonging to Thee, my God —

*Translator's Note — This very traditional doctrine of inequality of God's mercy and bounty is explained and defended on Scriptural and Patristic authority by Saint Alphonsus de Liguori (Sermoni Compendiati, serm. XV, which is translated on page 123 and following of Sermons of Saint Alphonsus de Liguori, published by Tan Books, Rockford, Ill., 1982).

Thy very Being as well as Thy deeds — all deserves our admiring praise. But yet nothing seems to me as much to deserve it as the special love Thou hast for me. Ah, and what is this love? Thou art an Infinite Being Who has had no beginning and will have no end. The history of Thy Life covers no less than an entire eternity into the past; and during that immense time there was never a moment in which I was not the object of Thy love.

Thou loved me with an eternal love. Thou loved me with a love more energetic, more powerful, than can be described. For where has Thy love for me not led Thee? Thou camest down from Heaven to earth and were born a poor Babe in a stable for beasts. Thou didst live a life of hard labor and earned Thy bread by the sweat of Thy brow, and Thou finally finished Thy days fastened to a cross like a criminal. What was it that moved Thee to do all this for me, if it was not love?

Thou hast loved me with a most patient love; and even though I had committed a countless number of sins and had made bad use of limitless means of salvation that Thou had prepared for me, and had treated lightly Thy numberless mercies — yet all these outrages of mine had not the power to extinguish Thy love nor even chill it.

And Thou lovest me even now, and lovest me with the fondness with which Thou hast loved me through all eternity. Oh how wonderful God is! O God of immense love and mercy! How truly dost Thou deserve my love — and deserve that I love Thee with all my powers! And if I could choose to love Thee with an infinite love, Thou would certainly deserve that I do so!

(2) Repentance and love — How ungrateful I have been toward God when I should have loved Him with all my heart! I recognize it. I admit it. O my loyal Lover and my God, my ingratitude is very great and I supremely detest it. I have loved those who have shown me a so-called generosity. I have not loved God, to Whom I am in debt for all that I am and all that I possess.

I have loved those who have done nothing for me, and I have not loved God, Who has gone so far as to die on the Cross for me. Yes, I recognize my ingratitude. I detest it and repent of it. I now have other sentiments and other desires.

Thou hast conquered, O Divine Lover, Thou hast conquered! My heart will no longer be mine. I give it irrevocably to Thee for always and for eternity. I will love Thee from this moment on. I will love Thee alone. And as I have been neglectful in loving Thee in the past, I will love Thee with all the more zeal and devotion in the future.

Second Point

God deserves to be loved because of what He stands ready to do for you in the future out of infinite goodness and love. What is it that God is ready to do for you, my soul? Ah! He would give Himself entirely to you. If you do not understand the greatness of this gift, of this marvel of love, then put to use all your intellectual powers and put what effort you can to the task of looking into the depths of a mystery which is the most comforting of the mysteries of our holy religion.

(1) To possess God is to gain the fulfillment of all our desires — At the moment when the soul

separates from the body (at death), a supernatural light, a sudden clear perception, makes the soul recognize that God is the Supreme and Only Good and is its supreme and only real source of happiness and well-being.

Following immediately upon this light, there is such a strong desire to enjoy this Only and Supreme Good, this Only and Supreme Happiness, that being without It causes the greatest pain that damned souls suffer in hell . . .

In fact, to satisfy this powerful desire, God joins the worthy soul closely to Himself, and as He makes it enjoy all the vastness of His Divinity, He causes it to feel in an instant a boundless satisfaction and to remain plunged deep in an ocean of delight.

(2) To possess God is to contemplate God and love Him — There will not be a moment in all eternity in which this soul does not see God and does not discover as it sees Him, the infinite treasures of His Almighty Power, of His Goodness, His Beauty, and His other perfections which charm it with a boundless delight. Throughout all eternity there will not be an instant in which it does not feel continually on fire with new flames of love which raise it to Divine heights of infinite joy.

(3) To possess God is to possess an infinite happiness — The happiness with which you will be blessed in Heaven, my soul, will be the very happiness with which God Himself is blessed. Understand this fact well. You will enjoy the very pleasures, the very sweetness, the very contentment that God enjoys. But to what extent will this be so?

Listen, my soul, to something amazing, which is

yet an undeniable truth. Just a faint ray from that eternal happiness would be enough to fully delight all the condemned souls with a joy greater beyond comparison, than all the painful punishments which they now suffer. Just a tiny sample of that boundless bliss would be enough to fill all those who are chosen for salvation, with gladness to an overflowing degree.

Just a little drop from that measureless ocean of joys would be capable of giving an eternal blessedness to all creatures together, even if a greater number were newly created than there are grains of sand on all seashores. In short, these joys are of such a nature and so great that they are enough to satisfy God Himself, Who is capable of experiencing infinite happiness.

(4) To possess God is to be loved by God with an infinite loving kindness — God never looks upon the good soul except as His tenderly beloved child, whom He wants to enrich with all the treasures of His goodness, like a bride in whom He finds all His delight and satisfaction.

There is no tenderness, no loving kindness on earth that can be compared with the tenderness of God's loving kindness. For, as God is an Infinite Power which infinitely surpasses all human powers, it is equally true that He is an Infinite Love which goes infinitely beyond all degrees of human tenderness and kindness. Yes, it is He alone Who can receive a soul into His Heart and give it a drink from the stream of those sweet delights which no creature can give and which the human mind hopes in vain to comprehend.

(5) To possess God means to live as long as God lives and to be happy as long as God is happy —

God's Happiness is a happiness that has no end and undergoes no interruption nor does it ever grow less. O my soul, your happiness will possess these same properties.

(1) Your happiness will be without end. As many years will pass as there are grains of sand on all seashores, atoms in the air, drops in all waters of springs, rivers, and oceans. But in all that long time not even half, not even the smallest fraction of this happiness will have passed away, for it will be eternal and without end.

(2) It will be a happiness without interruption; for in each moment you will always find in God new perfections. As God is Infinite Beauty, there will remain in Him an endless expanse to see which you will not yet have seen. As He is Infinite Goodness, always some other benefit will remain which you are yet to gain, and in each instant you will feel yourself burning with new flames of love for Him. As He is Infinite Delightfulness, always some other endless expanse will remain which you will not yet have enjoyed, and every moment you will meet new streams of joy and pleasure.

(3) It will be a bliss that never grows less. You will truly have very ardent desires to taste more of God, and it will be apparent to you that you are not overfed with Him; but you will always have the satisfaction of tasting Him fully and will always enjoy Him with total possession.

Affective Acts

(1) Love — O my Supreme and Only Good, how blind I have been until now! I have not known Thee nor Thy love. Now I know Thee and I know Thy

love. What can I do but try to duly respond to a love so wonderful and immense, and return another love which is small indeed, but more sincere than up to now? My God, look at me kneeling to pay Divine Honor to Thee, to offer the sacrifice of my whole heart. It is a sacrifice I owe to Thy boundless Goodness and Love. I love Thee, and I love Thee with all my affections, with all my soul, with all my mind, and with all my strength.

I hate and detest all those affections and inclinations which are not directed to Thee. . . I love Thee alone, my Sovereign Good. Only Thee do I want to love as long as I live; and I will prefer Thy Honor, Thy Will, Thy Good Pleasure, to all creatures, even those that I hold as dearest in the world.

(2) Desire to love God perfectly — But no matter how much I love Thee, no matter how much I do as I have resolved to do, what is such a love of mine in comparison with the love with which Thou hast loved me? It is really nothing. Ah! I wish I could squeeze into my heart all the love which all the saints have for Thee. I would wish, yes, I would wish singly to make the acts of love of all Angelic Spirits, so as to love Thee with their acts of love, O my Sovereign Good and Loyal Lover.

But of what use will these desires of mine be unless Thou, Who art the Supreme Good and thus deserve infinite love, enkindle in my heart a truly perfect flame of love? O God of Love, have pity on me and make me experience Thy Almighty Power today in my favor; for I crave nothing else and desire no more than to love Thee with all my being.

Now pray the Our Father and the Hail Mary and the Concluding Prayers as on page xi.

Meditation 31

On the Lovableness
of God in Himself

Preparatory Prayer as on page x

Composition of Place — Picture yourself in God's presence, and all angels and saints praising His Goodness and interceding for you.

Prayer of Petition — My God and my Lord, grant me a clear knowledge, as far as possible, of Thy Infinite Goodness, so that I may love and serve Thee with greater perfection.

"The more perfectly God is known, the more perfectly is He loved." - Saint Thomas Aquinas.

First Point

God deserves to be loved because He is the Supreme Good. Here we have, my soul, the foundation and basis upon which the perfect love for God is built. One rightly loves God because He is the Supreme Good Who, for His own sake, deserves to be loved with infinite love. Now do you understand what it means to be the Supreme Good?

It means that God is a Being which contains infinite perfections and contains and possesses them in Himself, by Himself, in the supreme degree, without being debtor for them to anyone. In order to conceive a faint idea of all this, my soul, merely consider some of these perfections of His.

(1) God is Infinite Beauty — Here it is suitable to use merely illustrations which, because of their greater vividness and expressiveness, will somehow resemble a child's ideas which he uses for consider-

ing the circuits of the sun and planets that shine in the sky.

Let this be the first illustration — The Blessed Virgin Mary perceives far more of God's Beauty than all the angels and elect together who are in Heaven. Now suppose God were to elevate Her understanding and enable Her to see as much more of His Beauty as She has perceived up to now; and that, a moment later, He gives Her a new enlightenment and She perceives twice what She had perceived in the earlier moment; and suppose this continued thus for a million years.

Would the Blessed Virgin ever perceive all that there is of God's Beauty? Ah! After the passage of so many years, as much of God's Beauty would yet remain to behold as would be left of water in the ocean after you had withdrawn what your hand would hold.

Let this be the second illustration — The number of angels is almost countless, and each of them is endowed with such rare beauty that no man could fix his gaze on him without fainting from the abundant joy that this sight would cause. Now suppose God created an angel who possessed by himself the beauty of all the other angels combined. Oh, what beauty would he not possess!

Yet this would be infinitely inferior to God's Beauty. Suppose furthermore, that God created at each moment in the course of a thousand years one million angels, each of whom surpassed in beauty all the others combined, as much as the highest Seraphim at present surpasses a man. Suppose that after that thousand years God again extended the arm of His might and drew out of nothing an angel who alone possessed the beauty of all the other angels combined. Could the human mind picture a beauty like that?

Yet all this would be nothing in comparison with God's Beauty and would be infinitely inferior to it. Proceed as much as you will, my soul, with these comparisons, for days, for years, for all eternity, and it will never be possible for you to envision a beauty so excellent, but that God's Beauty infinitely surpasses it.

(2) God is Infinite Power — Here again one needs to use the imagination in order to grasp something of this Divine perfection.

Let this be the first illustration — Suppose the number of men who, from the beginning until Judgment Day, have lived on earth and will live on it, amounts to two hundred thousand million. What a stupendous figure! Some of these men's souls are in Paradise, others are in Purgatory, others are in hell. Their bodies are reduced to dust. Now the final day is approaching and the angel's trumpet sounds in all parts of the universe. What will happen?

In the blinking of an eye, in a single instant those bodies will rise again, the souls will re-enter them, and two hundred thousand million men will again become alive. What a stupendous prodigy! To accomplish this, what will have been necessary? Nothing but these three words from an all-powerful Divinity: "Arise ye dead."

Let this be the second illustration — Suppose God, coming down from Heaven, paused on the bank of the sea, just as He tarried in the countryside of Damascus when He created the first man. Suppose that with His voice of authority He says: Let there be here as many men as there are grains of sand on the seashore.

At this utterance of Almighty Power, would there not appear, then and there, in an instant, as many men as there are grains of sand on the shores? Make, then, as many illustrations as you like. Increase, multiply them as much as anyone may wish. One can never find an example which God's almighty Power will not infinitely surpass.

(3) God is Infinite Goodness — There are three effects, my soul, by which you can know the greatness of God's Goodness.

The first effect is His patience in bearing with sinners. From Heaven God sees countless men who, letting themselves be dragged on by their disordered passions, surrender to all kinds of vice and daily outrage Him as they trample on His Holy Law and profane His Most Holy Name. God sees them continue this kind of life for twenty, thirty, forty years and longer.

In an instant He could rid Himself of them and punish all the wicked things they do against Him. Yet He remains silent as though He did not know of their evil behavior. Rather, He prolongs their lives, and as if they were faithfully serving Him He provides new benefits for them each day and speaks to their hearts, inviting them to His friendship as though He, the Lord, needed them and they did not need His Divine support. Oh what patience! What goodness!

The second effect is His lovable way of receiving sinners. Suppose, my soul, a man who has lived a hundred years continually offending God and who has never in his life done the least penance. If he were in a death agony and only a single moment of life remained, do you believe he could receive pardon from God for so many sins? Ah! Marvellous is the Divine Kindness! Realize that if this wicked man sent to Heaven a single interior act of perfect contrition, God would forgive all the iniquities of his bad life, would forget them forever, and would let him share in His glory. (This does not, of course, exclude some possible time in Purgatory.)

The third effect is the reward of the just. Picture, my soul, a man who, in the whole course of his life, had not done any other good but make with a contrite and humbled heart this single act, namely, "O my God, I love Thee above all things because Thou art the Supreme Good!"

And after this single good act, suppose he were to die and enter into eternity. What reward do you think God would give Him? Nothing less than the full possession of Heaven, the vision and enjoyment of all His Beauty, and both of these for all eternity. So wonderful, so infinitely grand, is God in His rewards.

Affective Acts

(1) Shame — O my God, I know well, and faith teaches me, that Thou art the supreme Good which has infinite perfections and combines them in Thyself to an eminent degree; that Thou art a God worthy of being loved with infinite love. But of what use is it, O my God, that a heart created by Thee only to love Thee and possess Thee, be with all this knowledge and with this faith, if it remains yet so insensible, so indifferent, so cold? I do not feel drawn to intimacy with Thee. Silence and recollection are distasteful to me.

I do not see in myself those effects which true love would be expected to produce in one who possesses it. And what does this mean? Ah! My God, I know my misery, and I must rot in it until the fire of Divine Love is enkindled in my heart. Oh, deliver me forever from my coldness and grant that for once I will begin to love perfectly Thy Divine Goodness and never cease loving it.

(2) Resolution and Repentance — But when will I begin to do this, O my soul? Do you wish to know? You will begin doing it when you die perfectly to yourself and to all creatures. Then your God will use His mercy with you and enkindle your heart with that holy fire . . . if that is so, my God, I hereby wish to strip myself completely of selfishness, to give Thee my whole heart and to love Thee with all my powers. I detest all the thoughts and affections that were directed to creatures exclusively and I repent whatever I have done in my life that has not been done out of love for Thee.

Henceforth Thy supreme good pleasure alone and Thy Love alone will be the object of all my thoughts, the aim of all my desires, the goal of all my undertakings . . . But, O my God, no matter how sincere I might be in this resolve of mine, I can never carry it out unless Thou stoop down to strengthen my weakness with Thy Grace.

Turn, then, Thine Eyes kindly toward me. Remember that Thou hast shed all Thy Precious Blood for this one purpose, namely, that I might love Thee. By that Blood I beg Thee to work in me one of Thy accustomed wonders of mercy, destroying in my heart all that is contrary to love for Thee and enkindling therein so great a flame that it will never go out for all eternity.

Second Point

God deserves to be loved because He is the only God — This is a very important truth, O my soul, and once it is well reflected upon, it has the full power to draw our whole heart to God. It consists in this:

(1) Neither in Heaven nor on earth nor in any other creature is any good to be found, no matter how little, that does not come from God. Look about the whole world: consider all the creatures to be found in it: note the great variety of trees, of fruit, of flowers and other plants, the variety of land animals, of the birds of the air, of the fish in the waters. From earth turn your eyes to Heaven and consider the marvels it displays.

Note the sun, whose brilliance brightens the world. Note the stars which shine in the firmament. Realize how incomprehensibly ample and lovely paradise is, the dwelling-place of those who are saved. From lifeless creatures turn your attention to the rational ones and ponder in man the many qualities that adorn him — his beauty, his wisdom, his love, his gallantry, his friendliness, and the like — natural qualities and supernatural ones.

Consider the angels and all the blessed who see God — their virtues, their merits, their holiness, the various things in which they excel . . . consider the glory wherein they are totally happy. And then, my soul, in entering within yourself, ponder as follows: Before the world was created, where were those noble creatures?

Ah! They were buried in the bosom of their nothingness, and would still be there if God, by His Almighty Power and by the bounty of His infinite goodness, had not drawn them into existence, as faith teaches. If, then, they have being, and have a being so lovely, they have it not from themselves; they have it from God.

(2) Everything that can be called good in creatures, is nothing else than a pure mercy that God has communicated to them — All the beauty of creatures is nothing more than a ray of this Divine sunshine. All their holiness is no more than a drop from the immense sea of God's Holiness. God alone is good, and the good that is found in creatures is only a merciful share of His Infinite Goodness. This is an Article of Faith and one must believe it.

But does our life agree with this Faith? Alas! How poorly we employ the noble affections of our heart! And consider well, my soul, the necessary consequences that follow from these stupendous truths. Penetrate them so well that they will not slip from your memory.

First Consequence — God deserves to be infinitely loved. Our reason teaches this. Everything good deserves love, and an Infinite Good deserves an infinite love. God, being infinitely Good, deserves then, to be infinitely loved.

Second Consequence — If God is an infinitely lovable Good, I, then, do not love Him as much as I ought if I do not love Him as much as I can.

Third Consequence — I, then, do not fulfill the obligation I have of loving Him with all my powers, if I admit into my heart any affection, even a fleeting one, which is not directed to Him; if I do anything that disagrees with His Divine good pleasure; if I only once oppose the designs His Sovereign Majesty has formed concerning me.

Affective Acts

(1) Shame — O God, Who alone are Good and are Supremely Good! I know too well what Thou deserves and what true love ought to be. A soul burning with love for Thee cuts off every attachment and does not tolerate any inclination which does not come from Thee and return to Thee. It does nothing but what is pleasing to Thee and does everything only to fulfill Thy Divine good pleasure.

It suffers all and does not oppose anything which Thou dost arrange concerning it. Wholly surrendering itself to Thee, it rests without fear in the bosom of Thy most loving Providence. Happy indeed is the state of this soul! O holy love, how beautiful, how desirable you are! How much of you is there in my heart?

How many hours can I count of my life during which I have loved in this way? How many deeds have I done, how many troubles have I borne, in the spirit of this love? How poor my condition is! Who will give me fountains of tears to weep day and night over this lack of love? . . .

(2) Love and consecration — But why do I afflict myself? All can still be done, all can be repaired with fervor. Away, then, with faintheartedness! Why can I, too, not do what so many youths, so many tender maidens, have done in the flower of their manhood and maidenhood? "I can do all things," said one of the greatest saints, "not of myself, but by Him Who strengthens me."

I say the same; and with this confidence in Thee, my God, my Strength, my All, I begin to love Thee and surrender myself entirely to Thee. Take, then, O Sovereign Good, my liberty, take my memory, my mind and my will. Whatever I have and possess, all is Thy gift, and I return it all to Thee. I desire and crave nothing else than Thy love. With that alone my desires are satisfied, and with that I am rich enough.

(3) Prayer of Petition — Come, then, Most Holy and Divine Spirit. Thou art Love by Thy Nature and are the Source of that Divine fire which burned in the hearts of the saints. Thou art holiness by Thy Nature and the Source of those effective graces which penetrate human hearts, captivating them to turn to God with all their affections.

Ah! Deign to come to my heart and to purify it of all imperfections and to enkindle it with Thy fire. I am ready to do and to suffer. Dispose of me, then, as Thou dost wish. I will offer no opposition in anything. I only ask Thee for Thy Love, with the purpose that It be the rule of all my conduct.

Now pray the Our Father and the Hail Mary and the Concluding Prayers as on page xi.

Meditation 32

Proper Devotion
to the Blessed Virgin

Preparatory Prayer as on page x

Composition of Place — Picture with Jesus, the Blessed Virgin Mary in Her Chaste Virginal Motherhood. You see Her with Jesus in Bethlehem, in Egypt, at Nazareth, at Jerusalem, at the wedding in Cana, at Calvary and in Heaven.

Prayer of Petition — God bless Thee, O Mary! Thou art full of Grace. The Lord is with Thee. Blessed art Thou among all women, and blessed is the Fruit of Thy womb, Jesus! Holy Mary, Mother of God, pray for us sinners, now and at the hour of our death. *Amen,* O Jesus!

First Point

One of the most powerful means which God our Lord has given us to gain and to increase grace and Divine love is, without doubt, devotion to the Blessed Virgin Mary. The reason for this is obvious. By Jesus we have everything, and as Mary is His Mother, She obtains everything She wants.

Jesus is, as it were, the reservoir of all Graces, and Mary is the conduit whereby they are brought to us. This precious conduit is always joined to the reservoir; that is, Mary is always with Jesus — in Bethlehem, in Egypt, at Nazareth, at Jerusalem, at the wedding feast in Cana, on Calvary, and in Heaven at Her Son's right hand, Who is King of kings and Lord of lords.

To make sure that devotion to Mary is true, you

need to consider three things; namely: Who is this Lady? What blessings are there that She has received and for which we should look to Her? In what does true devotion to Her consist?

Who is the Blessed Virgin Mary? Ah! A difficult question. Only God knows well Who Mary is, says Saint Bernardine. Yet you ought to know that Mary is a great Lady conceived without stain of original sin, full of grace and virtue, Virgin and Mother of God, Queen of Heaven and Earth, and One Who pleads for sinners.

(1) Mary is a great Lady, conceived without stain of original sin — She is a Lady indeed. The very word Mary means lady, and by this name the angel calls Her when he says, "Fear not, Mary, for Thou hast found grace with God." (Lk 1:30)

Thus it seems Her name comes not from a whim of Her parents, but is something decreed by the design of God, as the Holy Trinity, creating Her, imposed the name of Mary with a view of Her being Daughter of the Eternal Father, Mother of the Eternal Son, Spouse of the Holy Spirit, and Queen of all creation.

The dignity of Mother of God is an almost infinite dignity, says Saint Thomas; for this is to be Mother of an Infinite Being, Who is God. This is why, in creating Her, the Lord preserved Her from original sin, adorned Her with all graces possible for a creature to have, enriched Her with virtues and merits, confided to Her the treasury of His mercies and made Her dispenser of them.

(2) Mary is distinguished by God with all privileges and given all prerogatives — She is a Mother without ceasing to be a Virgin, a singular Virgin ...

and, as the Gospel says, the Virgin's name is Mary. She is Queen of Heaven and earth, Queen of Angels, Queen of Patriarchs, Queen of Prophets, Queen of Apostles, Queen of Martyrs, Queen of Bishops and Confessors, Queen of Virgins and of all the saints.

If someone presented to us here below a lady who was queen of all kingdoms and empires in the world, Ah! how she would be admired and honored! Even more you ought to honor the Most Holy Mary, Who is Queen of Heaven and earth. In Heaven, on earth, and in hell, knees are bent at the sweet name of Mary, inasmuch as She is Mother of Jesus; and what is owed to Jesus by nature and merits, the same is given (as much as any holy creature can receive) to Mary Most Holy by grace.

(3) Mary's role is to be a Mother to sinners and to plead for them — The Eternal Word took on flesh, became Man, became our Brother, and, as Brother, He wants us to have the same Father He has and the same Mother. He had already given us the Father. He had already said to us, "When you pray, you will say: Our Father Who art in Heaven." Later He gave us His Mother to be our Mother: "Behold thy Mother." (Jn. 19:27)

Yes, in Bethlehem Mary gave birth to Her first-born Son, and on Calvary to the second born, which we — all of us Jesus Christ's disciples — are, being represented by the disciple whom Jesus loved. He desires that His own Mother be our immediate advocate — be the One to whom we entrust our wants, and She shall present them to Jesus, Who is the One Who pleads for us before God the Father. Oh, what great confidence we ought to have!

Affective Acts

(1) Thanksgiving — May infinite thanks be given Thee, O Most Blessed Trinity, for having created Blessed Mary without sin, for having honored Her with so many graces and privileges, and for having given Her to be our Mother and advocate. We cannot, my God, give Thee the thanks we owe Thee for this great and wonderful favor, and we beg Thee, O Most Holy Virgin, our Mother and Advocate, to give thanks for us.

(2) Praise and Prayer of Petition — Hail Holy Queen, Mother of Mercy, Our Life, Our Sweetness and Our Hope. To Thee do we cry, poor banished children of Eve. To Thee do we send up our sighs, mourning and weeping in this valley of tears. Turn then most gracious Advocate Thine eyes of Mercy towards us and after this our exile, show unto us the Blessed Fruit of Thy womb, Jesus. Oh clement! Oh Loving! Oh sweet Virgin Mary!

Pray for us O Holy Mother of God, that we may be made worthy of the promises of Our Lord Jesus Christ. *Amen.*

Second Point

Gratitude is, without doubt, one of the virtues most pleasing to God and to the Most Holy Virgin and most useful for men. We see this truth demonstrated in the Old and New Testaments and by nature itself. When God used to deliver the Hebrews from evils and bestow blessings on them, He would demand a tribute of thanksgiving from them; and so that they would not easily forget, He made them keep the twelve stones which they collected in the Jordan (cf. Josue 4:1-7), and a portion of the manna was preserved within the Ark (cf. Ex. 16:34).

In the New Testament, we see that Jesus Christ showed Himself pleased with the foreigner who, finding himself cured of his leprosy, came to Him to thank Him, and He complained of the nine men who were likewise cured but were not grateful. We see that even in nature animals are grateful to one who does good to them. Trees bear fruit to one who plants them, and soil gives a generous response to the one who cultivates it.

Gratitude is so well appreciated that not only does one see a benefactor rewarding one for it, but we also see him feeling moved to grant new favors. Here we present reasons why we should all be very devoted to Mary:

(1) Be thankful and devoted to Mary for the many and great blessings we have received — Saint Bernard says that God has decreed that whatever we have, be through Mary. Saint Germaine adds that no one is saved except through Mary, Who intercedes for us and obtains for us the merits of Jesus Christ Her Son and our Redeemer and Savior. No one is delivered from evil except by Mary and no one obtains favors except through Mary.

Reflect that the lights and inspirations that you so often receive are benefits that come to you by Mary's intercession. If you have not fallen into mortal sin, or have not committed more and greater faults, this grace is from Mary.

If you have not died in sin and are not presently in hell, this grace is from Mary. If God is preserving your health and your life, if in every instant He is giving you new favors, realize that it is by Mary's intercession. There is no mother so watchful and careful about protecting her children as Mary is to protect those devoted to Her from all evil and misfortune.

(2) O my soul, it is not only the many benefits you have received from Mary that should induce you to be thankful and devoted to Her, but also the many favors you ought to look for and which the Virgin Mary will give you if you are faithfully and honestly devoted to Her. You cannot doubt Her power nor Her kindness nor Her willingness.

As Mother of God She is most powerful, and as your Mother, She wants everything good for you. Therefore rightly and truly, is She the Refuge of Sinners, the Consolation of the Afflicted, the Health of the Sick, the Mother of Mercy and of Divine Grace. She prays for you now and always, and She will especially pray for you at the hour of your death, and on every occasion She will obtain for you and grant you whatever you need.

With a special Providence Jesus Christ arranged that the first one whom He sanctified in the Law of Grace, the first one to whom He gave grace in the new order — namely, John the Baptist — as well as the first miracle He worked, was through the intercession of Mary, His Mother. These things happened when She visited Her cousin Saint Elizabeth, and when They assisted at the marriage feast of Cana where Jesus changed water into wine.

This was in order that the disciples and all men might know the compassionate Heart of Mary and might learn how powerful Her intercession is for gaining all graces for the soul, for the body, for time and for eternity. Let us go, then, with confidence, to our Mother Mary, as to a Throne of Grace, that we may obtain mercy.

Affective Acts

(1) Confidence — You have three reasons, my soul, to rely on the Blessed Virgin Mary: *First*, She is your Mother. The Creator has strongly instilled in every mother's heart the law of loving one's offspring. Now the greater the needs of her children, so much greater, so much more solicitous, is a mother's love and care for them. This we see by experience in all human mothers, and even among brutes.

Therefore what child of Mary, what devotee of Hers, will not trust in his Mother, Mary, inasmuch as She is such a good Mother and we Her children are so much in need, with needs so pressing, of such surpassing importance; for it is a matter of eternal salvation or damnation.

Second, Mary, even if She were not our Mother, possesses a very good compassionate heart, and merely this would be enough for Her to come to our rescue, just as we see certain good ladies relieving everyone by their kind corporal works of mercy. *Third*, She has a command from Jesus, a solemn charge He gave Her just before dying on the Cross. Even if She were not our Mother, even if She did not possess a heart so kind, it is enough that She have Jesus' command to be our unfailing rescuer and take care of us as very dear children.

(2) Resolution — My Mother, remember that Thou art my Mother, and make me mindful that I am Thy child. Yes, I will be mindful of this and will call upon Thee. I will run to Thee in all my wants and necessities of body and soul, and I put my hope in

Thee to assuredly provide for me in all situations.
Amen.

Third Point

True devotion to Blessed Mary is one of the surest
signs of predestination. But the devotion must be
true; for if it is false, it will serve no purpose. One
can compare it with money which, if not genuine, if
counterfeit, is worth nothing. To prevent any misun-
derstanding or deception in an affair of such surpassing importance, you should reflect very carefully to
see if your devotion to Mary has all the requirements
needed in order for it to be worthy.

*Devotion to Mary consists, first, in avoiding all
sin* — Love either finds or produces a likeness. If
you, my soul, love Mary, you ought to make yourself
like Mary. She was conceived without sin and never
consented to any sin. After your Baptism, in which
original sin was removed, in order for you to be like
Mary you must have a great horror for personal —
or actual — sin; you must never consent to it; and if
at any time you have the misfortune — which God
forbid — to fall into mortal sin, you must have no
rest until you rouse yourself and make a good confession.

You must not do as certain ones do who say they
are devotees of Mary, and have settled down in
mortal sin. They are not devoted to Mary. They are
Her greatest enemies; because, according to Saint
Paul, they are crucifying Jesus anew. If they are
crucifying Jesus, how can they love Mary His
Mother and be Her devoted clients? It is not possible.

*True devotion to Mary consists, second, in imi-
tating Her virtues* — Saint Bonaventure said, "If we

want to have devotion to Mary, let us imitate Her by charity, by modesty, by humility, by purity, by patience, and by love for God."

As a mother desires to have her children dress according to their status, likewise this Mother of ours wants to have Her children dress as She does — clothed in all virtues. And as a mother blushes with shame if her children go about in tattered clothes, dirty, unsightly, and in rags, likewise it shames Mary for Her children to go about soiled with vices, with bad habits and sins.

True devotion to Mary, third, endeavors to pay Her some homage and to receive the Sacraments often — It is impossible to keep free from sin in this life if one does not receive Holy Communion. Jesus Himself assures us of this, saying, "Unless you eat My Flesh and drink My Blood, you will not have life in You."

Where there is no life, even less can there be solid virtue. But if we frequent the Sacraments, then, receiving life from the Bread of the strong, our soul has strength and valor to conquer its enemies; we overcome difficulties, rise above self, perform the most heroic acts and even suffer martyrdom if need be.

True devotion to Mary, fourthly, takes care to perform well, with promptness, cheerfulness and perseverance, one's prayers and other duties belonging to Her service — Linger, my soul, on these words to perform well these duties. If, when one does something for a person of high rank, he is careful to do it well; how much more care should one take in what he does in the service of Mary, Who is so holy and is also Queen of Heaven and earth.

Oh, how blameworthy you would be if you did

your works and prayers with lukewarmness, laziness, and with little care! You should also do what belongs to Her service with promptness and as soon as you can. Imitate Abel and Abraham, who promptly offered God what they knew to be the Divine Will and good pleasure.

Do not imitate Cain, whose offering was of bad quality and tardy, and therefore God despised it and counted it worthless. Oh my soul, whatever you offer Mary, let it be the best you have to give, the best you can do, and do it promptly. Imitate Abel and Abraham, and carefully beware of imitating Cain and those bad Christians who offer Her what is of bad quality and who make the offering late and poorly.

They hear Mass but as something to do last; they pray the Rosary and other prayers and devotions, but as something put in last place and late at night, and they are performed badly because, having become drowsy, they do them with displeasure — and finally they neglect them altogether.

These are not children of Mary; they are deserters. Alas for them! Do not imitate them. On the contrary, make use of all the means that prudence dictates to you and experience teaches you to be best suited for making your heart zealous and fervent in devotion to Mary.

Affective Acts

(1) Means and Resolution — I know that the means I must make use of are:

(a) to keep a picture or image of Mary within sight to always remind me of Her. Likewise, I also propose that all that I shall do I will direct to God through Her most holy hands, and whatever gives me pain, I will suffer, remembering Her sorrows and the Passion of Jesus.

(b) Every day I will pray with attention and devotion at least one part (5 decades) of the Rosary without dozing or being distracted.

(c) I will pray my morning prayers, Noon Angelus and night prayers; also every time the clock strikes the hour, I will pray a Hail Mary.

(d) I will enroll in one or other of Her Confraternities (or a pious society approved by the Church and devoted to Her); I will wear the Scapular; I will go to Confession regularly and to Holy Communion frequently, even every day if possible, and at least once a month; I will read books that treat of devotion to Her and will get other people to read them too, and will exhort them to have devotion to Mary. Finally, I will do for me and for everyone what I know is more to the liking of my holy and sweet Mother, Mary.

(2) O my Mother, the fact that Thou art my Mother is enough for me. As a good mother, I know Thou wilt look after me. Sometimes a natural mother knows what her child needs and has no way to help him. But Thou art well acquainted with what I need, Thou hast a way to help me, and a good heart as well as a charge from Jesus to take care of me. Therefore I have certainty and confidence that Thou wilt take care of me and give me what I need.

Now pray the Our Father and the Hail Mary and the Concluding Prayers as on page xi.

Meditation 33

Love for Neighbor

Preparatory Prayer as on page x

Composition of Place — Imagine you see Jesus Christ in the company of His Apostles and disciples and saying to them: "Love one another as I have loved you . . . By this shall all men know that you are My disciples, if you have love one for another." (John 13:34,35). "As long as you did it to one of these . . . brethren, you did it to Me." (Mt. 25:40).

Prayer of Petition — Grant me, Lord, that spirit of charity whereby I would love my neighbor as myself — more than myself — that I may love him as Thou loved him, even to the extent of Thou giving Thy life for him.

First Point

You should know, my soul, that God is Love itself; God is Charity. This virtue is the greatest of virtues. It is greater than faith and hope. It is like the sun among the stars, like gold among the metals. It gives life to all the virtues. Without it no act has value for reaching Heaven — no, not even the most heroic works.

This Love, or Charity, is like the center from which rays emerge. It is like a vertex from which two lines originate, one of which leads to God and the other to one's neighbor. These two lines and these two Commandments contain whatever the Prophets and the Law have said.

If one truly loves God, that is proof that there is love for neighbor, and the love one has for his

322

neighbor discloses the love one has for God. He who says he loves God and does not love his neighbor, does not tell the truth, because it is impossible to love one whom we do not see, who is God, if we do not love one whom we see, namely, our brother.

Concerning this love, or charity, for your neighbor, my soul, you need to consider unhurriedly three things:

(1) What this charity is — Charity is an all-extensive virtue which embraces everyone; fellow-countrymen and foreigners, friends and enemies. It extends to everyone, embraces all, and does good to all. Therefore people who limit their love to those of their own area or those of their own nation, to those of their own sentiments, or to their friends or relatives, and are not careful to love the rest of men — such people do not have true charity.

(2) What the quality of this virtue is — The Apostle explains charity thus: "Charity is patient, is kind." (1 Cor. 13:4). It rejoices in another's good fortune as though it were one's own. It is resentful toward no one and speaks ill of no one. It does good to all and has sympathy for everyone. As much as is possible, it remedies the needs of all. It achieves and promotes what is good, and with all its power it hinders evil. In a word, charity encourages and cheerfully practices all the works of mercy — corporal and spiritual.

(3) By what spirit are you animated when you love your neighbor? — This is something you ought to examine, inquiring whether it is the love for God that moves you, or whether it is rather self-love. Perhaps you will find that you do not really love your neighbor. Maybe you will discover envy instead of

charity, spite in place of love. See whether you grieve at your neighbor's good fortune and are gladdened when he suffers ruin and trouble. "Out of the abundance of the heart the mouth speaks," says Jesus Christ.

Thus if your heart is full of love and charity for your neighbor, you will speak well of him; but if it has been emptied of charity and harbors some evil feeling of envy, spite or ill-will, you will be quick to speak ill of him; and sometimes you will grumble against him, another time criticize, another time ridicule, or exaggerate his faults, or you will downgrade his merits when you do not entirely deny them, or you might attribute them to a bad intention.

The person who is envious or uncharitable is like a spider which draws poison from the same flowers from which bees draw honey. Envious persons who are destitute of charity are like those large flying insects that are ever hunting for someone's sores, and when they come across one, they linger on it with pleasure to suck out the pus.

Thus envious, uncharitable people are recognized by the way they pry about their neighbor's faults and murmur about his failings. Such unhappy persons take pleasure and delight in going over such sordid affairs. You see, my soul, that you must have charity, and thus you will imitate the bee. Fashion a rich honeycomb which will be a great profit to you, an edification to your neighbor, and will serve God's greater glory.

Affective Acts

(1) Resolution — My God, I give Thee my word that I will do all the good I can for my neighbor by

offering alms, good counsel, prayers, and good example. And besides, I will meekly and humbly put up with his frailties, his peculiar traits and everything that can annoy me, and never will I grumble about offenses he may do to me. I will forgive him and pray for him, in imitation of Jesus Christ, Thy Son and My Sovereign Master, Whom I want to follow and imitate.

(2) Prayer of Petition — My Jesus, grant me grace that will enable me to practise the virtues that Thou hast vouchsafed to teach me by word and example, and in particular meekness and charity, which Thou hast so strongly recommended to us.

Second Point

The virtue of charity or love that we must have for our neighbor is something very noble and holy — so much so that it deserves to be practised for what it is in itself. But there are some other very powerful motives for it which neither pride nor self-love can resist. How deeply people would be moved if they would reflect upon them!

The trouble is that people do not reflect on them, and therefore we see the world in wretched condition, without charity or love for neighbor, since there is no one who ponders the powerful motives for practising this virtue. We will proceed, then, to meditate on them. They are the following:

(1) Charity is commanded by God — and this is itself an adequate motive — You ought to know, my soul, that after loving God above all things we must love our neighbor as ourselves, even if he be our enemy. Maybe self-love or pride will object, but the ready answer is: God commands it; and if an enemy

does not deserve to be loved, God does deserve to be obeyed, and for love of God and out of the obedience we owe Him, we must love our enemies.

(2) The second motive is human nature itself — There is a principle which says: Every living thing loves its own kind. To love is to desire and strive for someone's good. Hence we must strive for the good of one another. We all form one moral and social body, since man by nature is social. Thus, as members of the same body we ought to strive for the good of one another, just as we see is done by members of a physical body.

(3) Being Christians, we are taught by religion that we are all brothers — that we all have a common Father, Who is God, and a common Mother, Who is Blessed Mary, and that the greatest pleasure we can give Them is to love one another like good brothers. We have a common Redeemer and Advocate, Who is Jesus Christ. We are all created for the same end, which is Heaven. We all have the same commandments to keep and the same Sacraments to receive and the same truths that we must believe. We must put our hopes in the same promises and fear the same punishments.

(4) We are disciples of Jesus Christ — Who, by word and example, taught us this very important truth, and has done so with such earnestness and insistence that He went so far as to say that we know whether we are His disciples by whether we love one another as He has loved us; and He adds that whatever we do to our neighbor, He takes it as something done to Himself.

To emphasize the importance of charity, He reveals to us a wonderful truth. He told us that when

He shall come to judge us at the end of the world, He will glorify and reward those who have loved and served their neighbor as if they had done this to Him. But as for those who have not loved and helped their neighbor, He will disgrace them and publicly take them to task as though they had refused this love and help to Himself, and finally He will condemn them to eternal fire.

(5) The motive of good order — Even if this love had not been commanded by the Lord, one ought to love one's neighbor because of a need for it. Take a good look, my soul, at what happens in a home or town where there is no love of neighbor or fraternal charity, or where people do not love one another as brothers.

Oh, dear God! What disorder! What confusion! It seems more like a hell than a home or community. . . God withdraws His graces and blessings from it and leaves the people to themselves, and they become playthings of their passions; they do nothing good and are apt to do much evil — turning to rash judgments, suspicions, hatred, grumbling, fights, scandals, and many other great evils.

That is why Saint John says that one who does not love his neighbor as he ought, is dead. God is so fond of this love or charity that He is named Charity, and where charity is, God is, and there is peace and happiness. But where there is no charity, there is no peace nor tranquillity, laws are not kept, Commandments are not observed, obligations are not fulfilled, virtue is not practised, temporal goods are wasted, diseases afflict people, death is hastened, and the soul goes to hell after having suffered greatly in this world.

Affective Acts

(1) Resolution — I know that charity is such a necessary virtue that without it there can be no society. I am quite convinced that I have the strongest reasons to practise this virtue. Therefore, with God's help, I will practise it as much as I can.

(2) Prayer of Petition — Grant me grace, my Jesus, to be charitable to my neighbor, to help him as much as I can. May I never make him suffer from my disorderly or proud ways. May I always speak to him with friendliness and sweetness and never with unpleasant, rude or disparaging words. May I be sympathetic towards his pains and troubles and remedy them as much as I can.

Third Point

Consider, my soul, the means that you must take to suitably practise this virtue of charity or love for your neighbor.

(1) Do not of set purpose dwell on his faults and defects — On the contrary, consider the good with which God has favored him. If you do not see something in him that can move you to highly respect him, consider that he is an image of God, redeemed by the Blood of Jesus Christ and made for Heaven.

Consider that perhaps in Heaven he will have more glory than you, and that even if today he may be evil, perhaps he will become converted, will do penance, will become fervent, and will gain more merit than you will — as happened with Saint Paul, with Saint Mary Magdalene, with the Samaritan woman, and others.

(2) One must distinguish the sin from the sinner
— Sin should be abhorred, but the sinner should be loved. When you see someone who has committed a crime, reflect that if you had been placed in the temptation he was in, you might have committed the same sin as he, and that if he were in your position, assisted by the grace with which God assists you, he might be better than you are.

Therefore do not murmur about your neighbor. Fear God. Reflect that the weakness one person has, another can have, and that you will fall into the sin into which your neighbor has fallen if God does not help you in a special way. Moreover, not seldom does it happen that God permits us or our immediate kinsmen to fall into the same fault which we censure in others. Thus we should treat others as we would want to be treated if we had fallen into those faults.

(3) To preserve charity we must also fulfill the obligations called for by our state in life, our office, and our power to do good — It is not seldom that displeasure, quarrels, and abusive remarks come about from failure to meet obligations. In this way we trouble our parents and superiors, our equals complain, and people under us murmur and grumble when we do not fulfill the duties that pertain to us.

(4) We must also respect the interests of other people — One must not take nor desire what belongs to another. A man is more sensitive about the way he is treated as to his pocketbook, than about his blood. It not seldom happens that ties of close kinship are ruptured by a little property dispute. The same should be said about ties of friendship. Oh, how many friendships have been broken by petty property and money matters!

How many associations began in the name of God, and due to a sordid concern over temporalities, ended in the name of the devil, who engineered a thousand lawsuits wherein charity was abandoned, peace was forfeited, and even the wealth of the persons concerned was lost.

Therefore Jesus Christ tells us in His holy Gospel not to put up resistance to the injury. If someone wants to sue us and take our tunic, we are to let him take our cloak as well. If someone strikes us on our right cheek, we are to turn to him the other. Let all be lost rather than charity . . . Let us leave everything in God's hands, Who is well able to give us more than we give up and is just in seeing that our honor is restored. Let us not desire revenge. On the contrary, all who do us harm we should commend to God in imitation of Jesus.

(5) To preserve charity, not only must we respect other people's temporal interests and their persons, but also their honor — treating everyone with politeness and thoughtfulness, not offending anyone by rudeness, inappropriate speech, nicknames, and ridicule; for such behavior is not only against charity, but discloses a spirit that is cheap, ill-bred, and unworthy of human society.

Affective Acts

(1) Prayer of Petition — Grant me, my God, that patient charity which nothing changes, that accommodating charity that does good to all, that universal charity that makes no one an exception to it.

(2) Resolution — I will never be angry with my neighbors. If I might sometimes feel anger, I will be silent until the trouble passes. I will never speak ill

of anyone. I will not listen to those who speak ill of their neighbor. I will do what good I can to all, with the help of our Lord and the protection of the Blessed Virgin Mary.

Now pray the Our Father and the Hail Mary and the Concluding Prayers as on page xi.

Meditation 34

The Blessed Sacrament

Preparatory Prayer as on page x

Composition of Place — Imagine you see Our Lord Jesus Christ at the Cenacle with His beloved Apostles, that you are with them, that Our Lord washes everyone's feet, yours as well as theirs, and that He gives you Holy Communion.

Prayer of Petition — Ah, my Jesus! . . . That Thou would wash my feet! . . . that Thou would want it so! . . . Thy most holy Will be done. As Thou dost wish to wash me . . . do so, and I shall be whiter than snow.

First Point

Consider, first, that a gift is valuable and precious according to how great it is in itself, how great the giver's love is, and how useful and profitable it is for us. These three qualities are found together in a supreme degree in the priceless gift that the Lord gave us of His Body and Blood in the Most Blessed Sacrament.

The grandeur of the gift could not rank any higher; for it was like a seal of all blessings and is the greatest among blessings — bringing the things that are contained within Christ to each of the Faithful, namely, all of Christ's goods and treasures — His Body, Blood, Soul and Divinity, with all His merits, graces and virtues.

This gift is made with a resourcefulness so wonderful that for all eternity a prodigy so astonishing would never have occurred to the mind of the most enlightened Seraphim. And it comes with such lavish affection that, though God is infinitely wise, good and powerful, He cannot give us in this life a boon and a treasure that is worth more.

Affective Acts

(1) Thanksgiving — I give Thee thanks, my loving Lord and God, for Thy infinite generosity toward this lowly creature — myself. Thou dost shame me at the same time for my having been so stingy toward Thee up to now. But with sorrow and repentance I humbly beg that Thou add to this Sovereign Gift, the favor of granting me a new spirit and heart so that henceforth I may rightly value this Thy Gift and respond with total love and faithfulness to Something so precious and so priceless.

(2) Prayer of Petition — O Virgin Mary, when Thou heard from the angel that Thou wert destined for the great dignity of Mother of God, You were humbly baffled. How will my soul react on hearing and knowing that Jesus Christ, Son of Thy chaste flesh, Who is in the Most Holy Sacrament, wants to come into my poor heart. Obtain for me, O my Mother, a heart meek and humble like Thine, that I may be able to welcome Jesus in it, Who greatly delights in dwelling in hearts that are well disposed. Help me, assist me, and be present with me, my Mother.

Second Point

Consider, second, the greatness of the giver's love. Here is where properly is found the excellence of the favor; for Jesus was moved by a most ardent love — and this is to be valued most highly. The warmest flame of love one can conceive of burned in His breast the night on which He instituted for our good this Divine Sacrament.

At the same hour in which men were plotting His arrest and His infamous and cruel death, the Lord, knowing all this, celebrated this solemn occasion much as an eager bridegroom celebrates a wedding. Our Lord's celebration was to provide that He remain with men until the end of the world.

He gave Himself in the manner of a banquet, and took the appearance of bread and wine, in order to be our food and drink and to unite Himself with us spiritually and bodily in such close union, that just as no skill can separate food once it is changed into the body's substance, so no skill nor power nor anything else can separate us from Him.

But there is something else in which He revealed the fine quality of His Charity. He knowing all the injuries, irreverences and sacrileges that were to be done to Him in the Consecrated Host by infidels, heretics and bad Christians as long as the world would last, He went ahead with His whole design and did not hold back this favor to us. Through this gift He feeds us with His Own Flesh and becomes closely united to our souls and makes us truly blessed, in order to satisfy the desires of His loving Heart.

Who would have ever imagined something so wonderful, if Faith did not give us the certain assurance?

Affective Acts

(1) Self-accusation — And how is it, O my soul, that you react to this great favor with such coolness, or rather such ingratitude and lack of faith? How is

it that, though you have often had this Divine fire within your breast, no heavenly flame is now burning in it?

Recognize your unhappy condition, bitterly deplore it, lift up your heart with repeated Acts of Contrition, of Faith, of Hope and of Charity, and ask the loving Jesus to kindly visit you again with His presence, so that, united to Him intimately in Holy Communion, you will persevere until death in His friendship and grace and hereafter enjoy Him and bless Him forever in Heaven.

(2) Resolution — I see, Lord, that love is strong as death. Love obliged us to suffer everything, to bear everything. I resolve to surrender entirely to Thee. It will no longer be I who live, but Thou will live in me. I will be dead to the world and to myself. Praised be Jesus Christ!

Third Point

Finally let us consider, my soul, the benefits and advantages that this Divine Bread offers us. It is called, among other things, Communion, because in It the Lord communicates, or distributes, to each of the Faithful who receive Him in the 'State of Grace', the treasure of His virtues, gifts and merits that He earned by His holy life, passion and death.

At the same time He reveals with a fine tenderness not only the love with which He gave His Life for all, but the prompt and generous will whereby He would die again for the same cause if it were needed. As if to save us were a small thing to have offered once His Sacred Body on the altar of the Cross, He wonderfully multiplies His Body numberless times each day on altars by the ministry of priests for the same end.

Not satisfied with bringing us the gifts of His grace by the other Sacraments and other channels of His bounty and mercy, He comes in Person. And with His own hand in this Sacrament He is lavish with His heavenly riches, enlightening our minds, enkindling our wills, reducing the heat of our passions, reforming our feelings and depositing in us, even in our flesh, the seed of immortality, so that we may rise again one day to live eternally.

Affective Acts

(1) Admiration — O my God, in this sum of all marvels how wonderfully Thou hast shown us proof of Thy tender love with the sure pledge of eternal happiness! And I — how ungrateful and petty I appear toward One Who does not grow weary of being my most liberal benefactor! What small fruit I have obtained from the frequent sharing of this Source of all good things!

And what fruit — may I ask — if each time I am worse, each time more lacking in devotion, more vain, more impatient, more selfish, more anxious about pleasures of the world? I confess it with great shame, out of respect for Thy Divine honor. Ah! My ingratitude, my perversity, my hard-heartedness have gone far enough.

Help me with Thy powerful grace. Let Thy love triumph! O Jesus, Who already works so many miracles in this great Sacrament in order to become food for my soul, enkindle today within my breast, O Lord, the fire of Thy charity, so that my soul will always live in Thy grace and hereafter enjoy Thee in glory and praise Thee for all eternity. *Amen.*

(2) Prayer to Mary Most Holy — O my Mother,

336

obtain for me the wine of divine love which I lack. Say to Thy Son Who is in the Most Holy Sacrament: "My Son, this poor soul has no wine." I am sure that then Thou wilt obtain it. Obtain also for me the faith of Saint Peter, the love of Saint John, the zeal of Saint James, and the devotedness of the other Apostles. Adorn me, my Mother, with those virtues which Thou knowest I need in order to approach the Most Holy Sacrament in the best possible way.

> Soul of Christ, sanctify me.
> Body of Christ, save me.
> Blood of Christ, inebriate me.
> Water from the side of Christ, wash me.
> Passion of Christ, strengthen me.
> O Good Jesus, hear me.
> Within Thy wounds, hide me.
> Suffer me not to be separated from Thee.
> From the malignant enemy defend me.
> At the hour of my death, call me
> and bid me to come to Thee,
> that with Thy saints I may praise Thee forever and ever. *Amen.*

Now pray the Our Father and the Hail Mary and the Concluding Prayers as on page xi.

Meditation 35

On Perseverance

Preparatory Prayer as on page x

Composition of Place — Imagine that you see Christ and that He tells you: Remember what you have received and learned in this retreat, and observe it all faithfully. — "Behold, I come quickly: hold fast that which thou hast, that no man take thy crown." (Apoc. 3:11).

Prayer of Petition — My Lord and my God, grant me grace to perfectly fulfill the resolves I have made, and grant that I may persevere in them to the end of my life. *Amen.*

First Point

How fortunate you are, O my soul! Now you can truly be called happy. You have sought the Lord during these days of retreat and have found Him. He Who loves you has admitted you into His house, and opening the arms of His mercy, He has given you a place in the midst of His Heart.

He wants you to repay Him for this great love and the signs of affection which He has shown you, by opening to Him your heart and clinging to Him so firmly that you would never let Him go. You would do Him the most outrageous wrong if you would not accept this grace of a fond and favored familiarity with Him.

Then you would deserve that terrible woe of the Prophet Isaias — the woe against "apostate children;" "Woe to you, apostate children, saith the Lord, that you would take counsel, and not of Me:

and would begin a web, and not by My spirit . . ." (Is. 30:1).

Woe to him who does not persevere with the Lord!! Woe to him who quits His service! Alas for the ingratitude! Oh, what malice! Be astonished, ye Heavens! After God, in His overflowing love, has forgiven a sinner and has restored him to His grace, if the sinner is bold enough to gravely offend Him, he insolently declares to God, if not in words, at least by his actions: "I know not Thy favors. I am dissatisfied with Thy love. I am weary of serving Thee and so do not choose to serve Thee for the future. Satan will be my master. I put myself in his care and I am his slave. Down with Jesus! Long live satan!"

Do you not tremble, my soul, on hearing this language? Are you not filled with horror? Is it possible that you have no conscience about this deep in your heart? Where can we match an ingratitude so black, a treachery so unheard of, and a pride so mad? O Good God! It is not strange that those who know Thee not, run in the ways of wickedness.

Nor is it strange that they who have not experienced the pleasing taste of Thy sweetness would pursue the charms of their unbridled appetites, and that they who have not seen for themselves how sweet, how desirable is the yoke of Thy service, would serve Thy enemy. But that they who have known Thee, would leave Thee! That one who has experienced Thy lovable presence in his soul through grace, would offend Thee! That anyone would sin who has tasted the delightful fare of a good conscience and the enduring treat of peace of soul! How monstrous! What a profanation! What an insult to Thee, O Lord of Majesty!

An insult? Indeed, it is an insult to tell Thee plainly that sin is preferable to Thy grace, that it is more worthwhile to serve satan than Thee. That is what sinners do when they sin. They shut their eyes to Thy light in order to bury themselves in a pit of darkness. Alas for them!

In this very folly they have punishment. They have not wanted to see, and have remained blind. They have withdrawn from the source of All Good and have plunged into the sea of all evil. They have hated life and have fallen into the darkness of death. *"If the just man turn himself away from his justice . . . shall he live?* No, he shall not live." (Ezech. 18:24).

While the tree stays planted beside the running stream of water, it will keep its greenness and vigor and in season it will bear fruit in abundance. But if it is uprooted and removed from the spot, it will promptly start withering, will shed its leaves, will bear no fruit, will dry up, and will only be good for firewood.

The same thing happens to a just man who does not persevere. As long as he sits by the streams of Divine grace, he is rich in virtue and merit for eternal life. But as soon as he removed himself by sin from that fertile soil, he serves no purpose but to consume himself in vice and in the end to enter the eternal fire.

Do you understand this, my soul? If you want to be saved, you must persevere in the good way you have begun. You must do this at all costs; for it is not beginnings that count so much as the end. Saint Paul began badly and ended well. Judas began well and ended badly. Paul is blessed and one of the greatest saints in paradise. Do you wish to be Judas or Paul?

The reward is offered to those who begin, but, as Saint Bernard says, is given only to those who persevere. The crown of glory is hanging over your head. To come to wear it, you must persevere, for perseverance alone will be crowned, as Saint Bonaventure rightly declares: Persevere, and it will be given to you. Jesus Christ Himself has pledged His word for it.

Read chapter 24 of Saint Matthew's Gospel and you will see that these words have come from His Divine Mouth: *"He that shall persevere to the end, he shall be saved."* (verse 13). Be not deceived, my soul. The desire for salvation and an ineffective inclination to fulfill the means of salvation, are not enough. An effective will is necessary — one which goes ahead to perform the deeds needed for salvation.

Heaven and hell are full of men with desires, but with this difference: Those in hell stayed at a standstill with their desires, and those in Heaven put their hands to the task. The former were damned, and the latter were saved. You, too, should desire, proceed to the performance, and persevere, and you will be saved.

Here is where everything worthwhile for us lies. Therefore one must be whole-hearted, generous, and constant, without becoming frightened, no matter what the effort, the difficulty or the cost. The cost? Certainly it costs something. We should not hide the fact; for it has been written, *"The Kingdom of Heaven suffereth violence, and the violent bear it away."* (Mt. 11:12)

One must put down all evil cravings, conquer a rebellious flesh, subject a wayward will, be humble before God's Almighty Will, and submit to all of God's designs without giving any hearing to self-love or other enemies. Ah, this is the way, but a rough way, my soul.

One must keep following it, going ahead without turning back, without weakening. — As for you, what will you do, my soul? Will you perhaps turn back? Ah, no. You have generously left a world which, like another wicked Pentapolis (Wisd. 10:6; Gen. 19:25), is burning in the flames of every vice. See that you are not like Lot's foolish wife, who turned her eyes back, and after changing into a statue of salt, was left on the road. (Gen. 19:26).

Saint Augustine tells you, my soul, to consider well this salt. Keep yourself from a great misfortune. Salt is a sign of prudence. Know to be prudent and take a warning from another's experience. Through God's Providence you have put your hand to the plough.

Continue to work out your eternal happiness, without becoming frightened at difficulties, and trusting that the Lord, Who inspired your generous thoughts, will give you the strength necessary to carry on to the end. If you do this, you will not be among the number of those fools who "began in the spirit" and ended "by the flesh" — using Saint Paul's blunt language to the faithful of Galatia (Gal. 3:3).

Be mindful that people guilty of this folly are not few. "The number of fools is infinite," says the wise man (Ecclesiastes 1:15); and Saint Jerome and Saint Augustine add that they who begin are many, but they who persevere are few. Will you not be generous enough to be numbered among the few? Surely you have resolved to stand with Our Lord, and I trust you will persevere.

Affective Acts

(1) Confidence — My Lord and Father, I know the dangers and I am convinced of my weakness; but I hope in Thy Goodness, that from everything Thou wilt safely deliver me. Thou wilt not forsake me, my Father.

(2) Prayer of Petition — Most Holy Virgin, my Mother, pray to God for me now and always, so that I will persevere until death. Amen.

Second Point

But it is necessary, my soul, that you get ready for temptation, for you must walk a road that is narrow and rough, and where cruel enemies are on either side. The world, the devil and the flesh are hiding in ambush on both sides of the road to Heaven, which you are travelling. They have observed and learned your aims. They are preparing surprise attacks on you and will attack you at the first opportunity.

Oh, the scandals, the snares, the flatteries, the charms, which the world, even now, keeps preparing, to captivate your heart! And beware, for it is so skillful at this that it now reckons its victory to be a sure thing. But, ah! if the world fails in this ambush, what a shower of jeers, unkind jests, misrepresentations, cruel persecutions, it will cause to fall on you! You will be dragged before tribunals of criticism where you will be judged without a hearing and condemned without compassion.

On streets men will point you out with a finger. In gatherings and gossiping circles your honor will be torn to shreds. Perhaps you will be booed. You will be the butt of tales and the topic of amusement for worldlings. As for you, what will you do? Will you quit on this account? Will you know how to laugh in return at the world and resist its attacks?

But when you do this, are you unaware that the devil will spur on the worldlings and supply them with schemes to overcome you, and if he cannot, he will make them cruel toward you? He will use your father, your brother, your friends perhaps, as his most powerful instruments. He will rage by the mouth of all and will avail himself of everyone to devour you.

Oh, what heroic manliness, what constancy, you will need! And where will you get this? Do you not see how weak you are and how feeble your flesh is? This is the flank where the devil will doubtless attack and where he thinks you will surrender. Your good will shows itself, and it will do so quickly for "the spirit is willing" (Mt. 26:41).

But where will you get enough strength to be able to resist and conquer? Where? Listen: Be circumspect, be ever watchful and pray without ceasing, as Jesus Christ tells you in His Gospel (Lk. 21:36); because what is impossible for you, is very easy for God. If God is with you, what can all your foes do against you? But do not grow slack on your part.

Do what you can and in this way you will oblige the Lord to help you. Does the world hate you? Does it want to involve you in its ruin? You too should hate it and shun its supporters, who are the salt of Babylon, so that they will not envelop you in their darkness. Is the devil not roaring furiously, going about in search of a chance to devour you?

Live in perfect sobriety and continued watchfulness, as the Apostle Saint Peter tells you (1 Pt. 5:8 ff.), and, armed with the shield of faith resist him with firmness, for it is certain that the devil is very courageous against the faint-hearted, but with courageous and generous souls he is faint-heartedness itself. Does the flesh seek to overpower the spirit?

Strengthen the spirit, crucify your flesh and its concupiscences by mortification and penance, and you will subject it. In this way you will be fighting as God commands you to fight; and you will win, and will receive the immortal crown. *"Be thou faithful until death: and I will give thee the crown of life"* (Apoc. 2:10), says the Lord.

But, alas for me! Saint Augustine declares that when they are guilty of a careless look, lofty cedars of Lebanon fall, of whom one would not have feared this any more than of an Ambrose and Jerome! Persons have fallen who were as mighty as Samson, as just as David, as wise as Solomon, as determined as Peter to die with Christ.

And we who are weak, ignorant, faint-hearted, will we be over-confident? *"Your strength shall be as the ashes of tow"* (Is. 1:31), God tells you by the Prophet. Should we despair, then? Oh, no! Then where will our weakness lean for support? On Thee, Lord. I put my hope in Thee to deliver me from my enemies (cf. Ps. 7:2).

Prayer — May Holy Mary and all the saints intercede for us to the Lord, that we may be worthy to receive help and salvation from Him Who lives and reigns forever and ever. *Amen.* (Oration at Prime).

Third Point

Listen, my soul. Saint Paul defies tribulations, distress, danger, persecution, the sword, and has no fear of being overcome. *"Who . . . shall separate us,"* he boldly exclaims, *"who shall separate us from the Love of Christ?"* (Rom. 8:35). No one. Why? Because, as this Apostle assures us, while he was by himself frail and weak, he could do all things in the Lord Who strengthened him.

Trusting not in himself, he fully leaned on the Lord. He had been told that the grace of Jesus Christ was sufficient for him to fight the good fight, to finish his course, to keep the Faith, and to earn for himself the crown of justice which the Lord was reserving for him. Crown of justice? Is it not through grace he was able to acquire it? Yes, my soul.

Take note of this: God wanted Paul's cooperation, and Paul added to grace his cooperation; that is, with the help of grace he performed the work which God had commanded him, and for the performance of which God had promised an unfading crown of glory as a reward. Thus, by the merits of Jesus Christ he won the crown, and in justice the crown was awarded to him.

This is what we, too, must do: Have trust, and apply ourselves using all means conducive to obtaining final perseverance — something hard and necessary, yet possible. Very many, millions of saints have gained it. Can we gain it also if we use the same means? And what are these means? Learn the answer in the five following maxims, which are the principles which you should observe and conscientiously keep:

(1) Death rather than sin — this was the principle which gave Susanna courage to resist the two elders (cf. Dan. 13:23), gave chaste Joseph courage to despise the advances of his master's wife (cf. Gen. 39), gave the aged Eleazar courage to be worthy of his grey hairs (cf. 2 Mach. 6). With this principle the seven young Machabees became mighty and their tender mother became a heroine (cf. 2 Mach. 7).

These good people resigned themselves, suffered as they struggled against tremendous torments, until they conquered and by dying gained the crown of victory. Let us lose a short, wretched life, they said to themselves, and gain for ourselves another life which is eternal and full of blessing.

This was the language of the Holy Martyrs, who, acting by those sentiments, succeeded in gaining the palm of glory in wearing the white garments which they had washed in their blood and the Blood of the unspotted Lamb, Who became Chief of Martyrs and blotted out our sins and purchased life for us by surrendering to death, without counting the distress. He expected to suffer.

Oh my God, death rather than sin was the determined sentiment of all the saints, it is the resolution of all the just, and if it has not been mine up to now, it is now and will be until my death. This I promise and with Thy grace I will fulfill it. Neither pleasure nor delights nor pain nor death itself is to separate me from Thee. Alas! I am nothing more than weakness itself! But I put my trust in Thee, my Lord.

(2) Flee all occasions of sin — This is the second principle for persevering. He who loves danger will fall into it and will perish, says the Lord (Ecclus.

3:27), Therefore I will no longer love danger, nor hunt for the occasion; rather, I will flee from it. The slippery places where I have fallen will not harm me any more, because I will avoid them.

The Lord admonishes me to watch and pray, so that I will not fall into temptation, and I will watch and pray (Mt. 26:41). But how should I do this so that I pray with fruit? Let it be in the Name of Jesus and by His merits — so the Savior Himself tells us; and let it be by the Blessed Virgin's intercession — so all the saints cry out. Here you have the remedy, my soul.

(3) Prayer and devotion to the Blessed Virgin — Oh, who knows how to be truly devoted to Mary and to pray to Her without ceasing? Who knows how to win the heart of this great Mother of Mercy, this powerful Advocate for sinners? Do you want to win Her Heart, O my soul? It is a very easy matter: Have a horror for sin, consecrate yourself to Her service, practise all the devotions you can, not so that you can get by with your sins, but so that thereby you amend your ways; and above all manage to form in yourself, in Her honor, a living copy of Her virtues.

Ah! Never has anyone doing this been lost, nor will such a person ever be lost. Within that tower of refuge, what can the enemies do against you? Sheltered by that shield, what arrows of theirs can wound you? Mary will be a sure guide for you to walk without a stumble on the difficult road of your salvation, and a gateway ever open for entering the heavenly Jerusalem.

Follow Her steps and you will not go astray. Give Her your hand and you cannot fall. Now those truly devoted to Mary go to Confession and Holy Communion often. This presents the fourth principle for perseverance, which I am going to set forth.

(4) Frequent Confession and Holy Communion — Tell me, my soul, would your body live long without food? To enable it to live, do you think it would be enough if it took food one, two, or three times a year? And even if it were possible for it to live that way, would it be very strong and healthy? And will you try to have your soul live the life of grace without frequently taking the Divine and supersubstantial Bread of the Eucharist? Do you imagine that is less necessary than material bread is for the body? No. You foolishly deceive yourself. Do not seek miracles without necessity.

As God has given you material bread to nourish your body, He has likewise given you the Eucharistic Bread to maintain and increase the spiritual life of your soul. Therefore, receive Holy Communion often, as the saints counsel you and your spiritual needs indicate; and you will live forever. *"He that eateth this bread shall live for ever,"* says the Lord (Jn. 6:59). But you must eat it with the right disposition; otherwise this very healthful and Divine Food will become a poison to you.

Therefore take good care to cure your spiritual ailments with a healthful repentance and bathe yourself often in the heavenly bath of a good Confession, so that your life may be pleasing to the eyes of the heavenly Bridegroom of souls. Oh, if you do this, how lovable you will be to Jesus Christ! What a fondness He will have for you and you for Him! Then you can truly say: My Beloved is everything to me, and I to Him (Cant. 2:16).

Then the good Jesus will let you know Him, He will become always present to you, and you will never fail to see things with lively faith; and perhaps you may come to have the light of contemplation.

(5) The presence of God — Consider that God sees you. In whatever place you are, whether in your house or in your yard, whether in a church or on the street, whether in a public place or in a deep cave, God is always watching you.

And would you dare offend Him before His very Eyes? Does God not happen to be your Bridegroom, your Father, your Lord, your Judge as well as your God? And what bride, what son, what slave, what defendant, what creature would boldly venture so far? Consider, my soul, all God's claims on you — His claim to your loyalty, your piety, your respect, your fear, your gratitude and your love — all, all these cry out to you and plead that you sin no more.

Have you not gained a bit of light during these days of retreat? Have you not meditated, reflected, resolved? Have you not written down resolutions in your heart? Ah! Inscribe them now in your memory, or, if you wish, write them also on paper so that you may read them every day, or at least every month, so that you will never forget them and so that you will practise them faithfully, aiding yourself in this by the five very important principles which you have just seen. Oh, how useful, how necessary they are for you! Always remember them, keep them ever in view, count them off by the five fingers of your right hand, and you will never sin.

Prayer of Petition — O my God, God of my heart! Come to my assistance. By the merits of Jesus Christ, Thy Son and my Loving Redeemer, I ask of

Thee final perseverance in Thy Grace, and I ask that I die in Thy Love. O my Sweet Jesus! Do not permit all that Thou hast done to save me, to be fruitless in me.

By Thy weariness and sweat, by the humiliations and ill treatment Thou didst suffer, by the Precious Blood Thou didst shed, by Thy dereliction, Thy Agony and death, do not allow me again to plunge to my ruin. I love Thee, my Jesus, above all things, and I hope to be bound to Thee forever with new ties of love. O my Beloved, shackle me ever more and more with Thy chains.

I want to live always loving Thee. May I breathe my last breath for love of You, O Mary. You are called the Mother of Fair Love and are the Dispenser of the great gift of final perseverance. I beg that gift from You, and I hope for it from You; I am certain that I shall not be left eternally disappointed and confounded.

Now pray the Our Father and the Hail Mary and the Concluding Prayers as on page xi.

APPENDICES

Conclusion of The Holy Exercises with Hymns and Prayers

Ambrosian Hymn

We praise Thee, O God;
we acknowledge Thee to be the Lord.

Thee, the Father everlasting, all the earth doth worship.

To Thee all the Angels, to Thee the
Heavens, and all the Powers.
To Thee the Cherubim and Seraphim cry without ceasing:
Holy, holy, holy, Lord God of hosts.

Full are the Heavens and the earth of the majesty of Thy Glory.

Thee, the glorious choir of the Apostles,
Thee, the admirable company of the Prophets,
Thee, the army of Martyrs, in incandescent robes, doth praise.

Thee, the holy Church throughout the world doth confess: The Father of Incomprehensible Majesty;
Thine Adorable, True and Only Son; And the Holy Ghost, the Paraclete.

Thou, O Christ, art the King of Glory.

Thou art the Everlasting Son of the Father.

Thou, having taken upon Thee to deliver man, didst not disdain the Virgin's Womb.

Thou, having overcome the sting of death,
hast opened to believers the Kingdom of Heaven.

Thou sittest at the right Hand of God,
in the Glory of the Father.

Thou, we believe, art the Judge to come.

We beseech Thee, therefore, to help Thy servants, whom Thou hast redeemed with Thy Precious Blood.

Make them to be numbered with Thy saints in glory everlasting.

O Lord, save Thy people, and bless Thine inheritance.

And govern them, and exalt them forever.

Day by day we bless Thee. And we praise Thy Name for ever; yea, forever and ever.

Vouchsafe, O Lord, this day, to keep us without sin.

Have mercy on us, O Lord; have mercy on us.

Let Thy Mercy, O Lord, be upon us; as we have trusted in Thee.

In Thee, O Lord, have I trusted: let me not be confounded forever.

V. Let us bless the Father, and the Son, and the Holy Ghost.

R. Let us praise and exalt Him for ever.

V. Blessed art Thou, O Lord, in the firmament of Heaven.

R. And worthy of praise, and glorious, and exalted above all forever.

V. O Lord hear my prayer.

R. And let my cry come unto Thee

V. The Lord be with you.

R. And with thy spirit.

(This last verse is said only by a priest or deacon)

Let us pray — O God, of Whose mercies are limitless, and of Whose Goodness the treasure is infinite; we render thanks to Thy most gracious Majesty for the gifts Thou hast bestowed upon us; evermore beseeching Thy clemency, that as Thou grantest the petitions of them that ask Thee, Thou mayest never forsake them, but mayest prepare them for the rewards to come. Through Christ our Lord.

R. *Amen.*

Almighty and everlasting God, Who inscribe the justice of Thy law into the hearts of believers; grant us an increase of faith, hope, and charity that we may merit to attain what Thou dost promise, and make us love what Thou commandest.

O God, Who resists the proud and gives grace to

the humble, increase in us the virtue of true humility, which forms in the Faithful Thy Only-Begotten Son. He showed the Faithful, that we should never provoke Thy indignation, but rather we should always seek the gifts of Thy compassion.

O God, Who gives us fervor, turn us away from the vanity of the world, to a higher calling, pour forth Thy grace into our purified hearts, and make us persevere in Thee. Fortify us by the help of Thy protection, to fulfill the resolutions we have made, that we may obtain the joy Thou dost promise to those who persevere in Thee. We ask this through Our Lord Jesus Christ, Thy Son, Who lives and reigns with Thee, in the unity of the Holy Ghost, God, forever and ever. **R.** *Amen.*

A Daily Schedule for the Days of the Annual Retreat Made with Members of Our Family

5:00 a.m: Rising.
5:30 a.m: Morning Offering, Come Holy Ghost, and spiritual reading of the *Right Road*
6:00 a.m: Meditation.
7:00 a.m: Holy Mass.
7:30 a.m: Canonical Hours.
8:00 a.m: Breakfast, Rest.
9:00 a.m: Meditation.
10:00 a.m: Rest, visit with spiritual director.

11:00 a.m: Meditation.
Noon: Rest.
12:45 p.m: Examen.
1:00 p.m: Lunch, Rest.
3:00 p.m: Vespers, Compline, Rest.
5:00 p.m: Meditation.
6:00 p.m: Sermon
7:00 p.m: Dinner, Rest.
8:00 p.m: Rosary, Way of the Cross, examination of conscience.
10:00 p.m: Lights out.

Note:

1. Silence is to be rigorously kept at all times.
2. If the spiritual director approves, spiritual reading

may be employed before meditation.

3. During meals reading of the saints' lives appropriate to the Exercises takes place.

4. During free time one should examine one's conscience, confess, read, write down one's affective acts and resolutions.

5. With some slight variations, this plan can serve for Religious Communities and for those obligated to recite the Divine Office.

Proposed Daily Schedule For Those on a Closed Retreat for Ten Days

5:30 a.m: Rising.

6:00 a.m: Chapel, Morning Offering etc. according to the *Right Road*, Reading.

6:30 a.m: Meditation.

7:30 a.m: Holy Mass.

8:00 a.m: Breakfast, Rest.

10:00 a.m: Meditation.

11:00 a.m: Rest, Visit of the SpiritualDirector.

Noon: Way of the Cross, Rest, Examen. [30 minutes for the Stations, 15 minutes for Rest and Examen respectively.

1:00 p.m: Lunch, Rest.

4:00 p.m: Meditation, Sermon, Rest.

6:00 p.m: Dinner, Rest.

7:00 p.m: Benediction, Rosary, Joys and Sorrows of Saint Joseph, Examination of conscience.

10:00 p.m: Lights Out.

Note:

1. Rigorous silence must always be maintained.

2. During meals lives of the saints appropriate to the Exercises are read.

3. Free time is employed in examining one's conscience, Confession, reading under the Confessor's direction, writing down briefly affective acts and resolutions.

4. The examens of noon and evening will concern the Rule and its Observance.

Proposed Schedule For Those
who cannot go on a Closed Retreat

They are to meet twice a day in church

In the Morning

1. First act — Morning Offering, etc. through the *Right Road*, invocation to the Holy Ghost and other prayers.
2. The first point of meditation is read, followed by the Holy Mass.
3. After the consecration, the second point is read, and after the Mass, the third point.
4. After the Meditation, the Sermon.

In the Afternoon

1. Rosary, reading of the general confession and examination of conscience.
2. Meditation.
3. Sermon.

Note:

1. Since there are only two meetings in the church, there will be only two meditations in common, and thus they should seek to do the other two privately if there is a place, one in the morning, and the other in the afternoon or evening.
2. All are asked to maintain recollection at all possible times, and above all silence and keep the idea of the Presence of God.
3. That they write down all their resolutions for the entire year.
4. When going and coming, they should not allow themselves to be detained in conversation, but greet others briefly if necessary, all the time main-

taining recollection and the Presence of God.

5. In their home, office, or shop, they must keep all possible recollection, remembering what they have heard; if they have time they could read one of the books indicated in the Exercises. It should not seem strange that we insist on silence, for experience has taught us that breaking the silence is the most common fault during these Spiritual Exercises.

How To Make the Particular Examen for all the Days' Faults According to Saint Ignatius

It contains five points

1. Thank God for the benefits received. — I believe, my God, that Thou art present and I give Thee thanks for all the benefits which Thou hast showered upon me.
2. Ask for the grace to know our sins. — I beg Thee, my Lord and God, to give me light to know my faults and I ask for help to repent of them.
3. Ask for an account from the time of rising until the present examen, hour by hour, faults through thought, word, and deed.
4. Ask for forgiveness of Our Lord for our sins: My Lord Jesus, etc. or an Act of Contrition.
5. To resolve amendment with God's grace, and pray: the Our Father.

Practice — Tell me, my soul, what have you done? How have you done it? What have you failed to do that you should have done?

1. Have you risen punctually? Have you dressed modestly? Have you thought about God and about the meditation which you had to do?

2. Have you performed Christian actions and your meditation with fervor, reverence, and all the time indicated?
3. Have you heard Mass with devotion? Have you talked in Church?
4. Have you fulfilled the obligations of your state of life? Have you directed everything for God's honor and glory? Have you suffered with patience the pains, works, whims, malice and persecutions of your neighbors? Have you imitated the patience of Jesus, the good thief, of Job, etc., or on the contrary, have you acted impatiently or cursed, etc. . .?
5. Each time the clock strikes, have you prayed the Ave Maria? Have you put yourself in the Presence of God?
6. Have you said the Rosary every day with devotion? Have you prayed your other devotions?
7. Have you been temperate with food and drink . . . and in other matters?
8. Have you done your spiritual reading? How? For how long?
9. With what works of mercy have you occupied yourself? With what intention? How have you done them?
10. With what people have you dealt with? How have you treated them? What words did you use?
11. Have you made good use of your time?

How To Make The examination of Conscience

Particular Examen, daily Examination, according to Saint Ignatius, in order to amend a defect. It contains in itself three periods and two examinations.

The First Period — In the morning, upon rising, the individual should resolve to guard diligently against that particular defect or sin which requires correcting.

The Second Period — After eating, ask God what is necessary, that is, to know through God's grace how many times we have fallen into that particular sin or defect, and to help us overcome it in the future; consequently make the first examen asking an account of our soul concerning that resolution and of what we intend to correct, thinking over from hour to hour, from time to time, beginning with the time we got up until the moment of our examen. Then to resolve once more to correct ourself until the second examen.

The Third Period — After dinner the second examen is made hour by hour, beginning with the first examen until that moment.

Note:

1. Upon committing a fault, some light penance will be applied, e.g.: applying pressure of the hand to the chest. Also the ground could be kissed when alone, or an Ave Maria could be said.
2. Each day will be compared with another, each week, each month.
3. It is very useful to practise the virtue opposite the defect that one is trying to overcome.

Resolutions

Each year — I will make these holy spiritual exercises.

Each month — I will have one day of spiritual retreat.

Each week — I shall fervently receive Holy Communion every day. I shall confess at least once every 15 days. (Note: the original says Holy Communion each 15 days, but this was previous to Pope Saint Pius X's admonition to frequent Holy Communion.)

I shall keep holy Sundays and Holy Days as well as Feasts during the week. I shall not allow servile work in my home and I will assist at Mass and at other religious functions.

I shall occupy myself with reading good books and with the practice of the corporal works of mercy.

Each Day — In the morning and at night I shall make the spiritual exercises. I shall spend a quarter or half-hour in meditation.

I shall hear Holy Mass not only on feast days, which is an obligation, but on other days of devotion, if my occupations permit it.

I shall have a time for spiritual reading.

I shall make a visit to the Blessed Sacrament.

I shall pray five decades of the Rosary.

Always — I shall walk in the presence of God and make frequent ejaculations.

I shall have great devotion to the Most Blessed Trinity. I shall be strongly devoted to the Passion of Our Lord and to the Most Blessed Sacrament.

I shall have much devotion to the Most Blessed Virgin Mary and to the angels and saints.

I shall be devoted to the holy souls in Purgatory.

I shall be charitable to the poor.

I shall try by every means possible to bring about the conversion of sinners and the perseverance of the just.

These are the resolutions I have made and which, with God's help, I seriously propose to fulfill, and for them I sign my name today.

Day of Recollection

Each month — a day of spiritual retreat will be held.

This retreat will consist mainly of making a morning meditation and another in the afternoon or evening, according to one's opportunities. These two meditations will be like those made during the exercises, as seen in the table on page 363. Besides the meditations the resolutions made and written during the exercises will be read carefully and in detailed fashion.

This monthly day of recollection is very suitable to keep the fervor from cooling off; in addition it is a help for correcting faults not yet overcome, according to the proverb, *he who does not repair the leaky roof in time will have to rebuild his whole house*. The present month will be compared with the preceding months, and thus it will be recognized if progress in virtue is made and faults are decreased. On the same day or the next day, or at least as soon as possible, faults committed that same month will be confessed.

The day of Retreat, if possible, will be the 25th of each month, for the purpose of recalling the great events which have taken place at this time. We have no doubt that the remembrance of these same events will help a great deal to derive more benefit from the spiritual retreat.

On March 25, Adam sinned, lacking in obedience; on March 25, the Son of God obeyed the mission which His Father entrusted to Him[1] and He was made Man; and on March 25 He humbled Himself, becoming obedient unto death, even the death of the Cross.[2]

1. Lo, here am I, send me. Isa. 6:8
2. Philip. 2:8

On March 25, through sin, Adam became naked and God clothed him with lambskin and God said: *Behold Adam is become as one of us*[3] : In effect, as the Son of God who took the sheepskin of our nature; thus he was made man; Lamb of God Who takes away the sins of the world; with His merits may He clothe us with grace.

On March 25 Adam ate the fruit of death; and on March 25 Jesus Christ instituted the Most Holy Sacrament, which is the bread of life for our souls.

On March 25 Adam sinned eating of the fruit of the tree; and on March 25 Jesus Christ, the new Adam, died on the tree of the Cross[4] ; and thus Jesus defeated on the tree satan, who had defeated Adam.[5]

On March 25 Adam was driven out of the earthly paradise and on March 25 the Son of God entered the paradise of Mary, that is, He was made Man in the most Pure and Virginal Womb of Mary, and was born December 25.

See the schedule of these Meditations on page 363.

3. Gen. 3:22
4. The Hebrews counted the day from the first vespers to second vespers, as the Church does today in her liturgical prayers; thus what we say will be understood: that on the same day, March 25, both the institution of the Blessed Eucharist and the Crucifixion took place, although the former was at eight o'clock in the evening on the Thursday, and the latter was at 12 noon on Friday, for this day is understood liturgically between first and second vespers of March 25.
5. In the preface of the Mass.

Plan and Order of the Meditations
if used as a monthly day of Recollection

The Utility, Necessity and Manner of Making a General Confession

(1) One of the greater benefits resulting from these holy Spiritual Exercises is to pacify consciences through a good General Confession. This is what infuses a supreme quiet in the interior of the one doing it, because the soul is serene and the heart recovers peace. Oh what consolation belongs to the soul who has made a General Confession with some care! There is no longer anything which can disturb the serenity of its thoughts.

Certain apprehensions of death, of judgment, of hell and of eternity are no longer objects of horror for it, while resigned and conformed to the Will of God, it looks at them with holy tranquillity, as if for it they did not exist. It looks only at death as the end of its pains and labors and the beginning of a happy eternity.

Oh, what consolation it is to die and appear at the tribunal of God, Father of mercy Who has forgiven one and forgotten all his sins following the cleansing of all his faults from a General Confession! What sweet hopes blossom in his heart! Who, then, will not resolve to do it?

(2) Nevertheless, before treating of the way of making a General Confession, it would be beneficial to warn that it is of necessity for some souls and useful for others. It is necessary for those souls who in previous Confessions have been quiet and have maliciously hidden, through shame or fear, some mortal sin, or who thought it was a mortal sin, and for that reason believed that they had made a bad Confession, hiding it. Also requiring a General Confession are those souls who, although having confessed all their sins, but have lacked sorrow for their sins as well as the firm purpose

of amendment not to sin any more. If their Confessions have been without any purpose of amendment, if they have lived in a voluntary proximate occasion of sin, if they have always had hatred and rancor towards their neighbor, if they have held onto what belongs to others, and being able to make restitution, have not done it, if they have been remiss in fulfilling the main obligations of their state of life — those souls, then, who have made their individual Confessions with any one of those grave defects, must understand that these Confessions are null and sacrilegious, and that there is no other remedy than to repair their damages and harm and ensure their eternal salvation, by making a good General Confession.

(3) But for those souls who in all their individual Confessions have put forth all cautious effort on their part, and who have moral certainty that all their Confessions were good ones, nevertheless a good General Confession would be most useful, now in life and afterwards at the hour of death. I now say in life, since the General Confession has served many souls to begin a fervent and exemplary life, as experience teaches us that many, many souls following a General Confession, have not returned to sin, or at least, not for long, and if they do, they soon get up and they make many reforms.

Then happens to the soul who confesses generally, what happens to the person who clothes himself with a rich and new vestment, great care over a long period of time not to soil it; thus the soul, clothed once again with Divine Grace through a General Confession, lives more carefully not to dirty itself again.

(4) It is not possible to relate the multitude of souls who through a General Confession, have made a Christian reform of their life and have corrected certain vices, even those for which they no longer knew what

remedies to apply. From this it follows that the first advice usually given to one who wants to change his state, is to make a good General Confession, as is the practice with those who wish to embrace the religious life or Holy Matrimony.

This is also advised to those who have lived much time engaged in business of the world, and attempt to withdraw to a more quiet life, attending to their soul and surrounding themselves totally to God; they do not find any more efficacious remedy for this renovation of the spirit than a good General Confession. The reason for this is that because the soul who confesses in a general way conceives greater sorrow for its past sins and a greater purpose of amendment in the future. The soul on seeing all its sins together rather than one by one at various times, is presented with a different aspect; this is like an army of soldiers, when spread out at various places, cause no terror, but when they are together and placed in battle by command, they cause great terror. For this reason many saints made a General Confession during their life. In the life of the pious Archbishop of Valencia, Blessed John of Rivera, admiration of all Spain, it is told that he made six General Confessions throughout his life. Saint Charles Borromeo made a General Confession each year. Saint Teresa of Jesus, Saint Mary Magdalen of Pazzi and Saint Jane Frances Chantal made General Confessions. These saintly persons were not moved to make General Confessions through scruples, but rather they did it for its great usefulness which they reported in a practical manner, of greater confusion about themselves, of a considerable increase of sorrow for having sinned, and of a greater strength to correct themselves in the future.

From here Saint Francis de Sales, among other praises which he sings of General Confession, says:

"That it provokes us to a healthy confusion for our past life and makes us admire the features of the Mercy of God in order to love Him with greater fervor in the future."

It is the practice of every reasonable person who desires his eternal salvation, to make the exercises annually and include a General Confession of everything of that year, or from the last good General Confession of previous years; and it should be recommended to those souls who have never made it, that they make the General Confession at least once, when they are better acquainted with the gravity of their sins and of the goodness of God against Whom they have offended, as Saint Margaret of Cortona did by order of the same God, and He was so pleased that He said: "My child, Margaret, by virtue of the General Confession which you have made, I forgive you all your sins."

(5) Oh, blessed General Confession! Who will not be determined to do it faithfully, in order to be enriched with so many benefits which it brings? It revalidates past Confessions made lacking the required dispositions, excites the soul with greater efficacy to contrition for sins committed, it pulls out of the heart all the vices and sinful attachments, inclines the Divine Mercy to grant us a general pardon for all our evils, and finally, consoles the penitent soul and returns its baptismal purity, and besides it disposes it to receive new graces and favors in this life and eternal glory in the next life.

(6) In view of the great evils which are overcome and the great benefits which the General Confession brings, no one will be surprised that Saint Ignatius exhorts all those who wish to be perfectly converted to God, to make first a General Confession of all their sins. Nor should we find it strange that Saint Vincent

de Paul, from one General Confession which he heard, took as a motive for forming his first missions afterwards founding such a holy Congregation, in which an expressed profession is made to hear General Confessions. And thus we advise and beg all souls to make a General Confession: at least to two kinds of persons; to those who have never made it, and to those who have habitually lived in some vice, and have continued confessing from time to time with little or no purpose of amendment; these, then, should make a General Confession.

(7) The understanding convinced of the usefulness of General Confession, and the will resolved to make it then, it runs into the difficulty of the examination of conscience, looking upon this difficulty as an insurmountable mountain.

Courage; there is no reason to be frightened; here is a very easy method which is supported by these simple points:

(1) The first time you make a General Confession, confess only mortal sins which your conscience considers to be so, or those about which you are doubtful or have suspicion of being mortal.

(2) If you know precisely their number, for example, six, say that there are six mortal sins which you have committed.

(3) If you don't know if there are six or eight, say so.

(4) Whenever you have had some vice, examine the years such a fault has lasted, and the frequency with which you usually fell into it, computing some time connections, for example, two or three times a month, or two or three times a week, or once each day or whatever number of times.

(5) The individual who has sinned against purity will examine his conscience by his state of life, and thus he

will think first how old he was when he married, how many years he lived in a married state and how many lived as a widow or widower; next he will determine the number of times fallen in each state, since the sins of a married person are of a different kind from those of the unmarried.

(6) As for the rest of the sins, it is not necessary to make this distinction of state since it is as sinful in one state as in another. Nevertheless, to help the memory, it would be beneficial for the individual to better examine himself, running through the course of his life, beginning from his infancy, childhood, and youth; which year he changed his state and how long he spent in each state, places where he has been, positions he has held, relationships he has kept; and with this diligence his conscience will present like a faithful mirror all the sins he has committed throughout his life against the Holy Commandments of God's Law and of the Church, which for a better method and greater clarity, he will keep on following them in order, and in each Commandment he will examine every sin committed against that Commandment throughout his whole life, applying to this Commandment age, state, occupations, etc.

List of books St. Anthony Mary Claret recommends for those who make the Spiritual Exercises

Villacastin, or Luis de la Puente, *For Daily Meditation.*

Father Luis de Granada, *Prayer and Meditation.**

The Treasure of Protection, [For devotion to Mary]

The Glories of Mary, [For devotion to Mary]*

Thomas a Kempis, *Imitation of Christ.**

St. Francis de Sales, *Introduction to a Devout Life.**

The Gospel of St. Matthew, with a commentary by St. Anthony Mary Claret.

*Conformity to the Will of God.**

Granada, *Guide of Sinners.**

Madame Beaumont, *True Instruction of the People.*

Instruction of Youth.

Augusto Nicolas, *Philosophical Studies.*

Harmony of Reason and Religion.

Abbot J. Gaume, *The Catechism of Perseverance.*

Croiset, *The Christian Year.*

The Right and Safe Road for Getting to Heaven.

Our Little Works, The Catechism Explained by St. Anthony Mary Claret.

*Note — These books are available through the publisher.